IMAGES
of America

OREGON'S HIGHWAY 99

ON THE COVER: Art Lacey stands in front of The Bomber south of Milwaukie. Lacey purchased a surplus B-17 bomber in 1947 and flew it to Troutdale. He loaded it onto four trucks and moved it to its new home atop his service station on McLoughlin Boulevard. The Bomber was probably the best-known roadside attraction along Oregon's Highway 99. Lacey is in the dark uniform; the others are not identified. (Jack O'Donnell Collection.)

IMAGES
of America

OREGON'S HIGHWAY 99

Chuck Flood

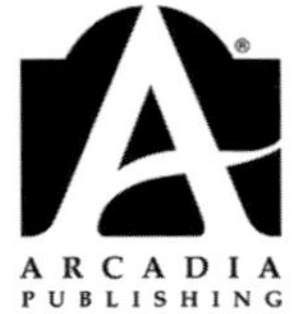

ISBN 978-1-4671-1534-6

Published by Arcadia Publishing
Charleston, South Carolina

Printed in the United States of America

Library of Congress Control Number: 2015948920

For all general information, please contact Arcadia Publishing:
Telephone 843-853-2070
Fax 843-853-0044
E-mail sales@arcadiapublishing.com
For customer service and orders:
Toll-Free 1-888-313-2665

Visit us on the Internet at www.arcadiapublishing.com

To Debbie (of course), Mike and Jennifer for putting me up,
and Jack O'Donnell for his continued support.

Contents

ACKNOWLEDGMENTS

Many thanks are due to the individuals and organizations that offered their support and assistance with this project:

- Addie Maguire, Albany Regional Museum, Albany (ARM)
- Mary Gallagher, Benton County Museum, Philomath (BCM)
- Devin Busby, City of Portland Archives, Portland (CPA)
- Karin Morey, Clackamas County Historical Society, Oregon City (CCHS)
- Jack O'Donnell Collection (JCO'D)
- Linda VanOrden, Junction City Historical Society, Junction City (JuncCityHS)
- Joan Momsen, Josephine County Historical Society, Grants Pass (JoCoHS)
- Cheryl Roffe, Lane County Historical Museum, Eugene (LCHM)
- Chris Peterson, Oregon Digital, Corvallis (OD-OSU)
- Oregon Historic Photograph Collections (OHPC)
- Austin Schulz, Oregon State Archives, Salem (OSA)
- Diana Painter, Oregon State Historic Preservation Office, Salem (OSHPO)
- Dave Hegeman, Oregon State Library, Salem (OSL)
- Original Pancake House Archives, Portland (OPH)
- Patty Chap and Bette Jo Lawson, Polk County Historical Society, Rickreall (PCHS)
- Jim Roake, Roake's the Hot Dog Folks (JR)
- Pat Harper, Southern Oregon Historical Society, Medford (SOHS)
- Sean Garvey, Tigard Public Library, Tigard (TPL)
- Karen Lange, Washington County Museum, Portland (WCM)
- Kylie Pine, Willamette Heritage Center, Salem (WHC)

Images with credit lines are courtesy of the organization or individual whose abbreviation appears in the above list, which should be used to determine the contributor's full name. Images without credit lines are from the author's personal collection.

INTRODUCTION

Highway 99 entered Oregon by crossing the Columbia River north of Portland and exited the state via the Siskiyou Mountains south of Ashland. That can be stated with certainty. Between those two fixed points, however, Highway 99 and its predecessor, the Pacific Highway, followed various and sometimes bewildering routes as it traversed 250 miles of fertile fields and forested hills. It was not until the 1930s that Highway 99's official alignment—including its major branches, 99E and 99W—was finalized. Today, almost all of the old highway still exists and is in daily use.

Like its neighbor states Washington and California, Oregon is bifurcated by the Cascade Mountains into a wet west side and a dry east side. In broad terms, agriculture, forest products, and the state's largest cities characterize the west side; the dry eastern side is more typified by mining, ranching, and wide open spaces. Both sides were well populated when Lewis and Clark made their famous trek to the Pacific Ocean.

Early post-contact overland travel into Oregon was from the east. The mighty Columbia River was a waterway for fur traders and explorers; starting in the 1840s, the Oregon Trail swarmed with emigrants on a one-way search for a new life. They reached their destination in the broad, level Willamette Valley. Within a decade, a sizeable population of settlers had grown up in the valley. Towns quickly followed; trading points for agricultural products, the earliest were usually along rivers, but inland settlements soon appeared.

Though home-seekers from the east continued to pour in, by the 1850s, north-south travel routes had developed in western Oregon. The Applegate Trail, an alternate route of the Oregon Trail that delivered settlers into the state via California, became a main thoroughfare for Oregon miners bound for the mother lode of gold discoveries in the foothills outside Sacramento. By 1859, several territorial roads had been established along the edges of the Willamette Valley, and towns became connected through a network of farm-to-market roads.

As population grew, so did commerce. Stagecoaches and freight wagons began operations, but few of the early roads were intended for long-distance journeys. Railroads handled that kind of traffic. By the mid-1870s, the locomotives of the Oregon & California Railroad were steaming up and down the Willamette Valley. As the 20th century dawned, road conditions were still primitive throughout most of Oregon.

Then came the automobile. Originally a plaything of the rich, autos rapidly became popular, safer, and affordable. In 1900, only 8,000 automobiles were registered in the entire country; by 1930, the nation's roads bulged with more than 23 million cars and an additional 3.5 million trucks. Commercial travel increased exponentially. Suburbs developed as workers realized they could live at a distance from their workplaces. Tourism was born. People traveled for the sheer fun of it, for the excitement of seeing sights and places they'd heard of but never dreamed they'd be able to visit.

It didn't take long to realize that existing roads were inadequate for the demand. Many early highways were no better than the wagon roads that preceded them; dust-choked in summer and mud-pits in the rainy season, they often got from point A to point B via points C, D, X, and Y. "Good roads" became a rallying cry among motorists. Major highway-building programs resulted from demands for getting from place to place faster and more directly.

In 1913, the Oregon legislature created a state highway commission with the power to raise funds for highway construction. Among its first projects was the Pacific Highway, proposed to run from Portland to Salem through Oregon City; then through Albany to Eugene, Cottage Grove, Roseburg, Grants Pass, Medford, and Ashland.

Planning had hardly begun before an effort was made to split the route into an East Side and a West Side Pacific Highway (not to be confused with Highways 99E and 99W, which came later). The East Side Pacific Highway won the contest for primacy and in 1927 was designated US Highway 99 as part of a national initiative to replace highway names with numbers.

For the first years of its life after being decreed into existence, the Pacific Highway simply followed the routes of preexisting roads. Beginning in the 1920s, improvements in the form of realignments, bypasses, paving, and new construction began to transform the patchwork of old roads into a unified highway. These improvements continued periodically and are still ongoing today.

The West Side Pacific Highway finally achieved national highway status in 1937 when it was redesignated Highway 99W. At the same time, the East Side Pacific Highway became Highway 99E. As they had since early days, the 99E and W came together at Junction City to form Highway 99 and continue on to California.

Though highway conditions had dramatically improved by the mid-1920s, services for the new breed of travelers were few and far between outside major cities and towns. Entrepreneurs saw a business opportunity in providing motorists with places to eat, sleep, and have their autos serviced. In-city hotels turned their faces toward the motor trade. Restaurants and cafés, tourist parks, auto courts and motels, gas stations, and roadside attractions started appearing along the highway.

Over the years, nearly 1,100 "gas, food, and lodging" businesses lined Highway 99, among them elegant hotels and rustic cabins, a hot dog stand shaped like a dog, and gasoline stations in the shape of a whiskey jug or with a B-17 bomber mounted above the pumps. Usually owner-operated (at least in the formative years), they often bore the owners' names (Jeff's Super Service Station) or took their names from local scenic, historical, or mythological entities (Rogue Haven Motel, Lithia Park Auto Camp, Noah's Ark Cabins).

Builders left individual imprints on their creations. Few standardized designs existed beyond the obvious: restaurants needed kitchens and tables; motel rooms had to have doors and windows. In some examples, the combination of design, colors, and setting approached folk art.

With the rise of the interstate freeway system in the 1950s, a different paradigm dictated how people traveled and were provided with services. Freeways changed the face of America. By limiting access and bypassing downtowns, freeways were often the death knell for long-established roadside businesses—and, in some cases, of entire towns. Rather than building through, freeways built around small towns, usually on the edges where land was cheap and there were fewer people to displace. New businesses sprang up at the access points to the freeways. Old, established traveler-oriented businesses located along the old highway or in bypassed towns could not compete. Some tried; many failed.

US 99 was decertified in 1968 with the completion of the freeway system. In Oregon, much of the old highway was renumbered State Route 99, though many portions of the highway go by their historical names. With the exception of a few stretches where getting on the freeway is necessary, Highway 99 (including 99E and 99W) can still be driven from border to border. Unfortunately, most of the roadside businesses pictured in this book have disappeared; only a fraction remain untouched.

One

Highway 99E
Portland to Junction City

The Columbia River: half a mile wide between Portland and Vancouver, Washington, it was not spanned until 1908. That year, the Spokane, Portland & Seattle Railway built the first bridge on the lower Columbia. A highway bridge followed in 1917, creating an important link in the newly established Pacific Highway. Suddenly, the river wasn't an impediment to travel. The old ferries vanished. In their place was a massive steel structure, symbolic of the automobile age.

Though a wagon road already led directly to Portland through Kenton, highway engineers decided that the Pacific Highway would proceed southeast from the Interstate Bridge to join Union Avenue. Major construction improvements extended Union Avenue and connected it with the new bridge. Southbound travelers followed Union to Broadway; turning left on Broadway and crossing the Willamette River on the Broadway Bridge took them into downtown Portland.

Several routes led south from Portland. The officially sanctioned route was Pacific Highway No. 1, the East Side Pacific Highway. It exited Portland on Terwilliger Boulevard, heading south to Oswego and crossing the Willamette River at Oregon City. An alternate route led east across the Hawthorne Bridge to Meridian Road (today's 82nd Avenue), then south to a Clackamas River crossing at Park Place.

The geography south of Oregon City challenged early road-builders. The old highway ascended the bluff at Oregon City and followed South End Road to Canby, then zigzagged into Aurora via Barlow. A relatively straight alignment from Aurora skirted the edges of Hubbard, Woodburn, and Gervais into Salem. Surface streets channeled traffic through Salem, and Sunnyside Road carried motorists out of the city. On flowed the Pacific Highway through Jefferson to Albany, then past Tangent, Shedd, and Halsey to Harrisburg and finally Junction City.

Realignments started early. The Oregon City/Canby/Aurora segment was straightened by 1930. Traffic through Salem was rerouted several times; S Commercial became the official route out of town. Albany was bypassed. One-way traffic couplets appeared in Portland and Salem. The biggest improvement was the McLoughlin Boulevard superhighway between Portland and Oregon City; eliminating the old Terwilliger route, it still carries large volumes of traffic today.

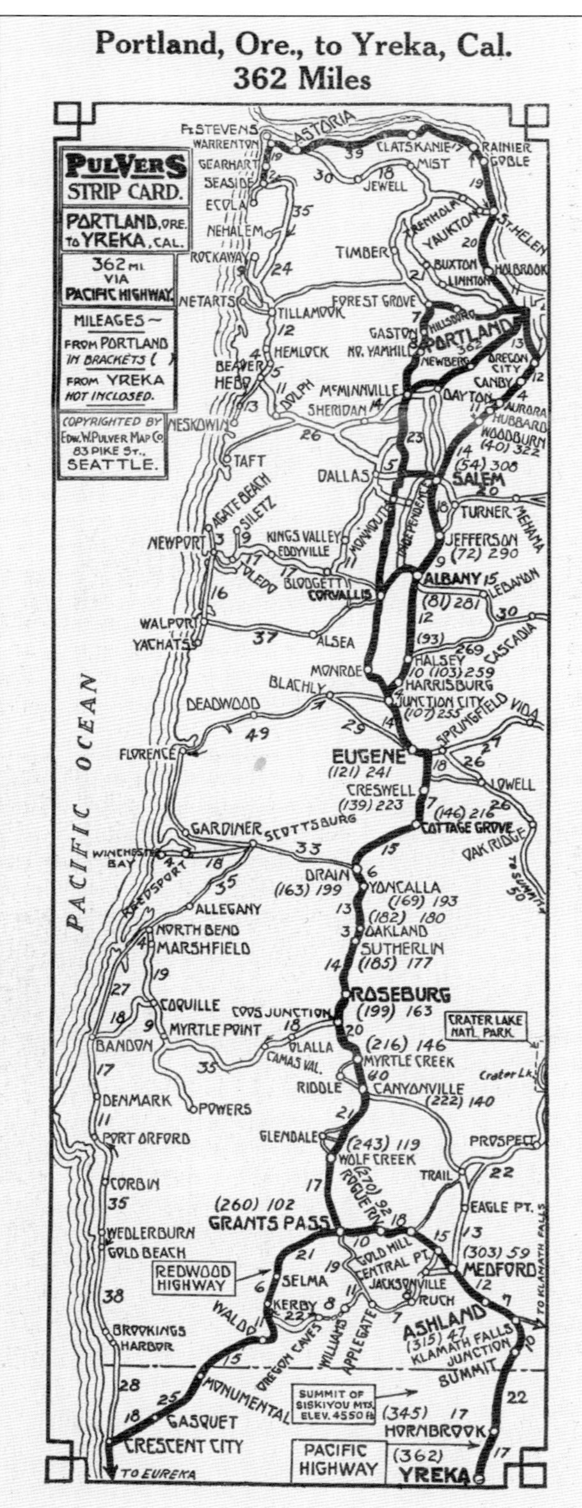

This "strip card," issued by the Edward W. Pulver Map Company of Seattle, depicts the early Pacific Highway between Portland and Yreka, California. It probably dates to the late 1920s, since major highway improvements completed in the 1930s—the superhighway (today's McLaughlin Boulevard) between Portland and Oregon City, and the upgrade of Barbur Boulevard out of Portland—are not shown. This map demonstrates how fluid the "official" routes of highways could be. The primary branches of the Pacific Highway, splitting north of Portland and reuniting at Junction City, are delineated; these became Highway 99E and 99W in 1937. But also shown are an alternate west-side route via Forest Grove and connectors between the east and west branches—one between Salem and Monmouth, another from Albany to Corvallis. These were also considered part of the Pacific Highway.

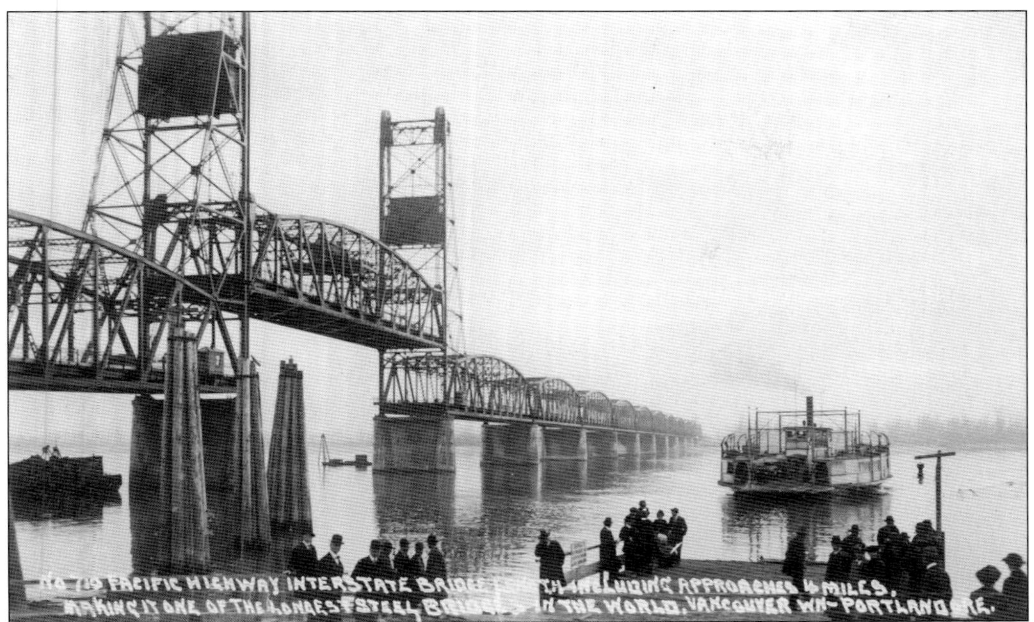

The Interstate Bridge, spanning the Columbia River between Vancouver, Washington, and Portland, Oregon, opened to vehicles in 1917 as a single bridge carrying two-way traffic. The bridge consisted of 13 steel spans, one of them being a lift span to allow river traffic to pass under it. Its construction ended the longtime ferry service between Portland and Vancouver.

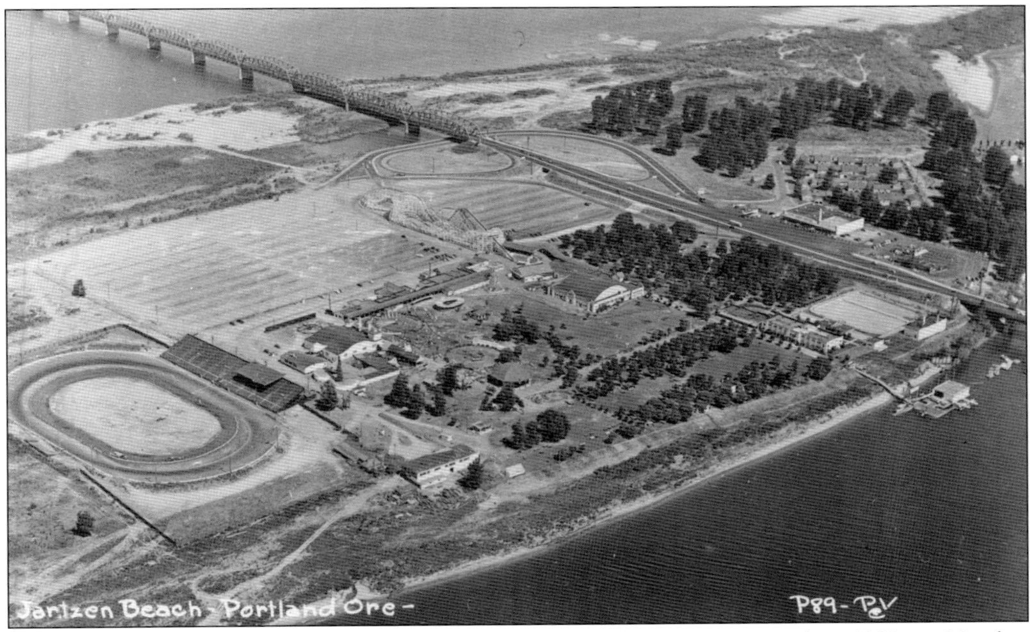

Jantzen Beach Amusement Park, "the Coney Island of the West," opened in 1928 on Hayden Island south of the Interstate Bridge. This aerial view shows the expanse of the park, claimed to be the largest in the country at the time. With roller coasters, carnival rides, and four swimming pools, Jantzen Beach was a magnet for fun-lovers of all ages. It was demolished in the 1970s for a shopping mall.

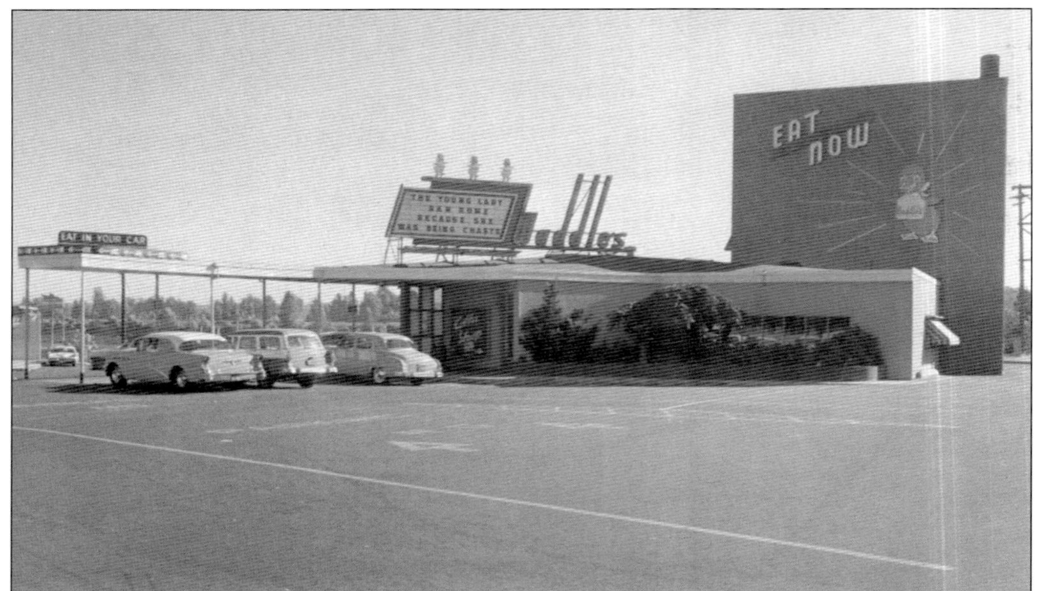

For over half a century, Waddle's Coffee Shop, with its huge sign and duck mascot urging motorists to "Eat Now," was a familiar landmark just south of the Interstate Bridge. Gene and Natha Waddle opened the restaurant in 1945, later expanding to other locations and a string of Taco Houses. Waddle's underwent several remodels, including one designed by Portland architect Pietro Belluschi. Closed in 2004, it is now a Hooters.

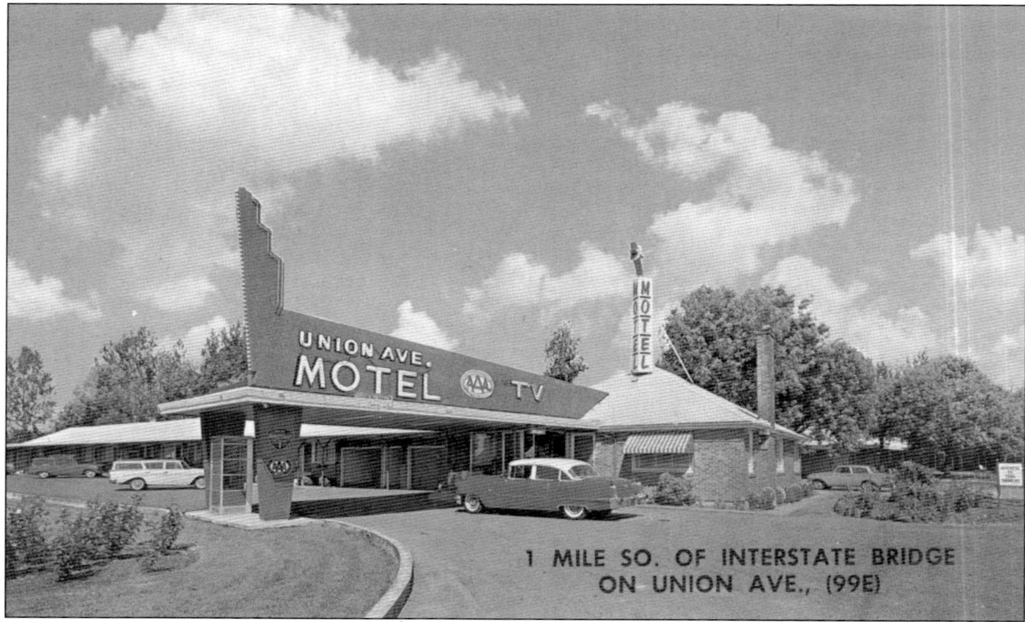

Located on Gertz Road just off Union Avenue (today's MLK Jr. Boulevard), Ken and Judy Gustin's Union Avenue Motel offered 18 one- and two-room units with kitchenettes. The motel, built in an L-shaped configuration with the office at the knee of the "L," was sited amid lawns and shade trees. Overnight rates in 1941 were $1.50 to $3 for two persons. The motel was severely damaged by fire in February 2015. (JCO'D.)

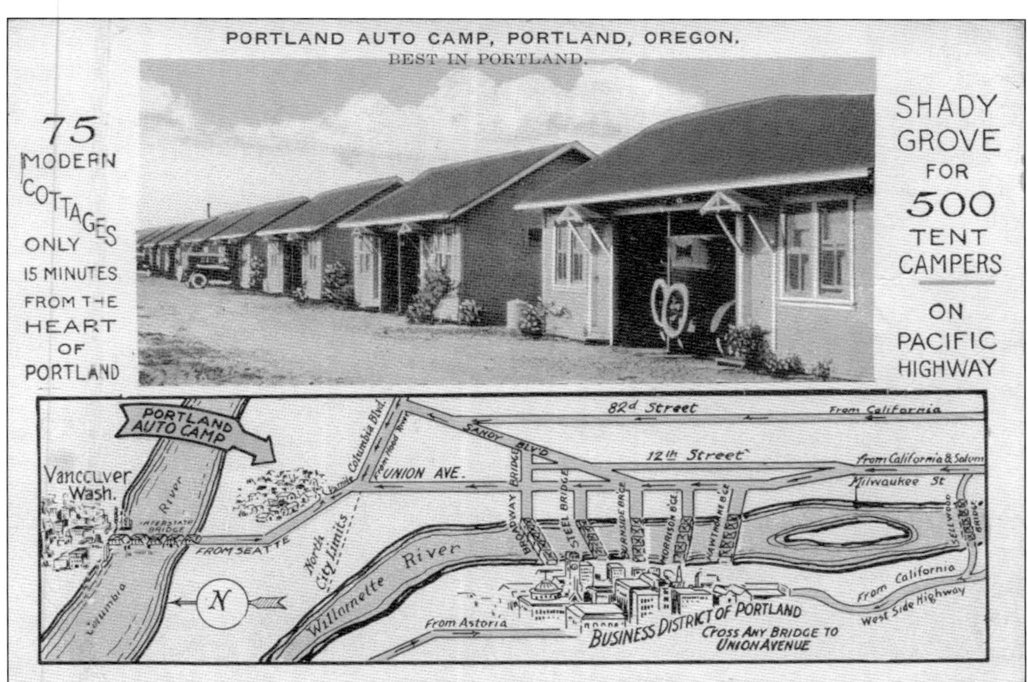

The Portland Auto Camp opened in 1925 on 40 acres adjacent to Union Avenue. Duplex cottages in parallel rows provided 40 units (later increased to 75), each with folding bed, gas heater, private toilet, and kitchen. Completing the facilities were 500 tent spaces under cottonwood trees; a community house with fireplace, radio, and phonograph; a shared laundry/bathhouse; and an on-premises store stocked with groceries, meats, and vegetables.

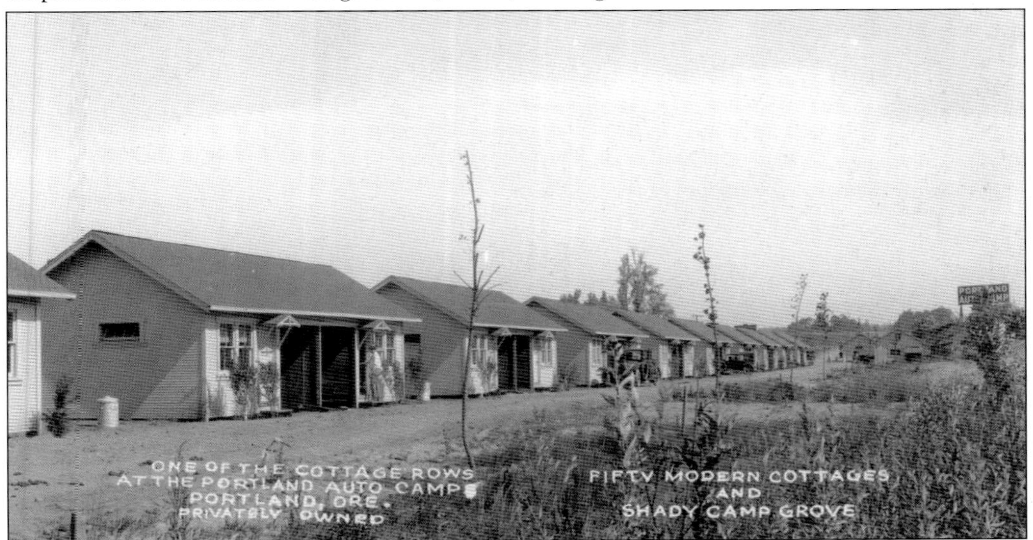

Long rows of cottages at the Portland Auto Camp presented a neat, tidy appearance in this 1926 photograph. Originally focused on the traveling motorist, by the 1930s, the cabins became homes for long-term residents. Sited as it was in the lowlands along Columbia Slough, the camp was inundated by the great flood of 1948. Water-damaged cabins were offered for sale that September, and the camp soon disappeared. (CPA, A2004-002.631.)

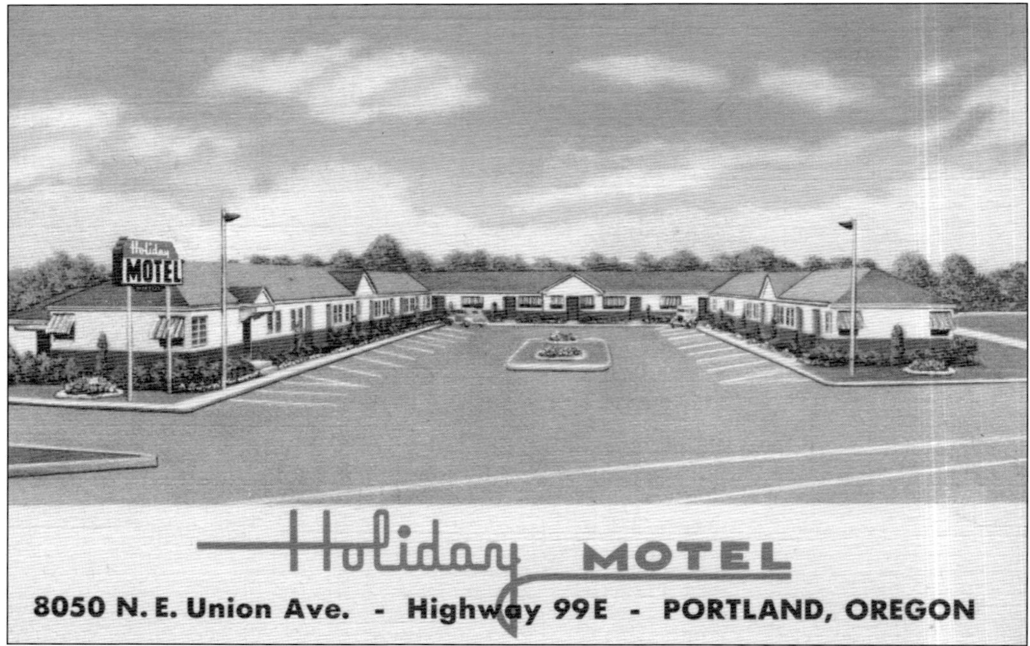

The Holiday Motel is perched atop the high land at the south end of the Union Avenue Viaduct, just north of Columbia Boulevard at 8050 NE Union Avenue. Opened prior to 1948, it was owned by Mrs. R.B. Harris and managed by Mr. and Mrs. Cecil Rose in 1954. Its 23 units featured Simmons Beautyrest mattresses, automatic electric heat, and tile baths and showers. It is still in business.

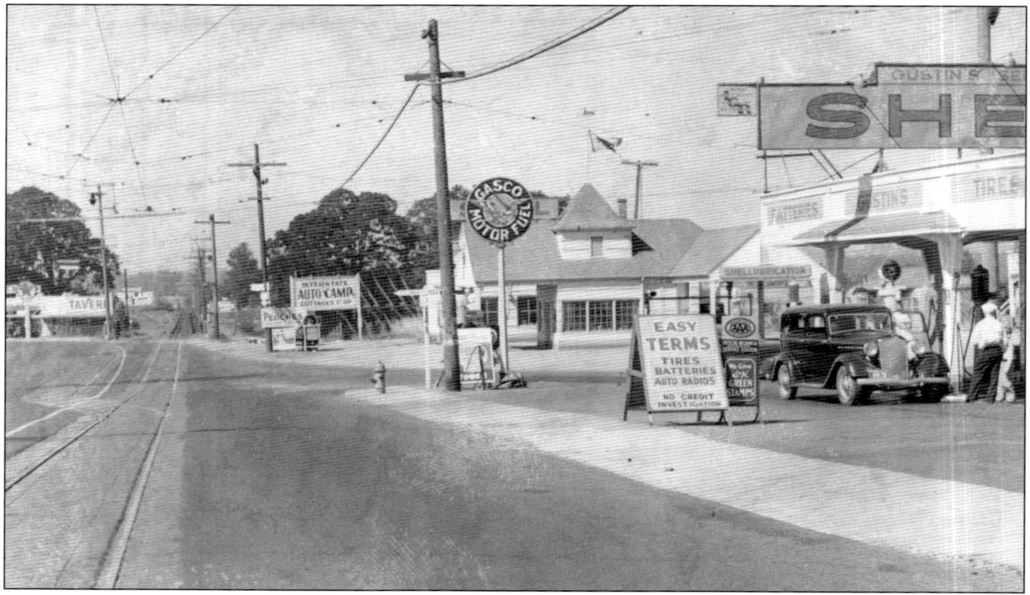

In 1937, the Columbia Boulevard–Union Avenue intersection was bustling with roadside businesses. This view looks north on Union with a Shell gas station on the east side and a Texaco station visible where Union curves to drop down to the flatlands at Columbia Slough. The Interstate Auto Camp occupied the northeast corner of the intersection; the trees behind it indicate where the Holiday Motel would later be constructed. (CPA, A2005-001.735.)

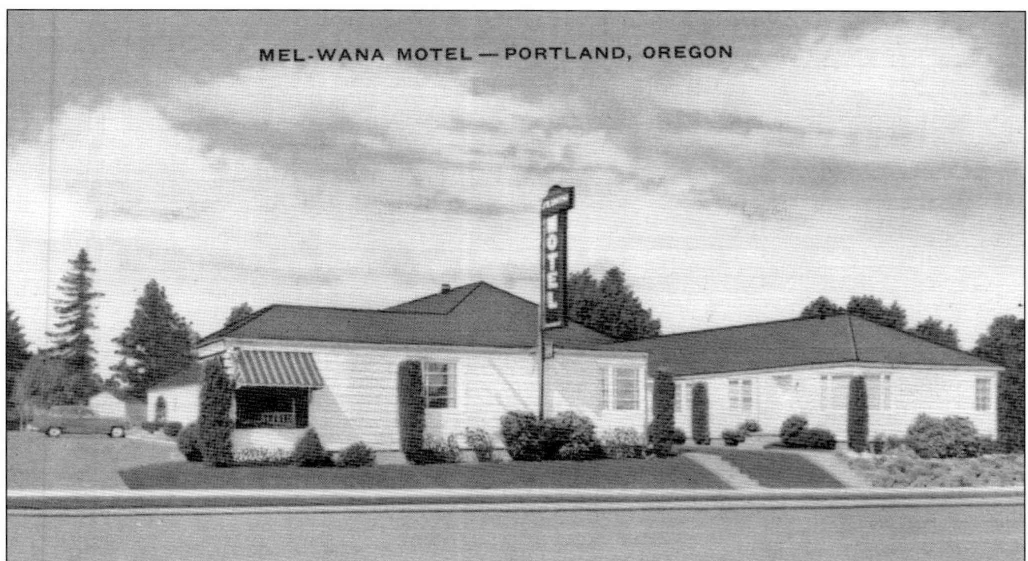

Melvin and Juanita Wolf combined their names ("Mel" and "WAN-ita") to christen their Mel-Wana Motel, which opened in 1949 at 7057 NE Union Avenue. Units offered deluxe accommodations with the customary electric kitchens and tile baths and showers; television became de rigueur in the 1950s. Steps leading down to Union Avenue invited guests to hop a city bus for a trip into downtown Portland. An apartment complex occupies the site today.

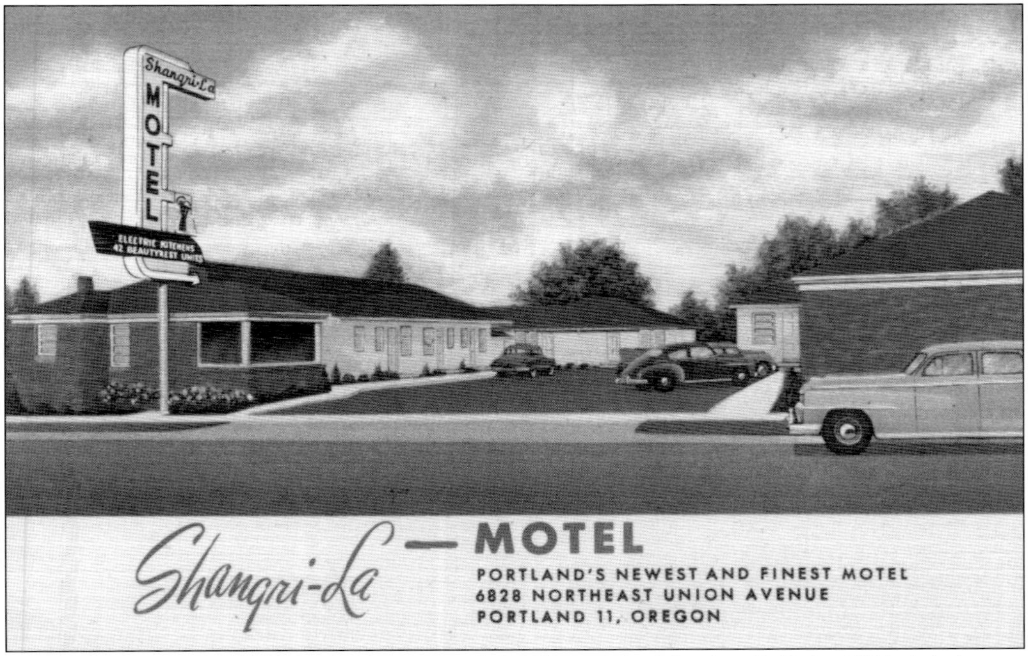

Lester Asbahr and Donald Smith constructed the Shangri-La Motel in 1950; by 1954, Asbahr was sole owner. The motel offered 42 units (with or without electric kitchens), tile showers and tubs, radios, and wall-to-wall carpeting. The address was listed as 6828 NE Union Avenue, though the main entrance seemed to be via Grand Avenue, a block east. Its entire contents were sold off in May 1978. The building is still standing.

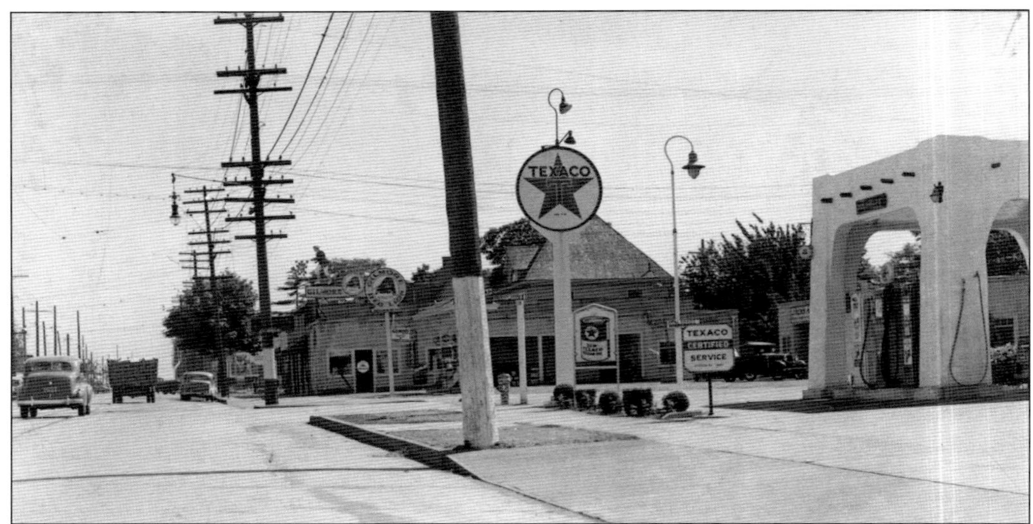

In 1933, Norval Phelp's Texaco Service occupied the northwest corner of NE Union Avenue and Ainsworth Street; in this 1937 view, it was rebranded as a Texaco Certified Service Station. Across the way at 5945 NE Union was Fred Holman's Gilmore outlet and Jack Carey's auto repair. The site of the Texaco station, 6003 NE Union Avenue, is now a Starbucks; the Gilmore station is a Popeye's Chicken. (CPA, A2005-001.1.)

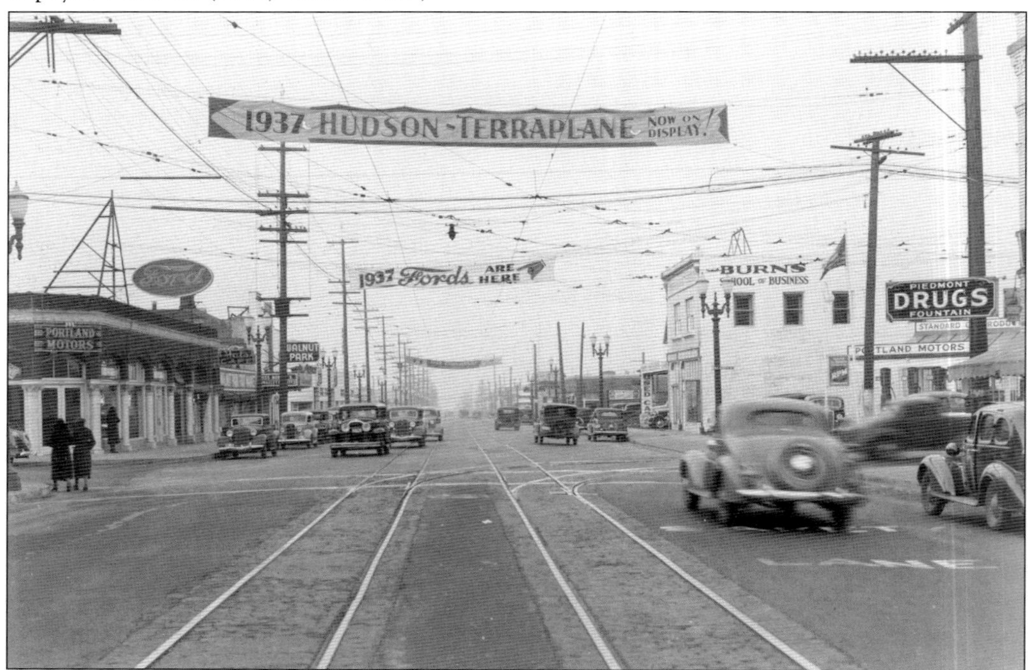

There is not much doubt about when this photograph was taken: banners flying above Union Avenue welcome the arrival of the 1937-model Fords, Chevrolets, and Hudson-Terraplanes. Visible are signs for the Portland Motors Ford dealership and service station, Hal's Cafe, the Walnut Park theater, the Burns School of Business, and Piedmont Drugs and Fountain. Rails of the soon-to-be-obsolete trolley head north on Union and curve east onto Alberta Street. (CPA, A2005-001.667.)

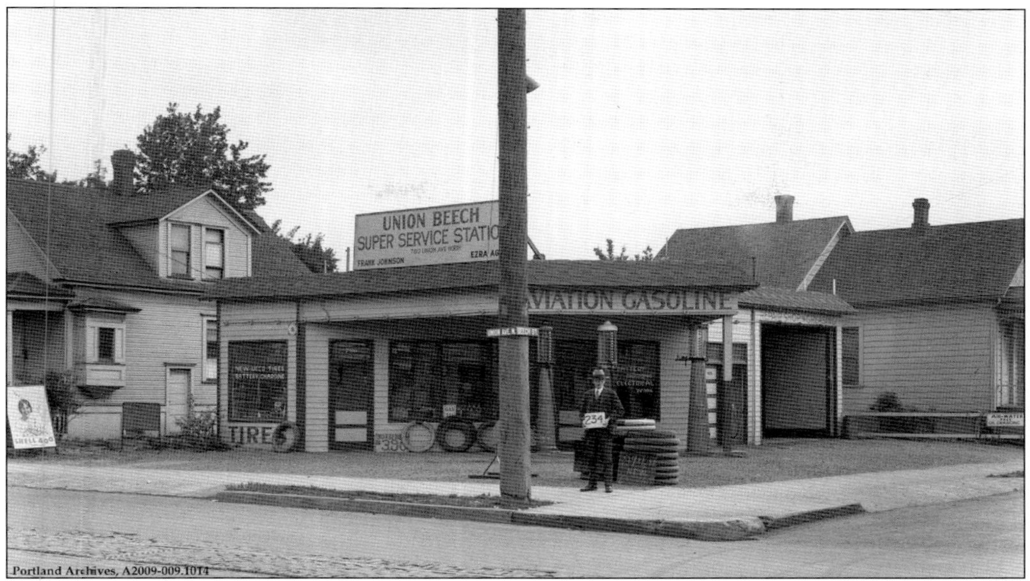

Frank Johnson and Ezra Agee owned the Union Beech Super Service Station at 3780 NE Union. In addition to three gravity-feed pumps delivering gas for 21¢ a gallon, they offered a full range of auto service, including tire repair and replacement, greasing, battery charging, and electrical work. In this 1929 photograph, the man holding the numbered card is a property assessor. The station was gone by 1937. (CPA, A2009-009.1014.)

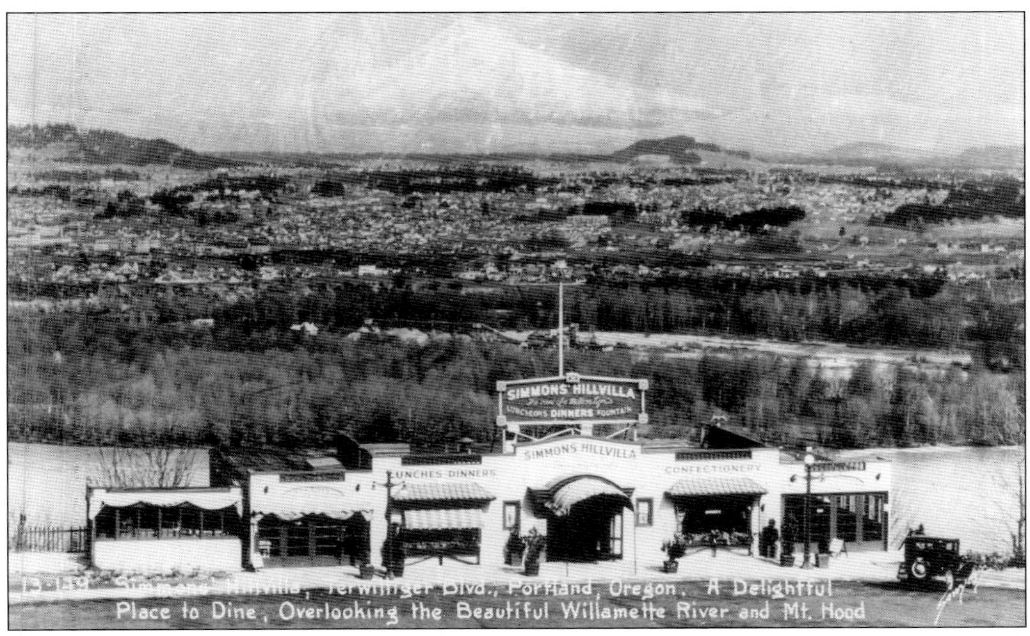

The early Pacific Highway took motorists past Simmons' Hillvilla at 5700 Terwilliger Boulevard. Perched on a hill with a spectacular overlook of the Willamette River and Mount Hood, the restaurant billed itself as "The View of a Million Lights." Rolla Simmons owned the Hillvilla as well as Simmons By The Falls at Multnomah Falls on the Columbia River Highway. The Hillvilla operated into the 1950s; it is the Chart House today.

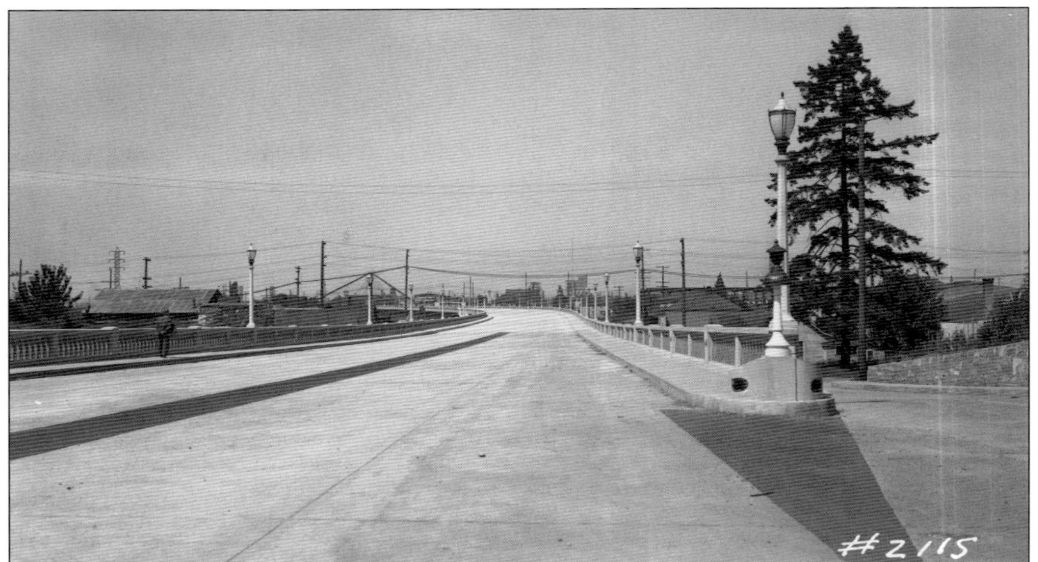

By 1934, the McLoughlin Boulevard superhighway was open all the way from Oregon City to 17th Avenue and Schiller Street in southeast Portland, but how to connect to the existing Pacific Highway was still debated. The winning proposal included two miles of highway and viaduct connecting 17th and Schiller to the south end of Union Avenue. This 1937 view of the newly completed viaduct looks south from Stephens Street. (ODOT.)

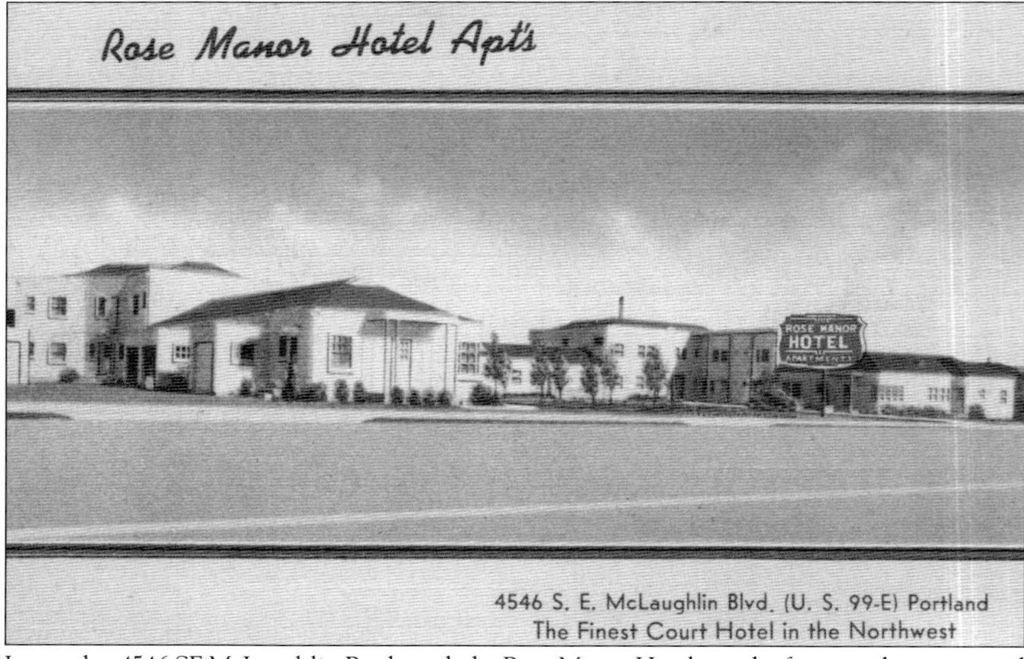

Located at 4546 SE McLoughlin Boulevard, the Rose Manor Hotel was the first motel encountered by travelers southbound out of Portland on the new superhighway. A combination of motel units and monthly rental apartments, the Rose Manor opened in 1941 with 27 deluxe two- to four-room units; by 1960, it had expanded to 61 units set on 3.5 acres of park-like grounds. Today, an LA Fitness occupies the site.

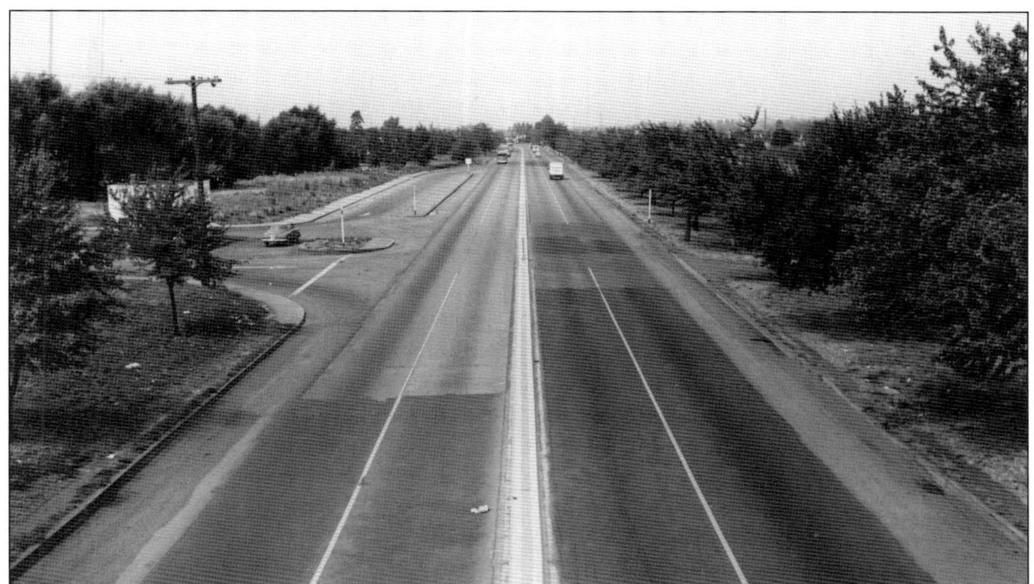

The four-lane superhighway proposed in 1929 to connect Portland and Oregon City east of the Willamette River was under construction by 1932. Completed in 1937, it was named McLoughlin Boulevard to honor Dr. John McLoughlin, the "father of Oregon." It became Highway 99E in 1937, replacing the Portland–Oregon City route via Terwilliger Boulevard. This 1951 view looks north from SE Bybee Boulevard. Traffic is heavier these days. (CPA, A2005-001.424.)

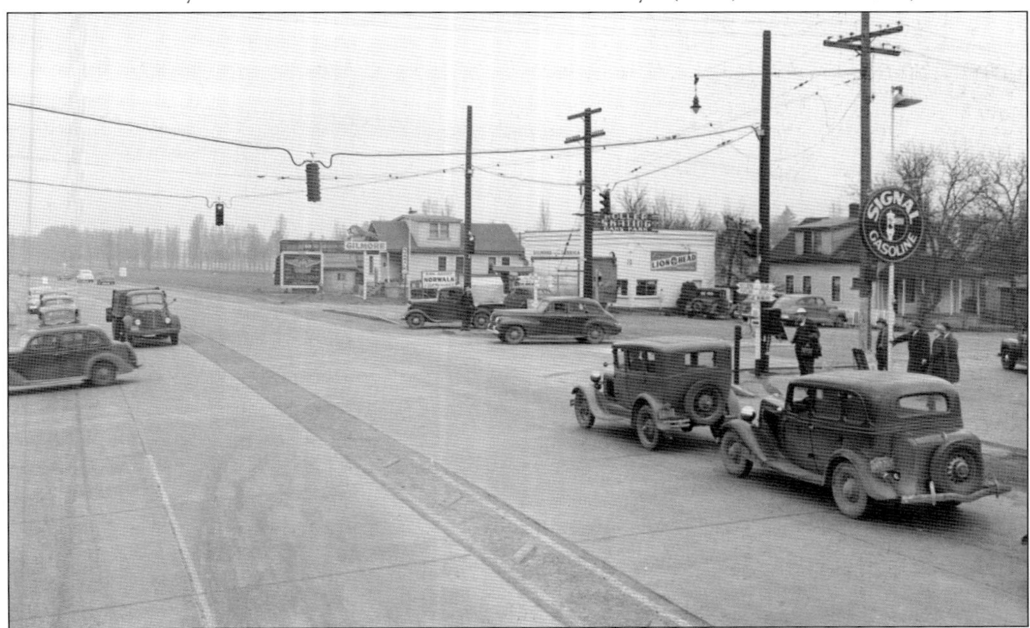

The intersection of SE McLoughlin Boulevard and SE Tacoma Street was a busy place, as this 1942 view shows. Two service stations—Signal Gasoline and Gilmore—face each other across Tacoma Street; a sign points to the Oaks Park roller-skating rink a mile west. The trees in the left-center background shielding Eastmoreland golf course from the highway are still a familiar sight along McLoughlin Boulevard. (CPA, A2005-001.422.)

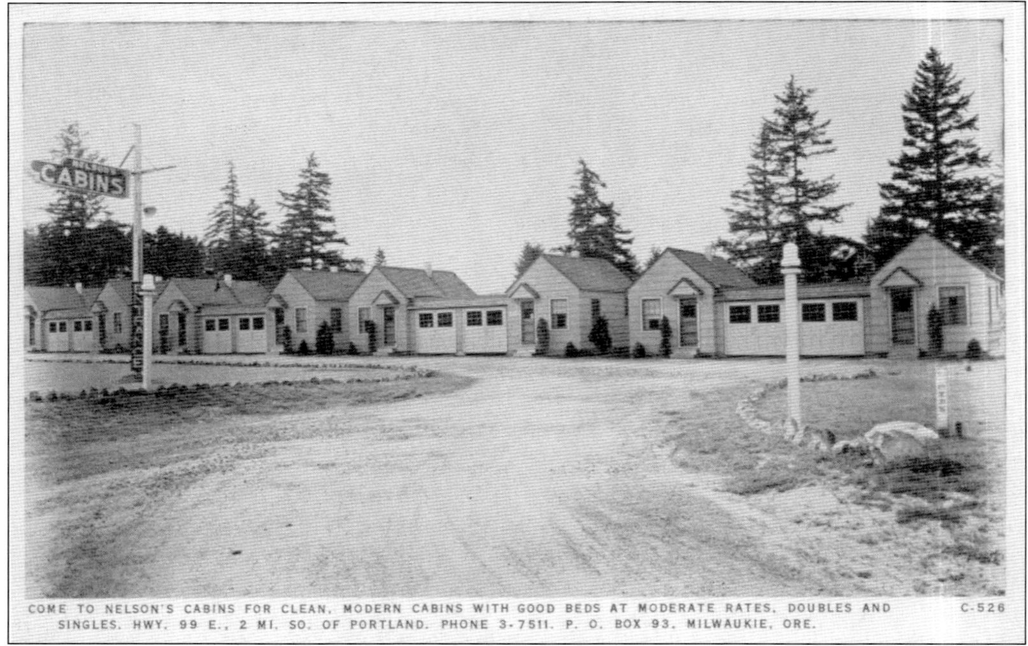

Nelson's Cabins date to at least 1939, when they were purchased by L.R. Roestel. In 1948, the 14 cabins rented for $3.50 to $7 single and $5 to $8 double. Cabins were equipped with hot and cold running water and private toilets and baths; units with kitchens came with cooking utensils and dishes. The cabins were built in pairs separated by locked garages, providing occupants some privacy.

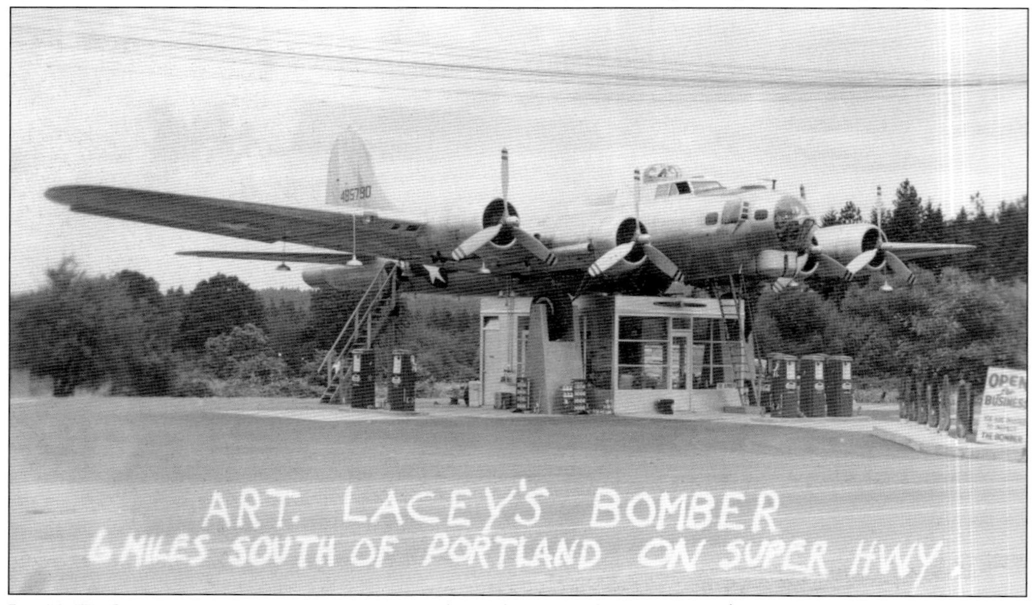

In 1947, Oregon native Art Lacey purchased a B-17 bomber for $13,000, flew it home from Oklahoma, and installed it atop his service station on McLoughlin Boulevard in Oak Grove, five miles south of Portland. Growing to 40 pumps, The Bomber claimed to be the country's largest volume independent service station. The Bomber stopped pumping gas in 1991; the plane was removed for preservation by the B-17 Alliance in 2014.

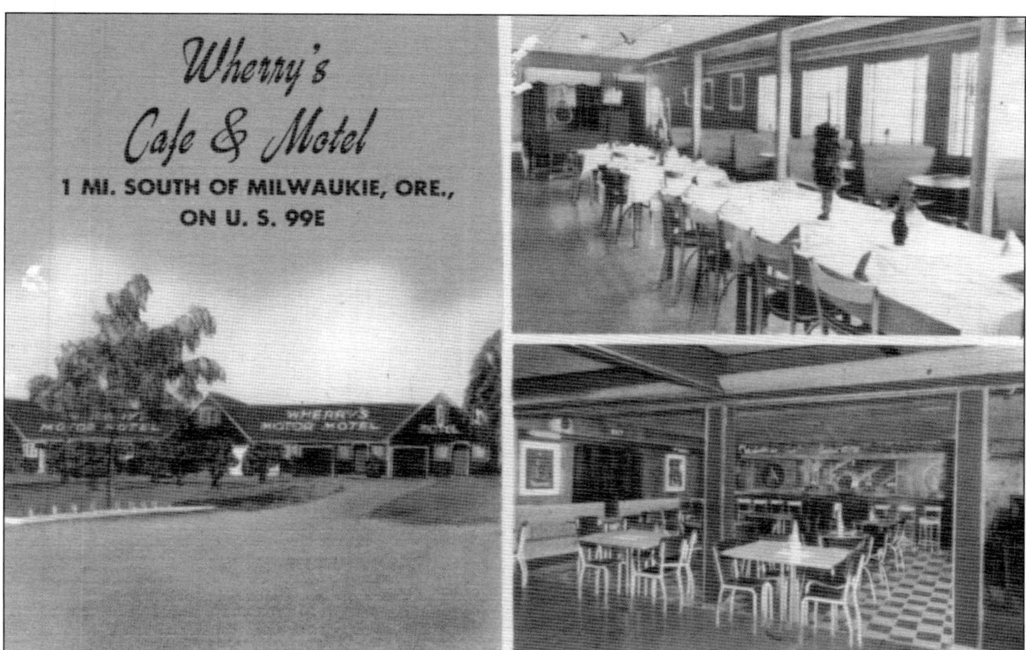

In 1934, A.C. and Emma Wherry opened Wherry's Tavern, which soon became a well-known roadhouse on the new superhighway. A motel opened in conjunction with the tavern (by then transformed into a respectable eating establishment) in 1941. The Wherrys sold out in 1945 but the new owners retained the name, and by 1950 were billing Wherry's as "Portland's Only All-Around Tourist Center." Wherry's was located directly across from The Bomber.

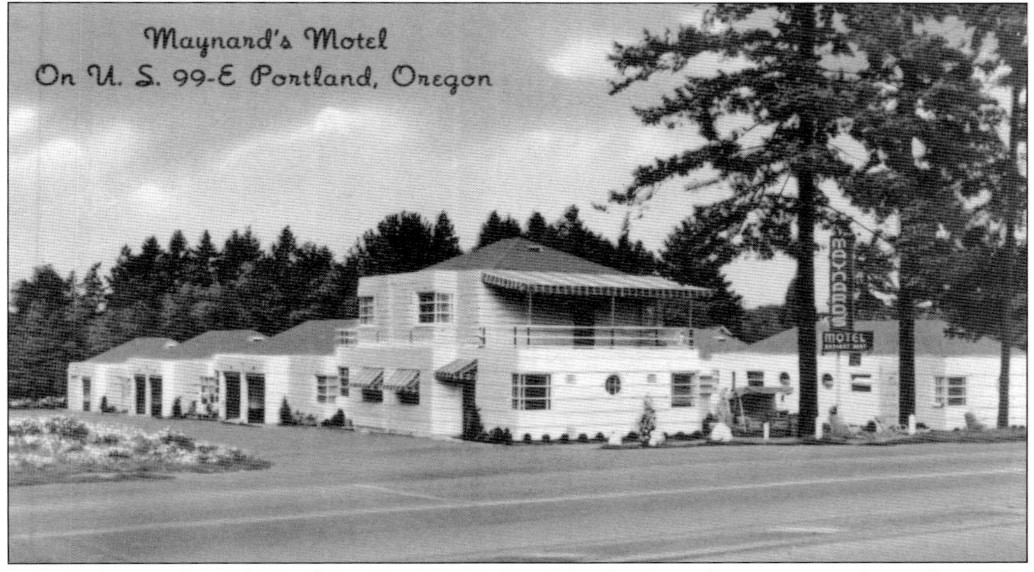

Maynard's Motel was located at 14015 SE McLoughlin Boulevard, a quarter-mile south of The Bomber. Douglas Q. and Anona Maynard opened the motel in 1946, offering 15 elegantly furnished "roomy motel units," all with private baths, radios (a vital source of entertainment in pre-television days), kitchenettes, and locked garages. Maynard's was still known by that name in 1984; today, it is operating as the Milwaukie Inn.

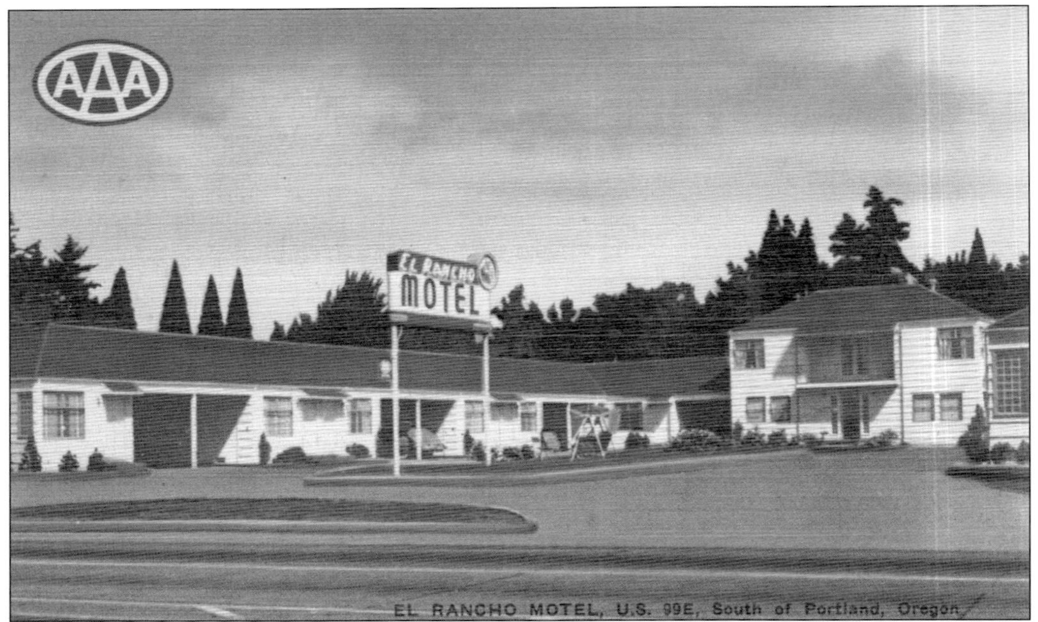

The El Rancho, open by 1949, changed ownership three times in the next few years. Located at 14110 SE McLoughlin Boulevard, the El Rancho contained 14 units in a U-shaped configuration around a grassy courtyard. Each unit featured Sealy mattresses, tiled baths, and wall-to-wall carpeting; four units had fully equipped kitchens. The prominent central building contained the office and manager's apartment. The building still stands, though not in use as a motel.

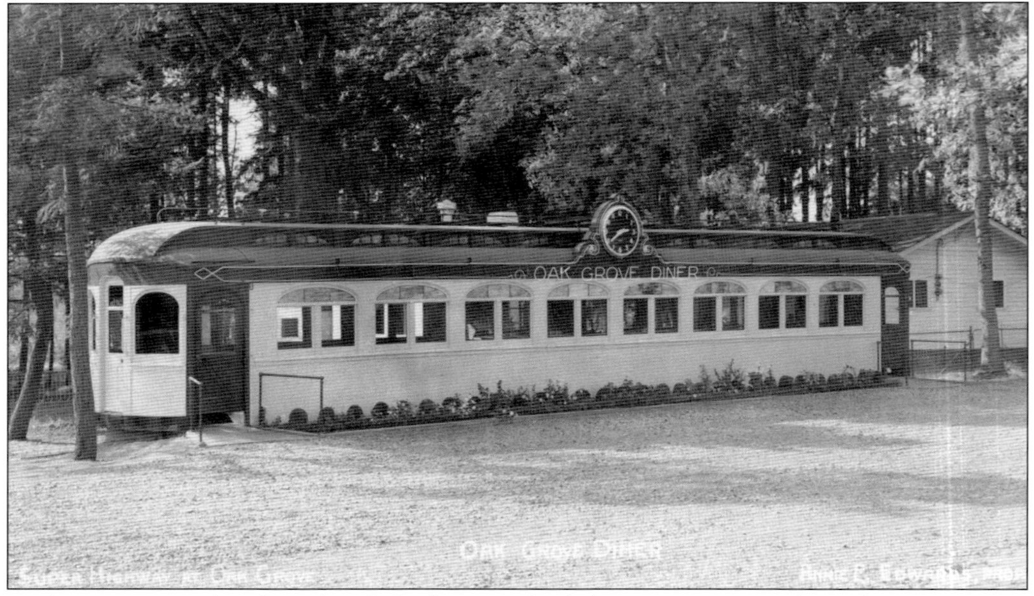

In the 1930s, as railroads replaced obsolete wood-sided passenger cars with steel, entrepreneurs purchased and repurposed the old cars as roadside businesses. Among them was Anne E. Edwards. She had an old railroad car transported to 14715 SE McLoughlin Boulevard and positioned at an angle facing the highway. With the addition of an ornate clock and neon signage, the Oak Grove Diner opened for business in January 1937. (CCHS.)

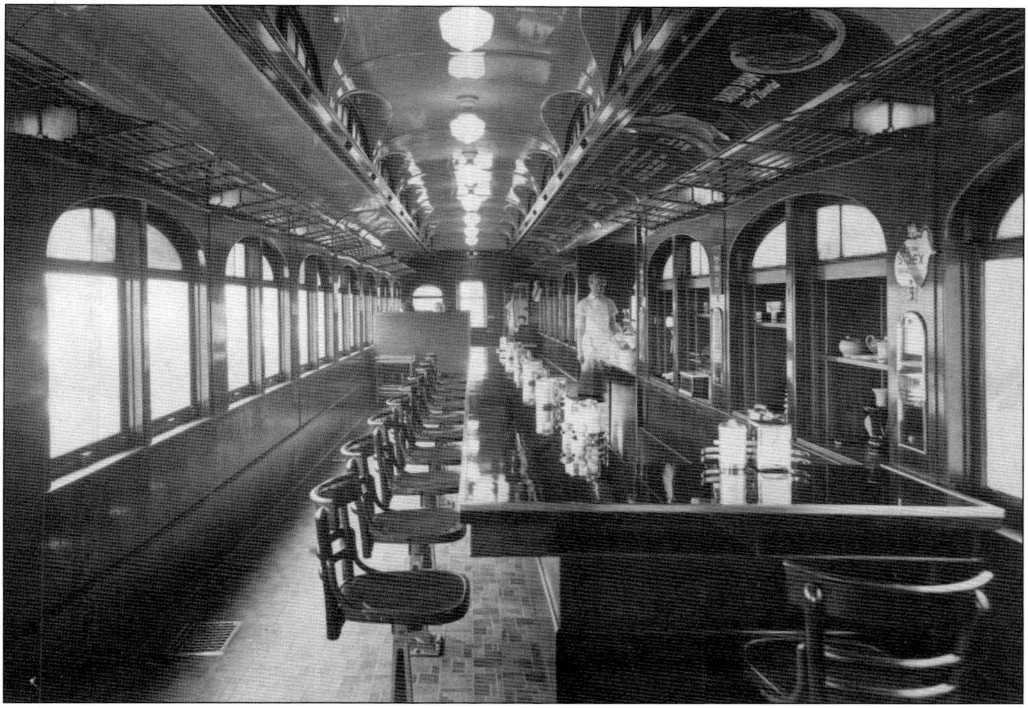

Behind the counter, a woman—probably owner Anne Edwards—is pictured surveying the gleaming interior of the Oak Grove Diner. Signs advertising chili (15¢ a bowl) and other specials line the walls; the cash register and other utensils sit in window alcoves of the railroad-car-turned-diner. Owned by Jack Horner in later years, it was offered for sale in 1964—to be moved—and has since disappeared.

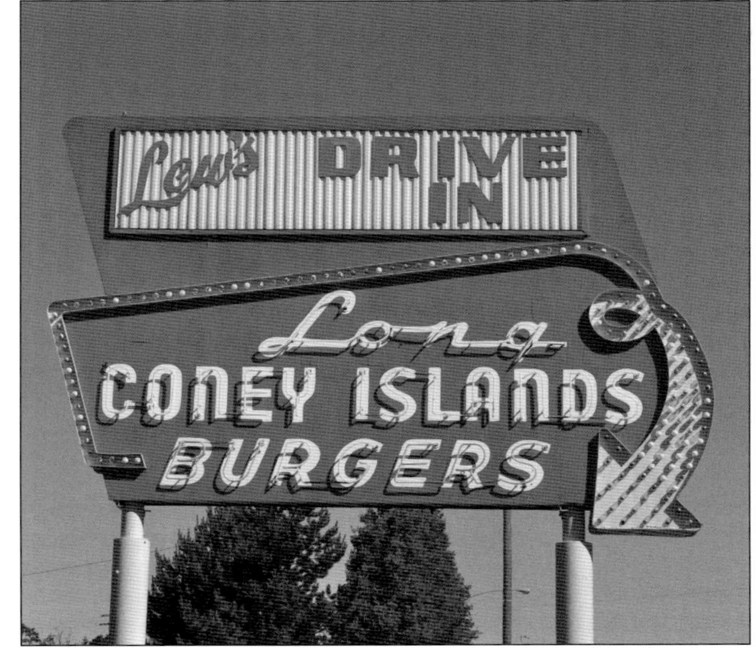

Lew's has been a southeast Portland fixture since 1957, when Lew and Betty Johnson bought an old restaurant at 14911 SE McLoughlin Boulevard and transformed it into Lew's Dari Freeze. A new building and the giant sign went up two years later. Famous for 11-inch Coney Island hot dogs topped with "secret mix sauce" and classic burgers, Lew's menu also features everything from breakfast to wraps and nachos.

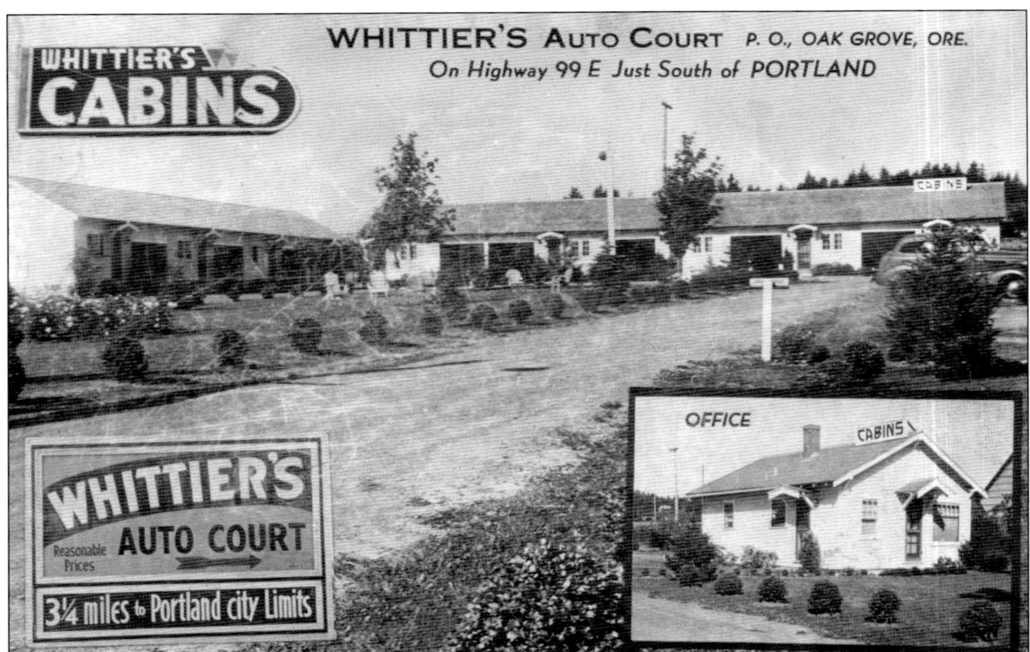

Whittier's Auto Court was located at 15018 SE McLoughlin Boulevard in Oak Grove. Its nine units—featuring private toilets and showers, hot and cold running water, kitchenettes, and carports—rented for $3 to $5 a night in 1948. Mr. and Mrs. Joseph W. Bouska purchased Whittier's in 1954. Four years later, they were tied up by three gun-wielding men who robbed them of $400 in cash and jewelry.

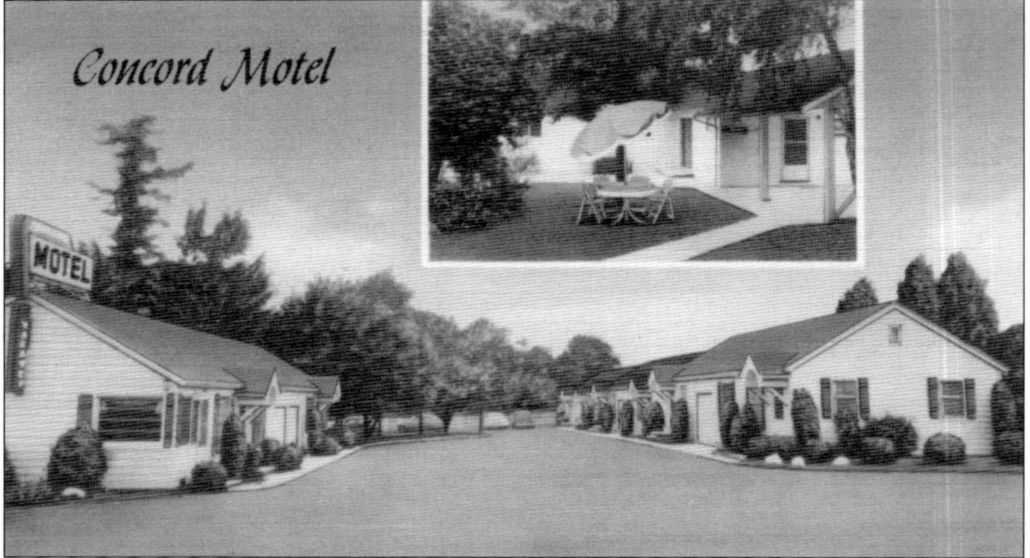

The Concord Motel dates to at least 1939. Owned by Mr. and Mrs. George Dougherty, the Concord offered "hotel accommodations" in a motel setting—eight units, all with such modern luxuries as automatic heating, insulation, and tile baths, at nightly rates of $2.50 to $3.50 single, $4 to $4.50 double. Gabled entrances to individual units added a nice touch. The two rows of cottages still stand at 15717 SE McLoughlin Boulevard.

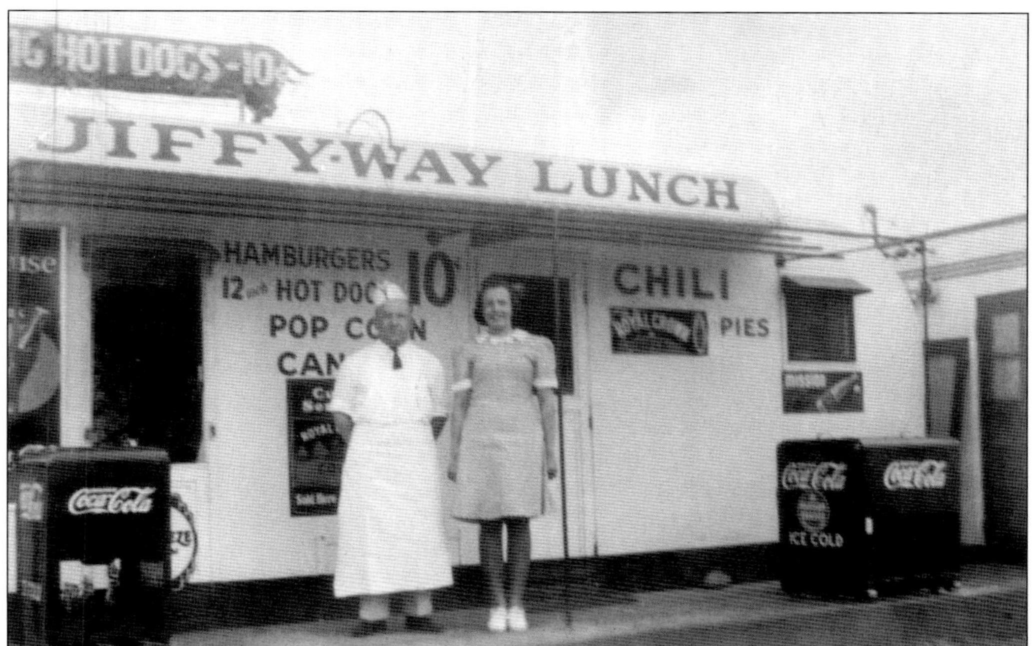

Envisioning a chain of Jiffy-Way Lunches throughout the Pacific Northwest, Roy Dowell custom-built trailer-style lunch wagons complete with counters and kitchens. Charles Doud bought the first unit in 1937, installed it at Jennings Lodge, attached a sign (a neon-lit dachshund) on the roof, and sold foot-long hot dogs for 10¢. At that time, Doud's Jiffy-Way was the only lunch stop along the superhighway between Portland and Oregon City. (JR.)

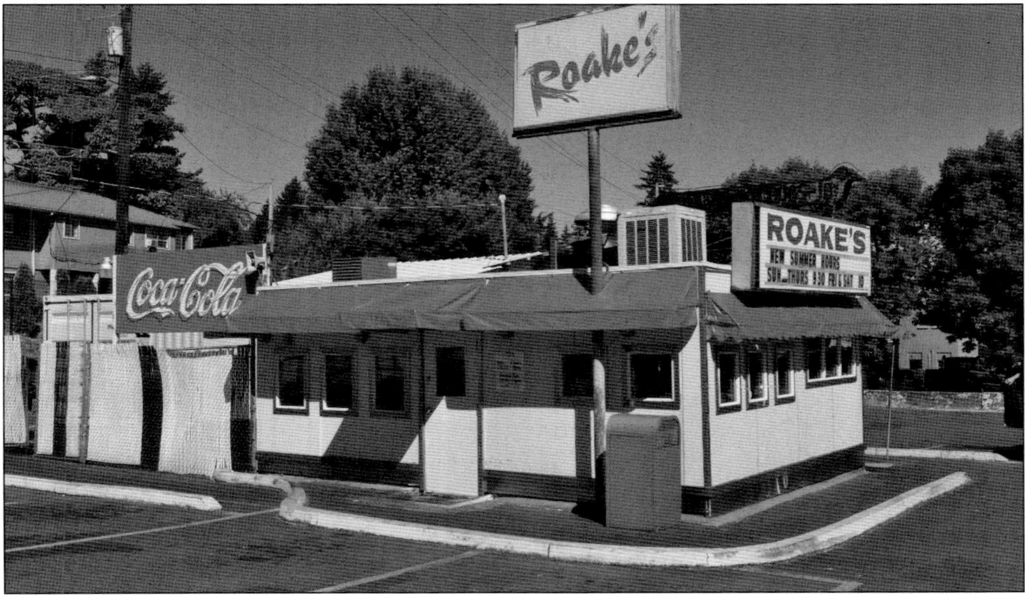

By 1939, Doud had sold out to Ed Berdine and headed south to open additional Jiffy-Ways in Roseburg and Grants Pass. Berdine and son-in-law Dale Ficken continued to operate the original Jiffy Way for nearly three decades. Jim Roake purchased the place in 1976 and renamed it Roake's. It has been a Highway 99 institution ever since, serving as many as 100,000 hot dogs per year.

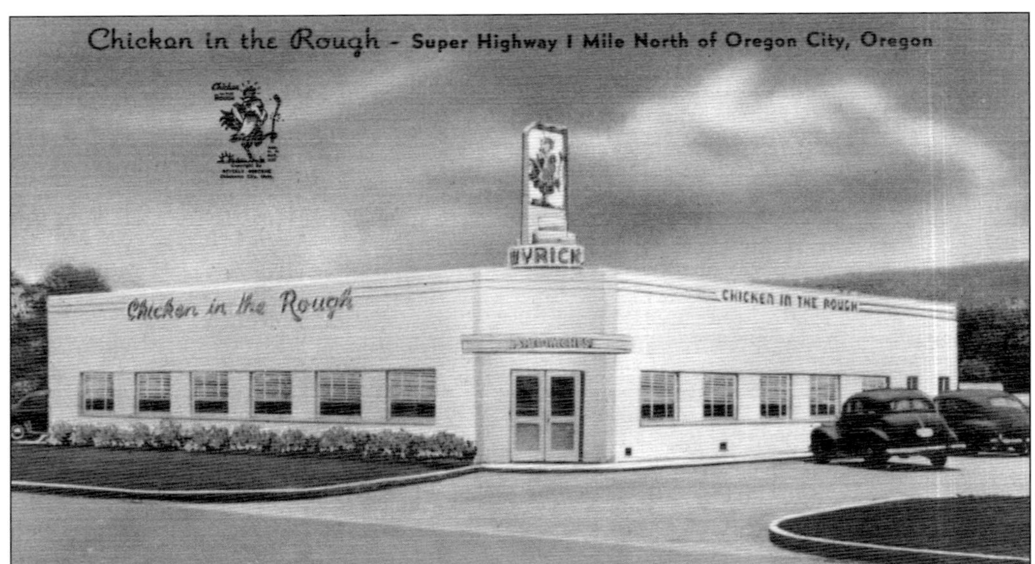

Chicken in the Rough was a franchised chain of restaurants originating in Oklahoma in the 1930s. Its specialty dish was half a fried chicken served unjointed without silverware (thus "rough"), accompanied by shoestring potatoes and honey. The restaurant's mascot was a golf-playing rooster. Wyrick's Chicken in the Rough, the local outlet, was located on Highway 99E just north of the Clackamas River Bridge. The building now houses Stanley's Corner.

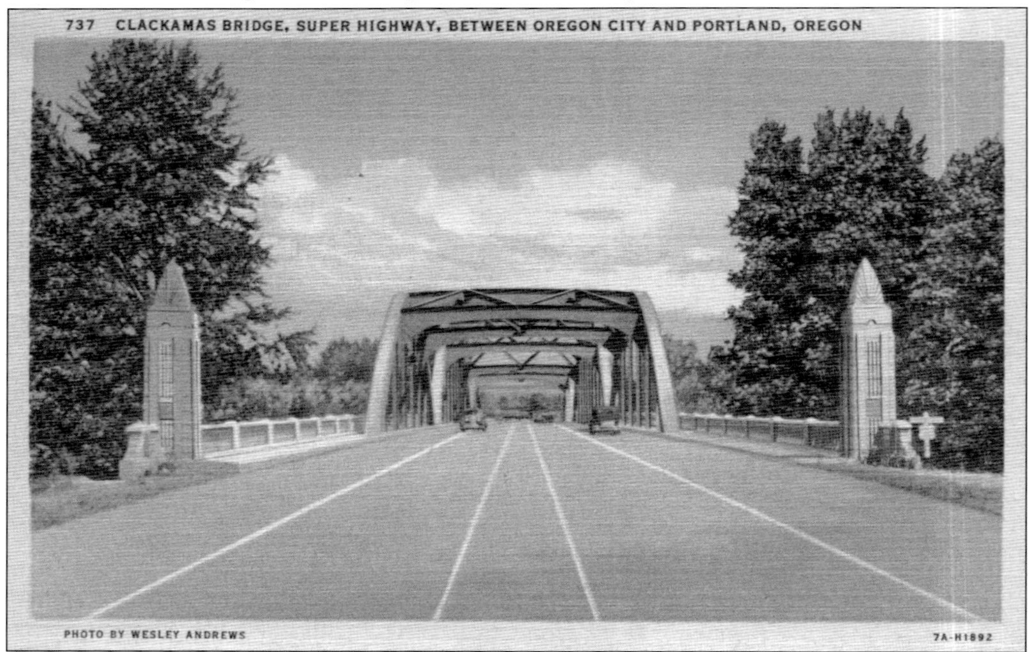

A major component of the proposed east side superhighway was a new bridge across the Clackamas River. The early bridge, still standing at Park Place, was a traffic bottleneck. A bridge of modern design and four lanes capable of handling large volumes of traffic was needed. Construction began in early 1932. It opened for traffic in July 1933 and was formally dedicated as the McLoughlin Bridge that August.

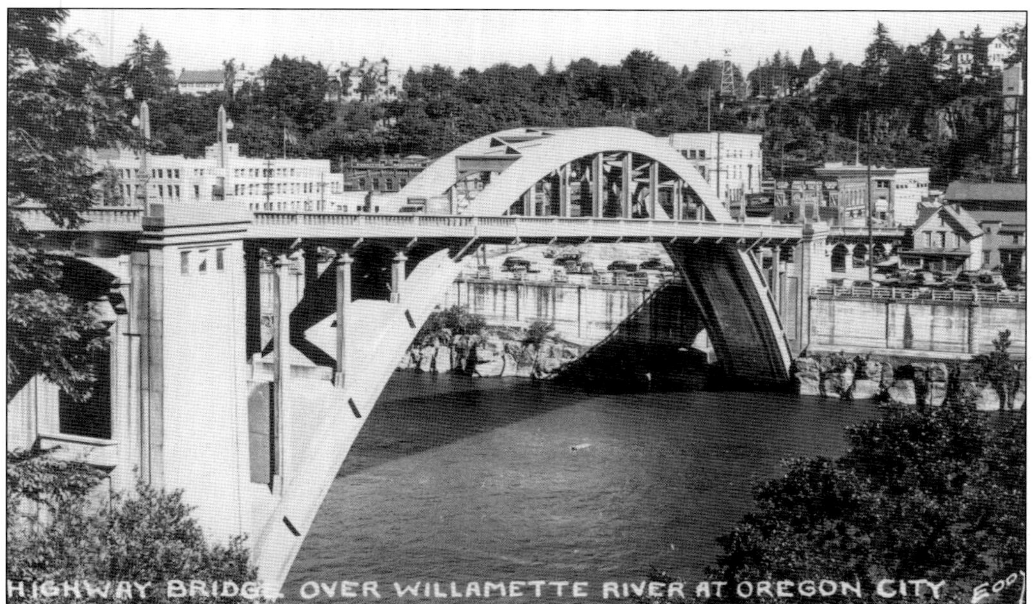

Terwilliger Boulevard, the early Pacific Highway route south from Portland, crossed the Willamette River between West Linn and Oregon City on the bridge shown here. Designed by famed architect Conde McCullough, when constructed in 1922 it was encased in a sand-and-concrete mix called Gunite for protection against caustic air pollution from nearby paper mills. Fully restored and reopened in 2012, it is listed in the National Register of Historic Places.

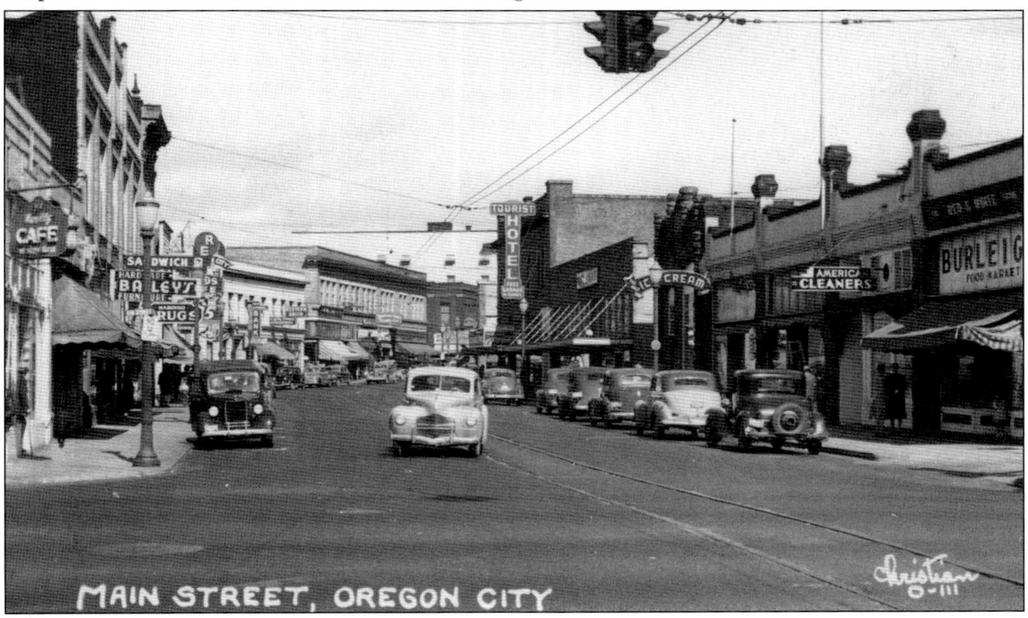

Once across, the Oregon City Bridge traffic flowed east on 7th Street to Main Street, then south on Main through downtown Oregon City before jogging left onto 5th Street and curving along the bluff southward and on to New Era and Canby. Signs abound in this photograph: Bailey's Hardware and Furniture, Harding Drugs, First National Bank, the Tourist Hotel, The Malt Shop, and American Cleaners, among others.

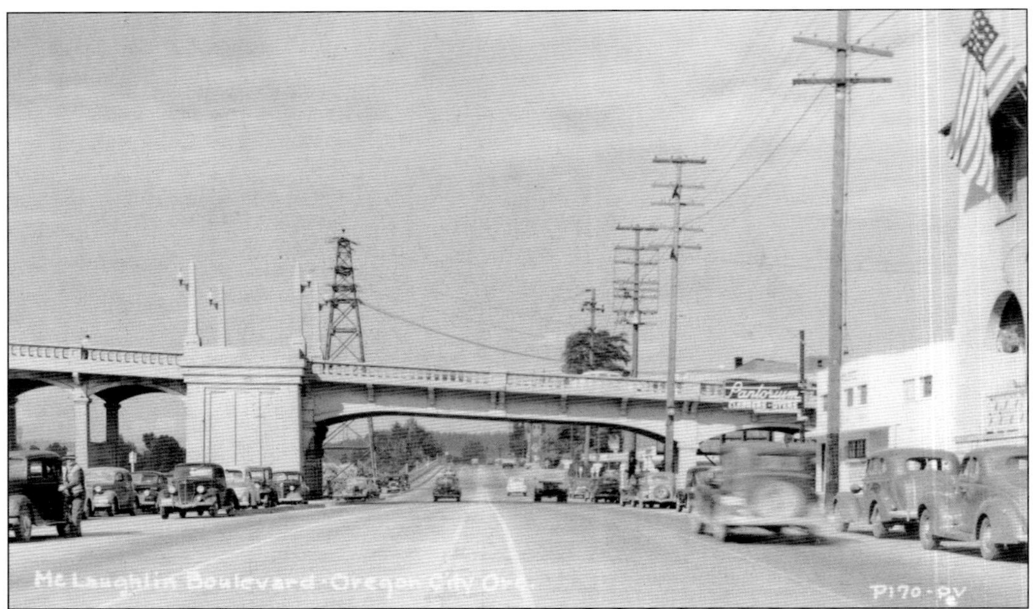

With four-lane McLoughlin Boulevard pouring increased volumes of traffic into downtown, by the mid-1930s, Oregon City was a major bottleneck for motorists. Several years of discussion culminated in a 1936 state highway department decision to reroute the Pacific Highway around downtown via Water and 5th Streets. The new segment opened in late 1940. This view looks north, with McLoughlin Boulevard passing beneath 7th Street and the old Oregon City Bridge.

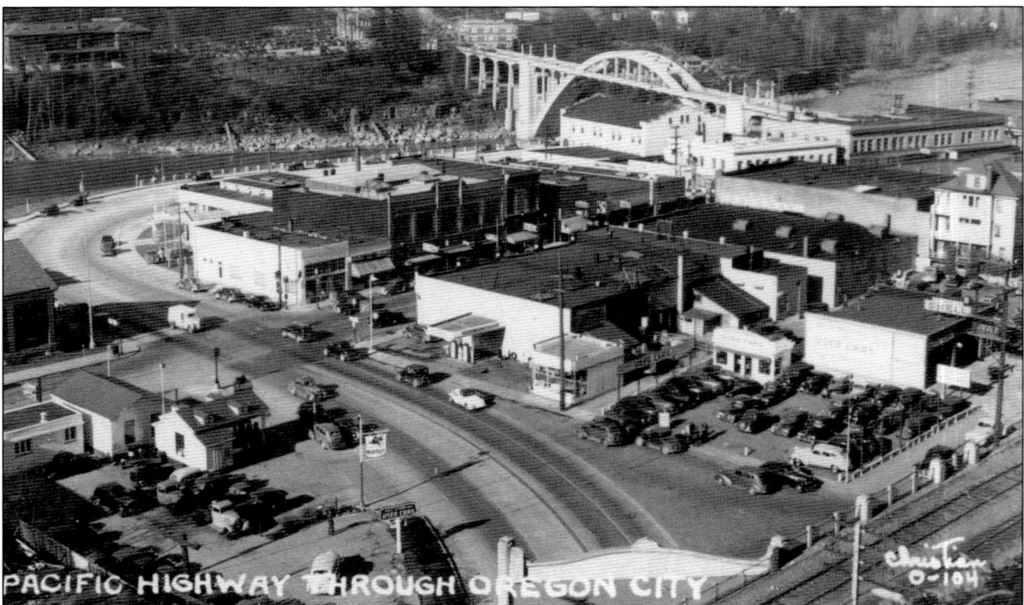

This north-facing view lays out the highway alignments in Oregon City. At the top, the Oregon City Bridge, the original route of the Pacific Highway, carried traffic onto 7th Street (hidden behind a building) with a turn south onto Main Street. The prominent intersection at left center is 5th and Main Streets. The Highway 99E bypass follows the river, curving to that same intersection before passing under the railroad tracks.

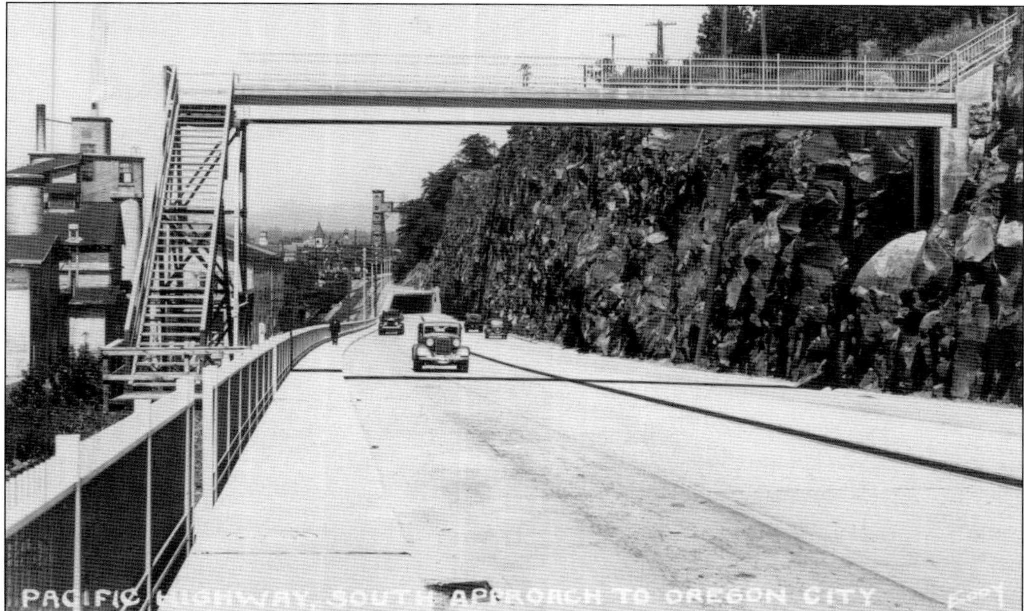

Oregon City's south end, constrained by 50-foot-high Willamette Falls, railroad tracks, and a 130-foot bluff on the east, has long been occupied by heavy industry. To overcome this combination of geography and industrialization, the Pacific Highway (and later Highway 99) carved an angle up the face of the bluff to gain sufficient elevation to exit (or, as shown here, to enter) the city.

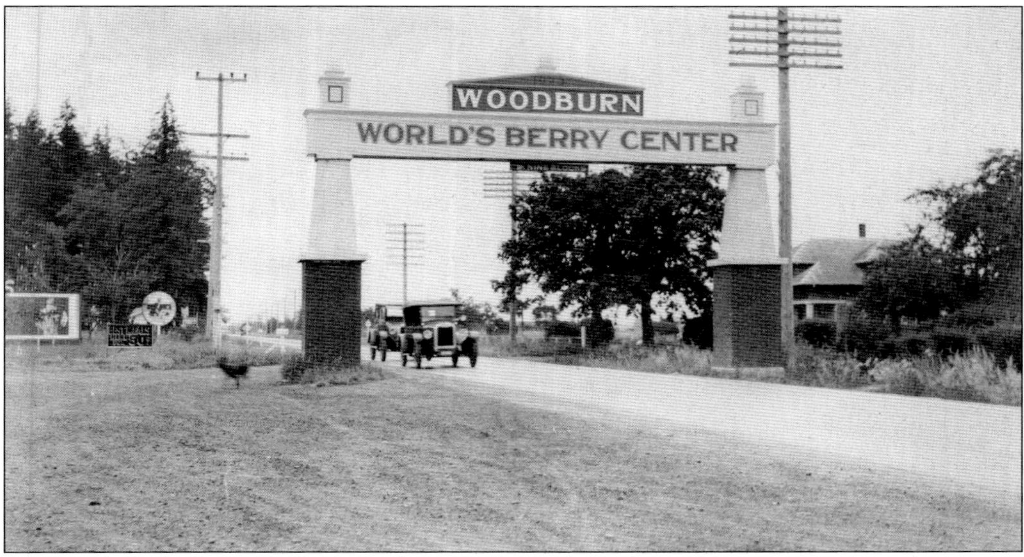

In 1923, Woodburn erected its famous arch across the Pacific Highway, proclaiming itself the "world's berry center" and directing motorists to downtown, nine blocks west. In just a few years, traffic had increased so much that the brick columns supporting the arch became a traffic hazard and it was ordered removed. Highway widening in 1933 included efforts to move and preserve the arch, but it was irreversibly damaged. (OSL, 43556.)

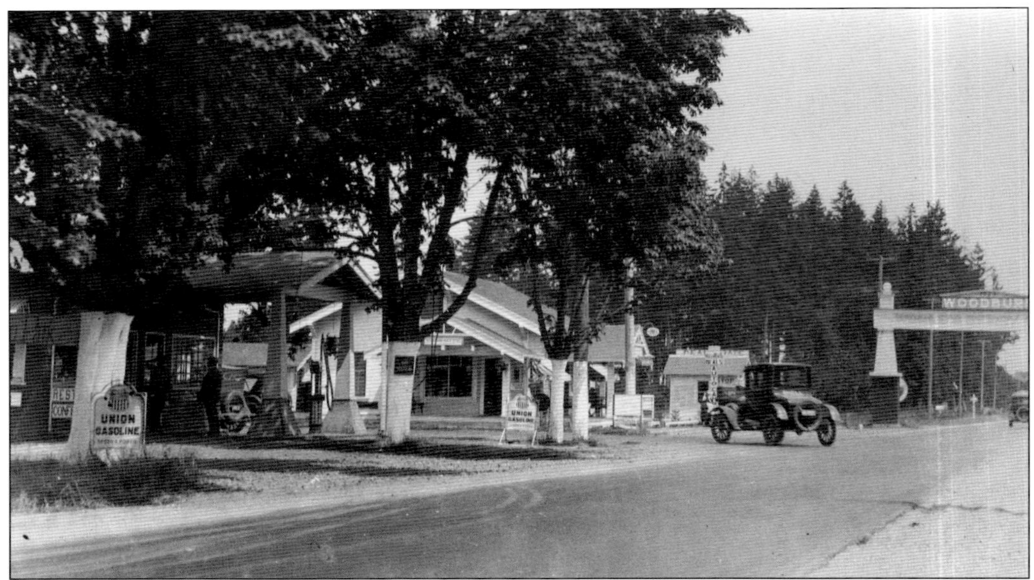

A cluster of roadside businesses were built up around the arch, including the Woodburn Arch Store. A combination grocery–restaurant–bus depot with an auto camp immediately adjacent, the Woodburn Arch Store outlasted the arch itself, surviving until at least 1942 when it was relocated 200 feet to the north. This 1923 view looks north along the Pacific Highway from its intersection with Young Street. (OSL, 43411.)

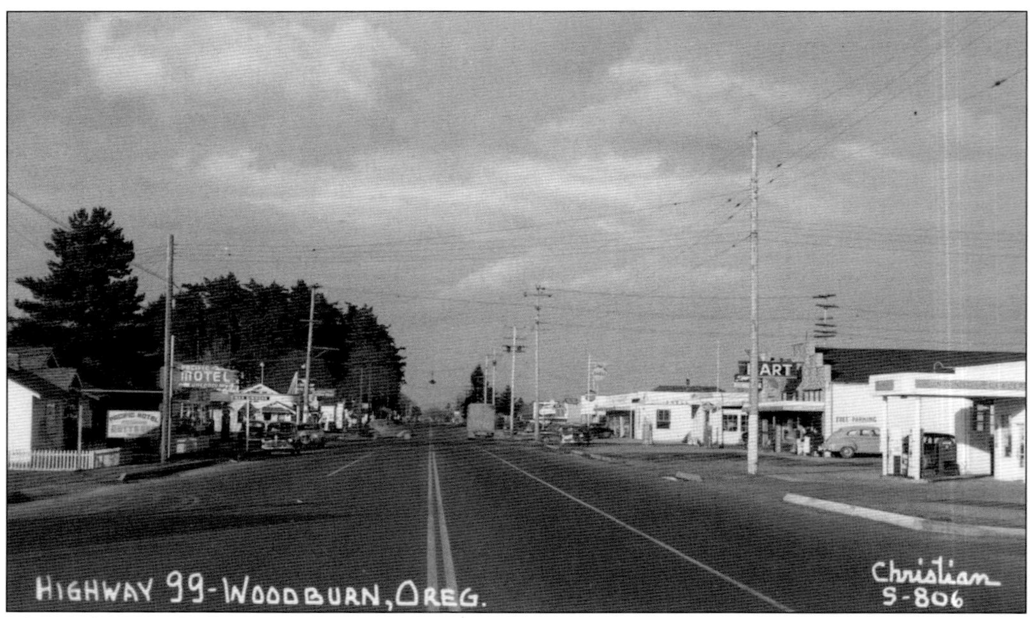

This is the same location looking north on Highway 99E, 30 years later. The Woodburn Arch stood about where the hanging blinker light is in this view. Signs for the Pacific Motel and Cottages, Max Simmons Chevron Service, and a coffee shop lined the left side of the highway; across the road were a grocery store and Shell station. Other than the Pacific Motel (now apartments), very little of this scene exists today.

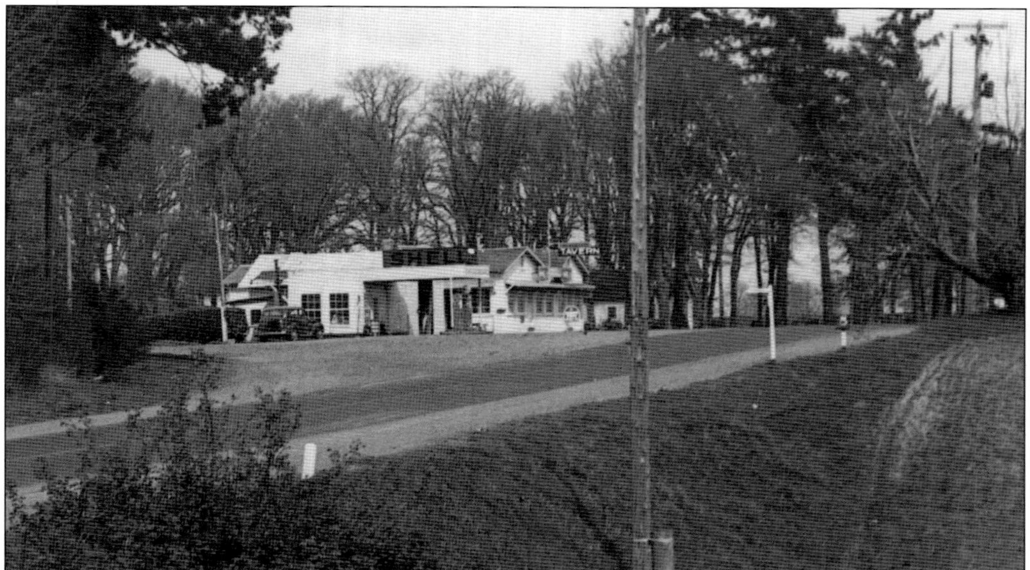

J.H. Campbell's Checker Board Tavern, Auto Camp, and Shell Service Station was located on the Pacific Highway about a mile south of the turnoff to downtown Gervais. In 1928, Campbell added a new dining room with old English–style booths and a hardwood floor for dancing. He expanded again a few years later, building cabins for his growing tourist trade. Today, the building is the Last Chance Tavern. (OSL, 23018.)

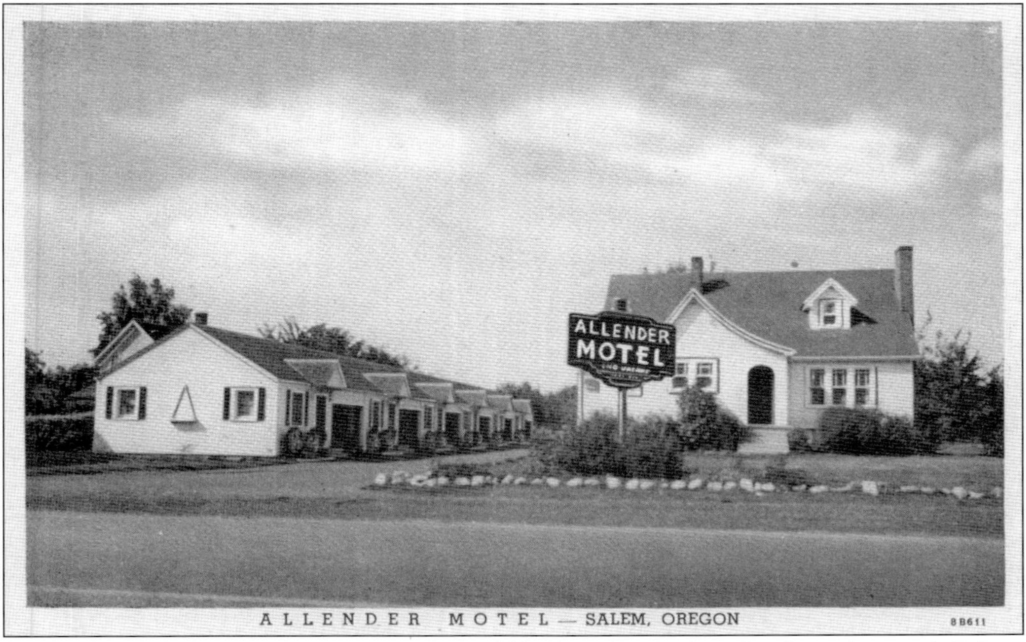

In 1946, the six-unit Spencer's Auto Court could be found at 4195 Portland Road in north Salem. When Clyde and Anna Allender assumed ownership two years later, they renamed it the Allender Motel. After Clyde died in 1956, Anna operated the motel until 1959. It later became the Ila V. Motel and was sold in 1963 for service station construction. There is a Jack in the Box at that address today.

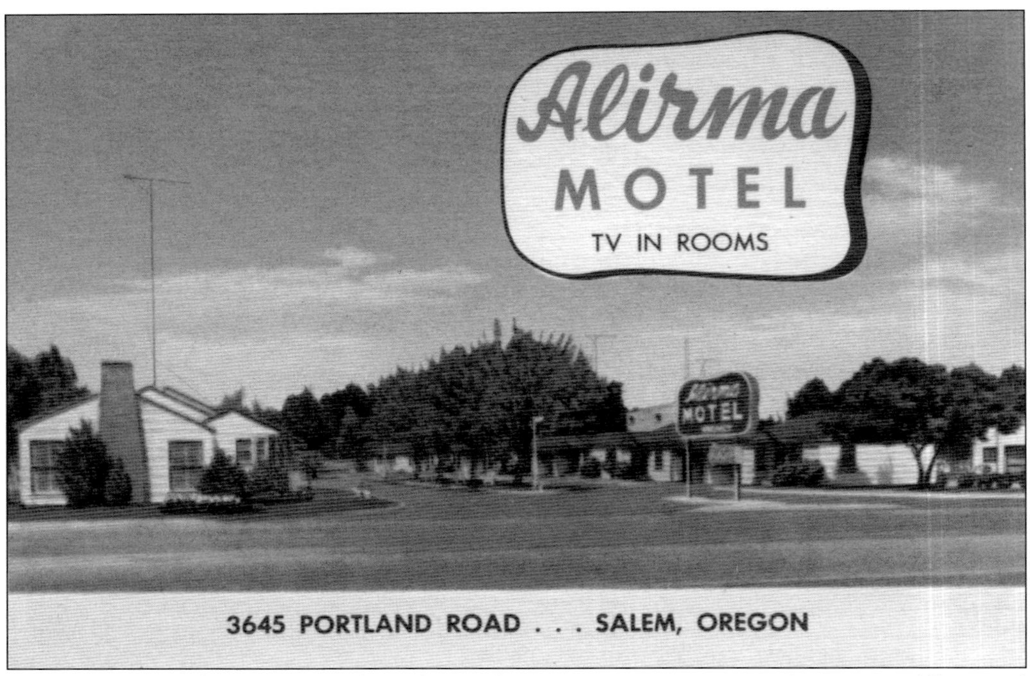

The Alirma Motel's name came from those of its owners. Longtime motel operators Albert and Irma Sauers, who had previously operated the Nod-A-Way Motel a quarter mile farther south on the highway, constructed the Alirma in 1946. Its 11 units were arranged in two parallel rows flanking a shaded greenspace. Located at 3645 Portland Road, the Alirma survived into the 2000s; the site is a business complex today.

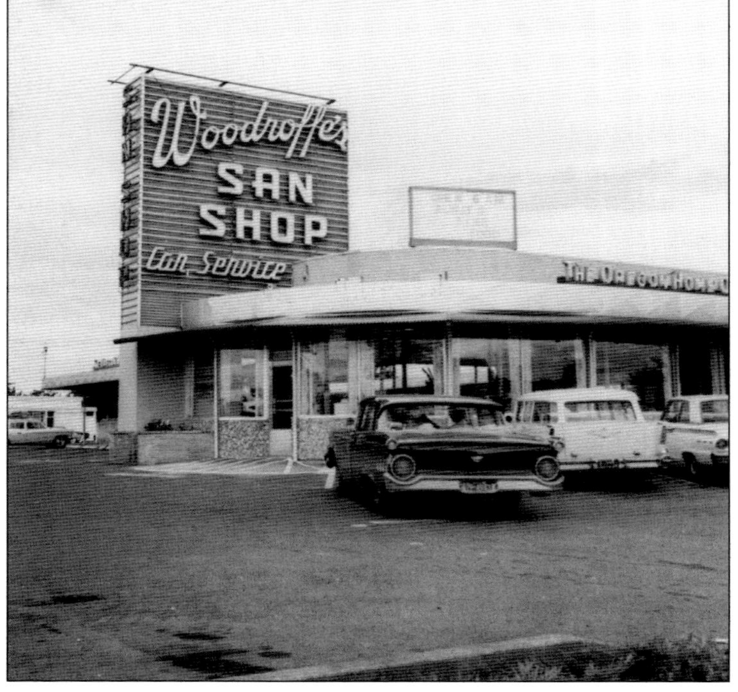

Paul and Helen Woodroffe opened Woodroffe's San Shop, at 3400 Portland Road, in 1950. Breakfast, lunch, and dinner were on the menu, with featured items such as broiled Sanburgers, a special roast turkey dinner for 85¢ on Sundays, and their own brand of ice cream. After a remodel and grand-reopening in 1959, "Woodroffe's" was dropped from the name. It continued business as The San Shop into the mid-1960s. (OSA, OAG0192.)

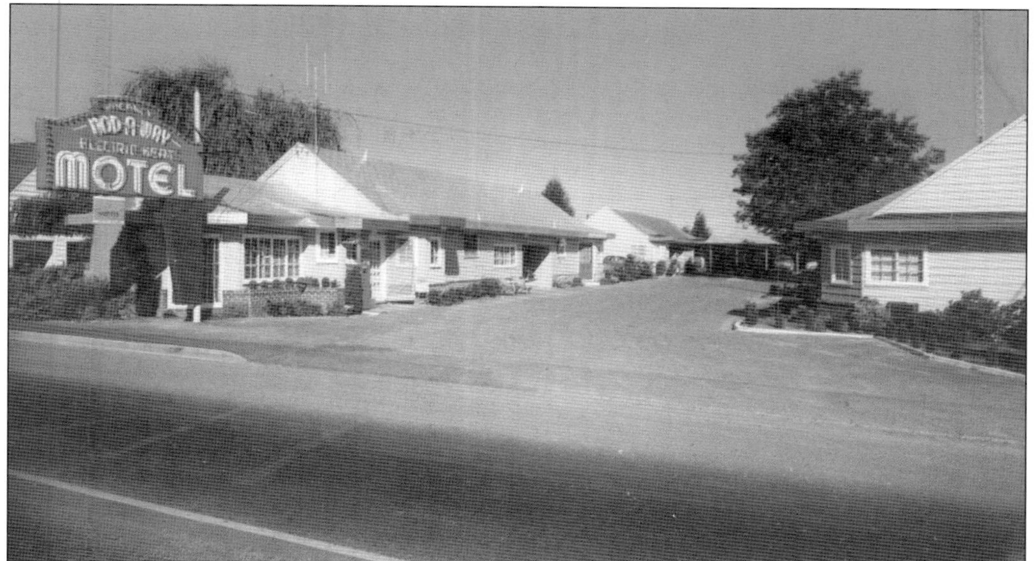

Albert and Irma Sauers operated the 12-unit Nod-A-Way Motel for several years before opening the Alirma back up the highway. After the Sauers departed, the Nod-A-Way changed hands frequently—four times in three years—before Clarence Bartell took over in 1945. Located at 3355 Portland Road, it was known in later years as the Mar-Don Motel. It is in use today as the Alder North Cottages apartments.

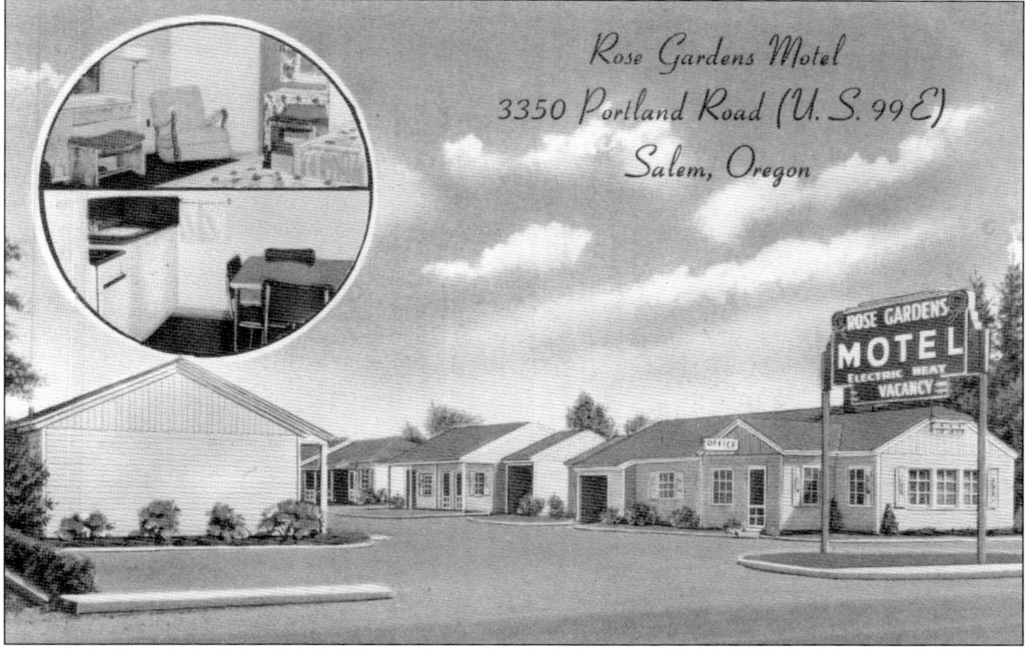

Halvorson Construction Company broke ground for the $75,000 Rose Gardens Motel in November 1945. When it opened a year later, the motel consisted of 14 one-room and 6 two-room cabins with kitchens, baths, and dressing rooms, as well as a dwelling and office for the manager. A rose garden fronted each cabin. The Rose Gardens survived into the 1990s, but the site at 3350 Portland Road is now an empty lot.

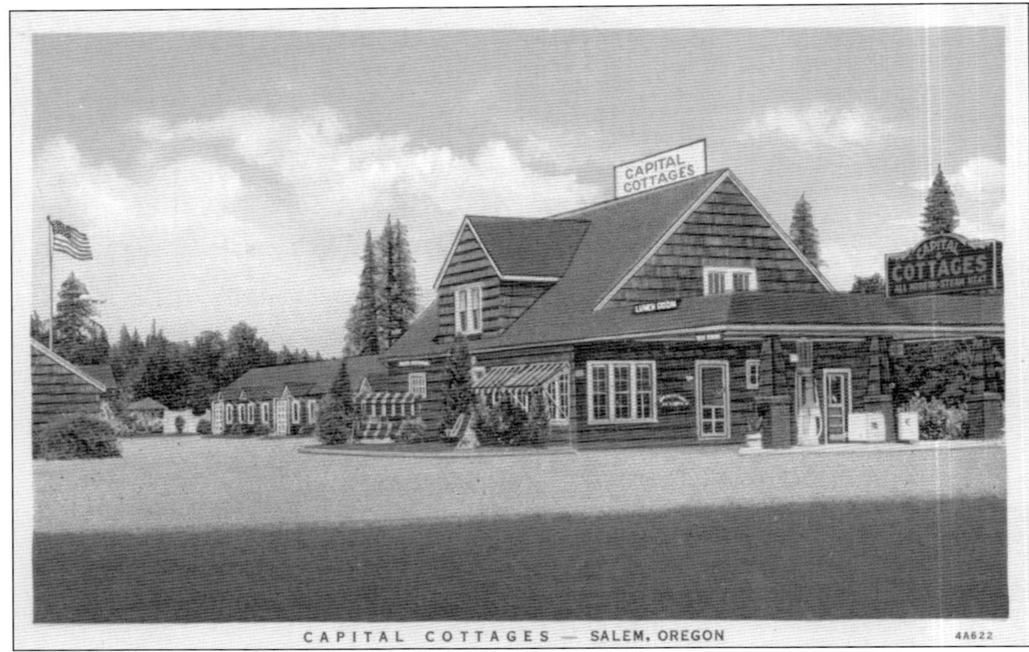

James and Mabel Kriesel billed their Capital Cottages as "a distinctive automobile tourist hotel." Opened in 1932 at 3305 Portland Road, the court consisted of 16 cottages (eight with kitchenettes; all with Beautyrest mattresses, steam heat, and private garages), a gas station, and a combination coffee shop/lunchroom/beer parlor. In 1948, room rates were $3.50 to $6 single, $7 to $8 double. Still in business in 1964, the site is now a vacant lot.

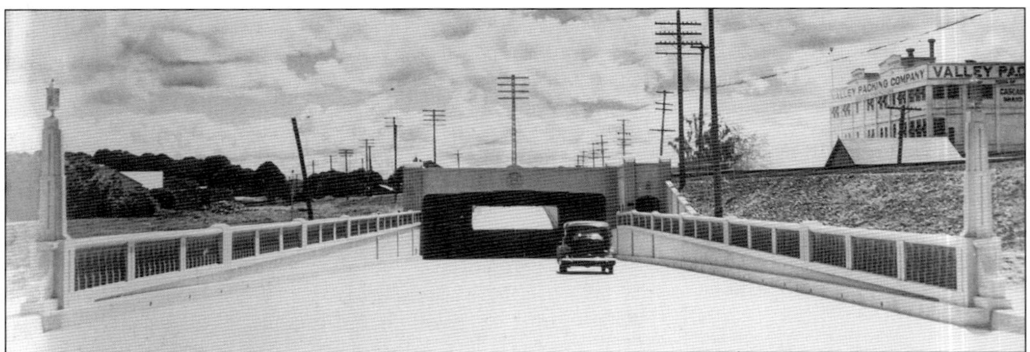

A mile and a half north of Salem, the Pacific Highway crossed the Southern Pacific Railroad tracks at ground level until 1936. That year, construction of a $300,000 underpass eliminated one of the state's most heavily traveled grade crossings. At 44 feet wide with four traffic lanes, pedestrian tunnels edged by concrete handrails, and retaining walls sporting lighting stanchions, the underpass was a remarkable example of utilitarian elegance. (OSL, 26662.)

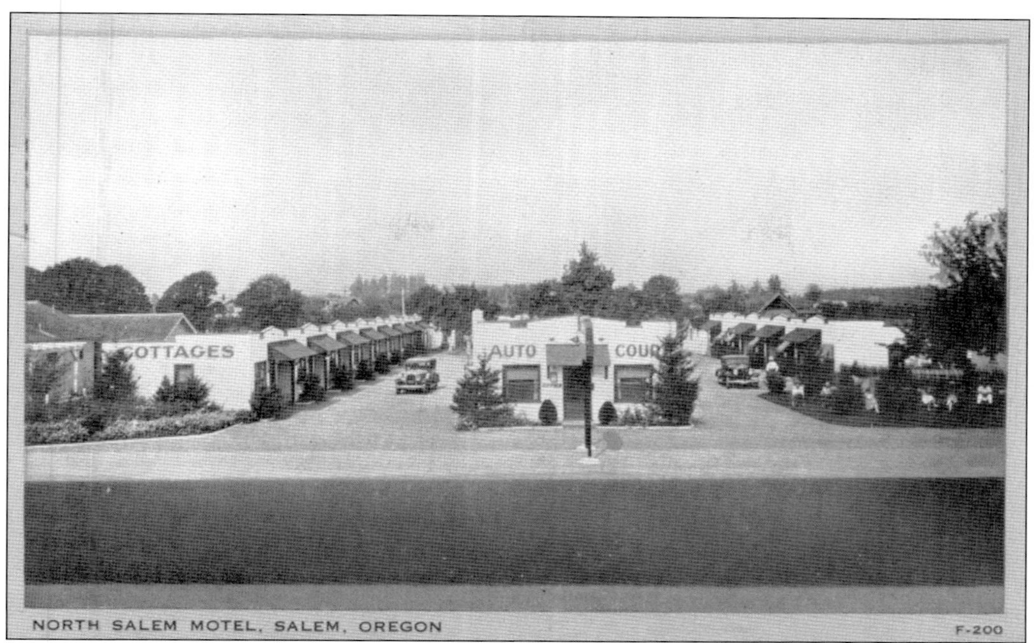

The North Salem Auto Court, among Salem's oldest, dated to at least 1932. The court consisted of 20 stucco cottages set in a U-shape around a central office and lawn. Each unit was "luxuriously furnished and ultra-modern in every detail" with colorful tiled baths. It went through a succession of owners over the years before disappearing around 1960. The site, at 2673 Portland Road, is now a used car lot.

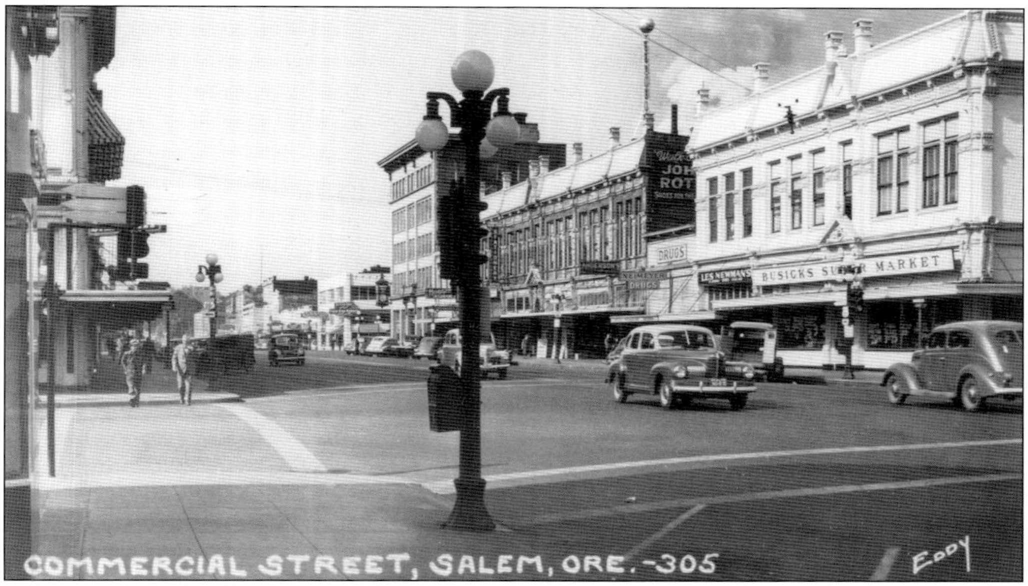

Salem's early business district focused on the Willamette River. By the dawn of the auto age, Commercial Street, carrying the Pacific Highway through the city, was the heart of downtown. This view looking south from Court Street predates 1951, the year a one-way couplet was created: southbound motorists traveled on Commercial while northbound traffic followed Liberty Street, a block away. Many of these buildings are still standing. (WHC, 2011.006.0324.)

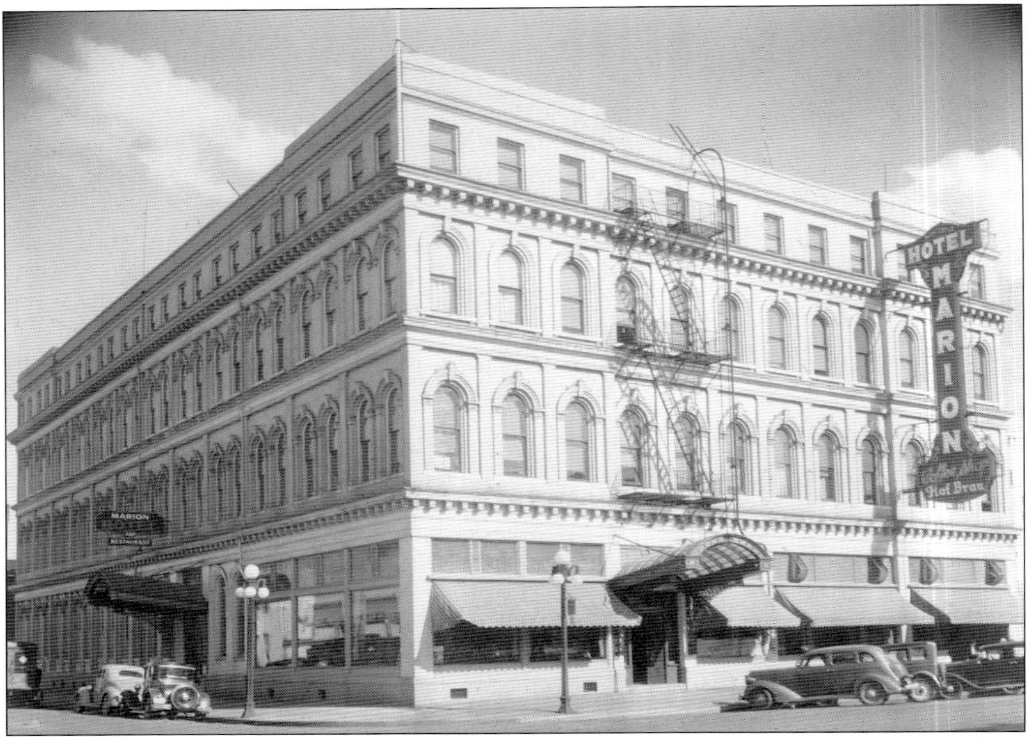

Opened in stagecoach days as the Chemeketa House, this grand old establishment had been renamed the Marion Hotel by the time of this 1939 photograph. The nightly rate for its 124 AAA-approved rooms was $1 and up, and its restaurant, the Hof Brau, was billed as "Salem's newest, most modern eating establishment." Located at Commercial and Ferry Streets, the Marion was destroyed by fire in 1971 after a century of service. (OSL, 22272.)

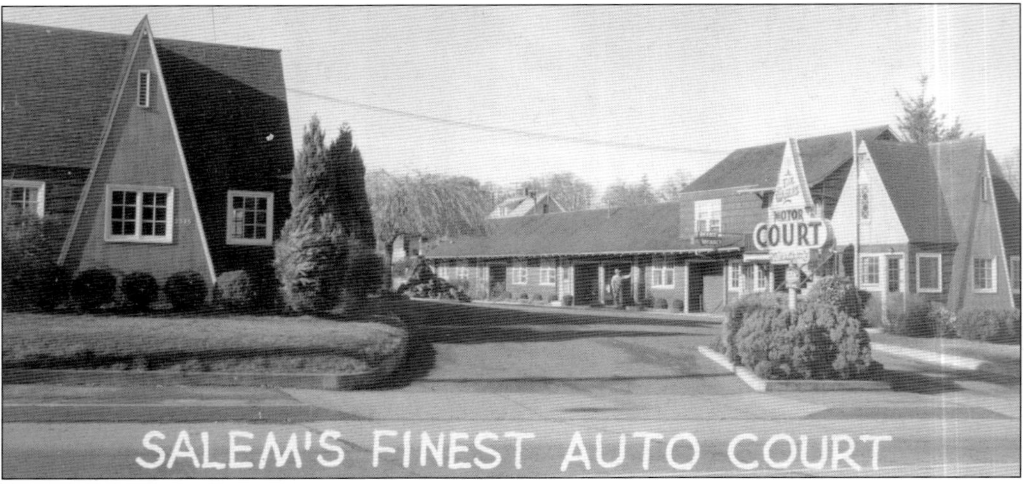

Only the entrance buildings were gabled at The Gables Motor Court. The nine AAA-approved units were equipped with Beautyrest mattresses and tile baths; some units had fully stocked kitchenettes including dishes and utensils. In 1948, an overnight stay cost $3.50 to $4 single, $5.50 to $6 double. A mid-1950s remodel changed the name to Gables Motel and added television and wall-to-wall carpeting to each unit. The location, at 2375 S Commercial, is now a Wendy's.

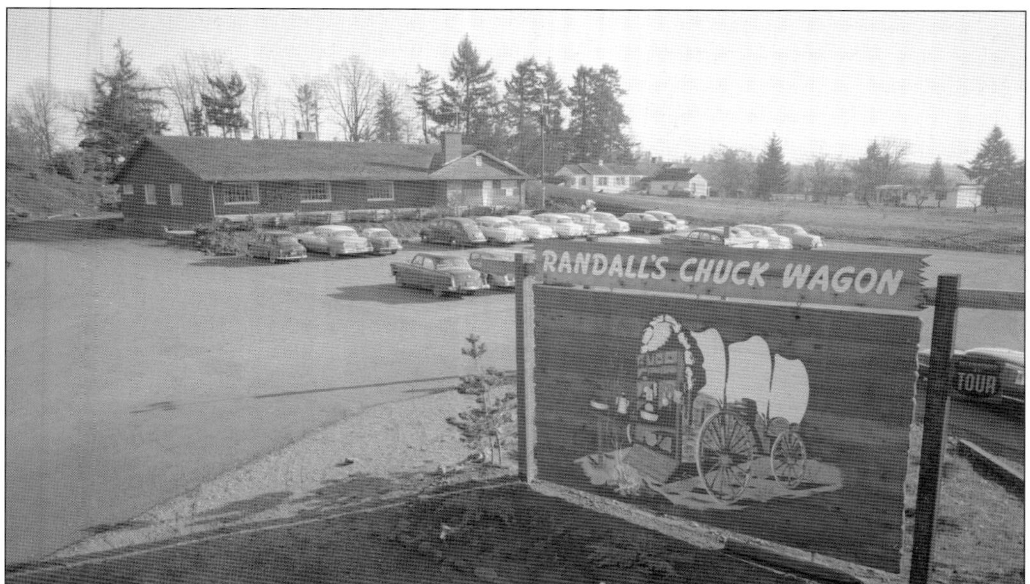

In 1951, Joe Randall retired from 25 years of owning the Golden Pheasant in downtown Salem. A few years later, he was back with plans for a restaurant-motel complex on Highway 99E just south of town. Randall's Chuck Wagon opened in 1954 with ranch-style construction, early American decor, seafood bar, dance floor, and three-tier backyard patio. The original (though remodeled) building is still in use at 3170 S Commercial. (WHC, 2006.002.1930.002.)

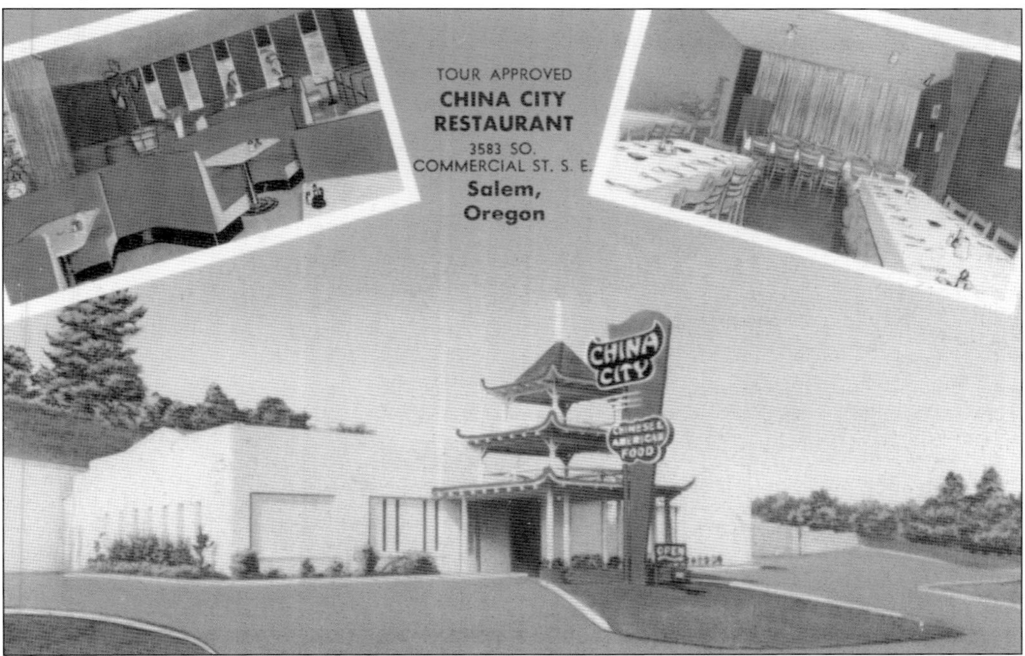

In August 1953, business partners George Chinn, Timmy Yup, and Donald Yee opened the China City Restaurant at 3583 S Commercial in the rapidly developing south Salem district. An immediate success, the restaurant served "rare Chinese delicacies and delicious American foods . . . in quiet Oriental luxury." It was later known as Chinn's and is still in business as the Hong Kong House.

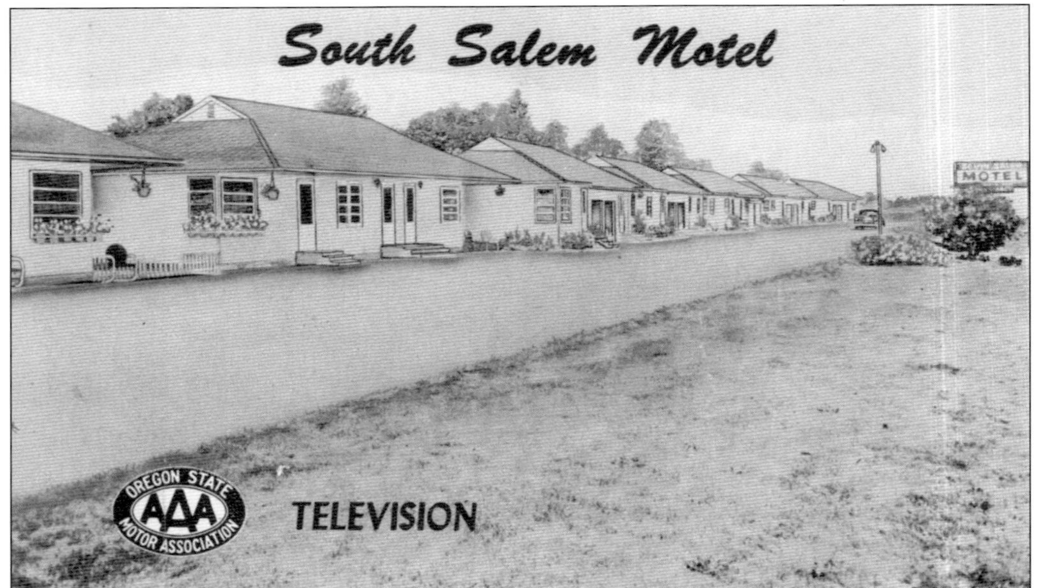

The South Salem Motel, at 3581 S Commercial, opened in late 1946 with 10 apartments and 8 sleeping units. Owners A.A. and Mary Larsen sold the motel to S.H. and Ruth Domsted for $90,000 in March 1953. Tragedy struck later that year when Frances Hardman was strangled in cabin 13 by her husband, Jack, who later committed suicide. It is a parking lot today.

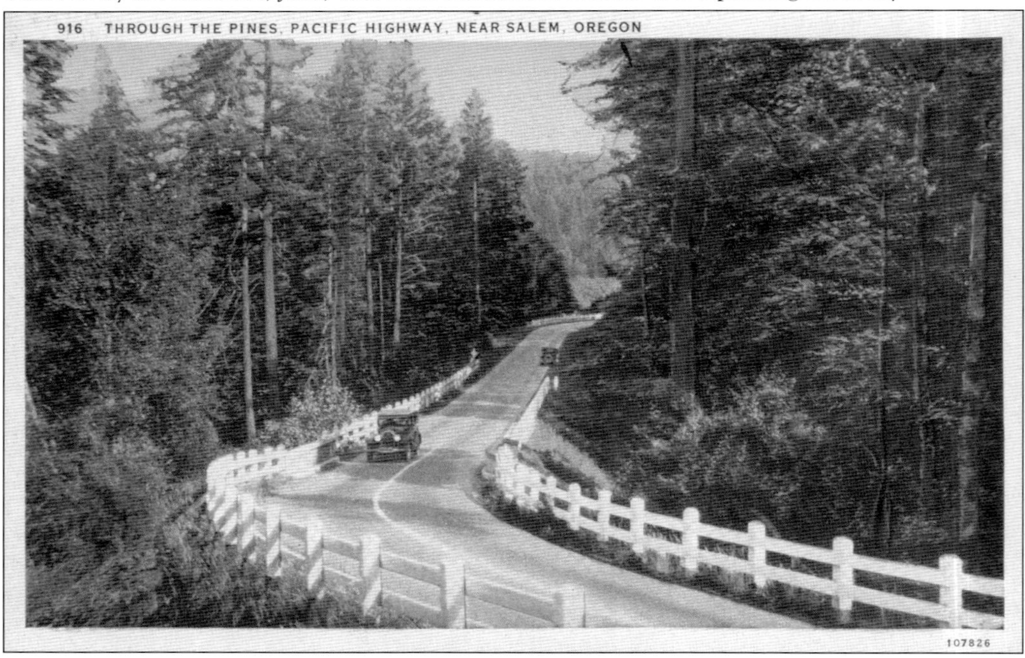

Sunnyside Road, the original route of the Pacific Highway, branches off today's S Commercial about two and a half miles south of Salem. This early view was probably eight miles out of downtown, where the highway entered a band of forested hills on its way toward Jefferson. This section of road was narrow, twisty, and downright dangerous in places, and in 1936, planning began to relocate the highway to the east.

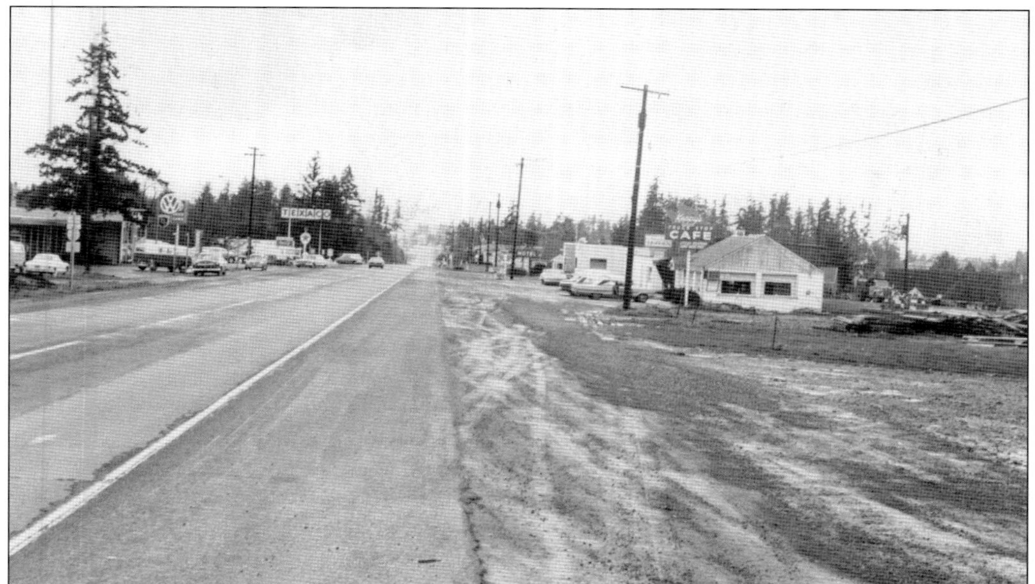

By the 1950s, Sunnyside Road was reduced to back-road status and a newly extended S Commercial had become Highway 99E. Businesses lost little time building up along the new route. This photograph, looking north from the vicinity of Crowley Avenue, shows the newly established Eyerly Volkswagen dealership at 4525 S Commercial, a Texaco station, and Keppy's Truck Stop Cafe. Sunnyside Road splits off from Commercial just beyond the Texaco sign (WHC, 1997.007.0007.)

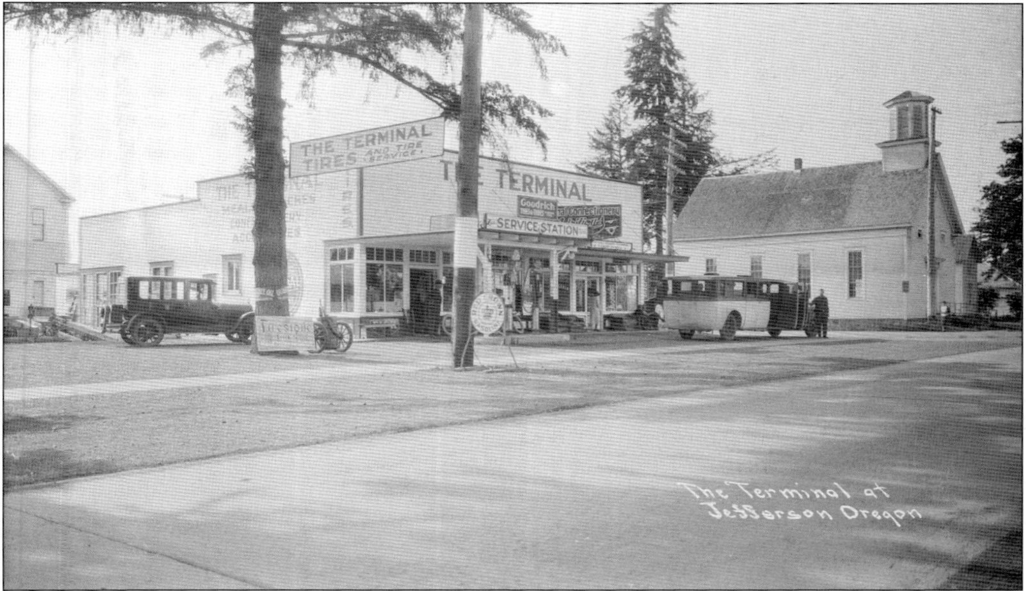

The Terminal Service Station was located at the corner of Church Street and the Pacific Highway in Jefferson. Joe and Paul McKee started the business in 1924. By the time they sold out to John Korenian in 1941, they had added fountain service, a lunchroom, and tourist cabins. A 1945 fire nearly destroyed the place, but portions of the original building survive and are used by Cafe 99. (LCHM, CS800.)

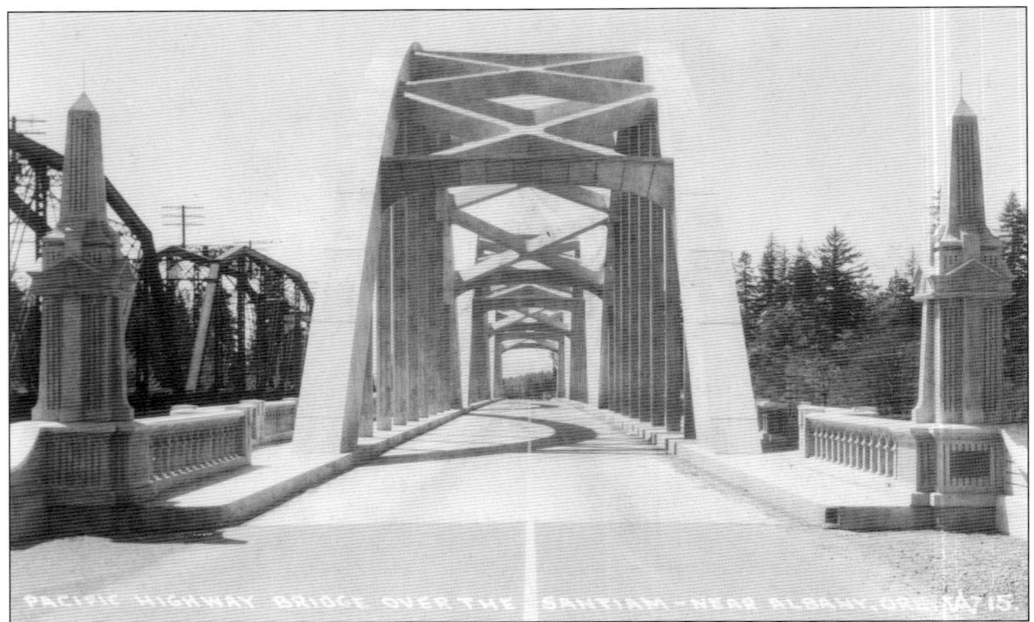

In 1853, pioneer Jacob Conser was operating a ferry across the Santiam River at Jefferson. A wood bridge replaced the ferry; a steel span was built in 1910 but proved inadequate for Pacific Highway traffic. In 1932, construction began on the $150,000, 700-foot-long, 24-foot-wide concrete bridge shown here. When it opened in August 1933, it was dedicated to Conser.

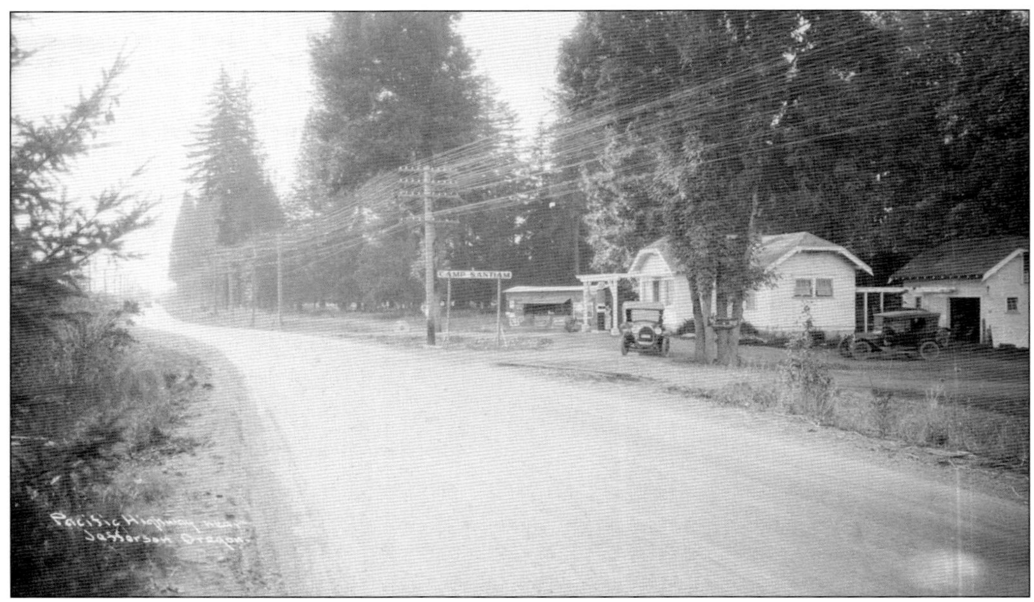

Camp Santiam, on the Santiam River just south of Jefferson, was operated by James Blackwell. Opened in May 1922, it quickly became popular with campers and picnickers. Within a year, Blackwell had established a gas station, grocery store, open-air tea garden, and lunchroom featuring chicken dinners. By 1935, five cottages had been added. The camp has disappeared; residences and small farms occupy its site today. (LCHM, CS804.)

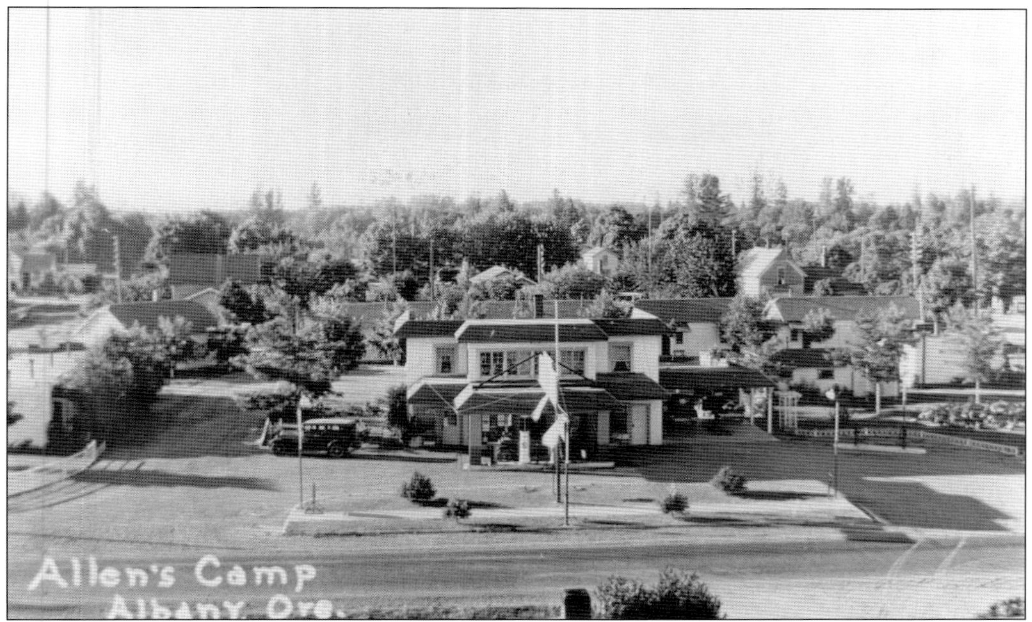

Founded by brothers Dodge and Neil Allen, Allen's Camp opened in the 1930s. The large central building contained a service station and a grocery store; the row of 14 cottages behind it rented for $1.25 to $2.50 a night in 1936. In later years, it was known as the Woodland Square Apartments. Demolished in 2007, the site at 1415 Salem Road is an empty lot today. (ARM, 2008.260.Transport.0259.)

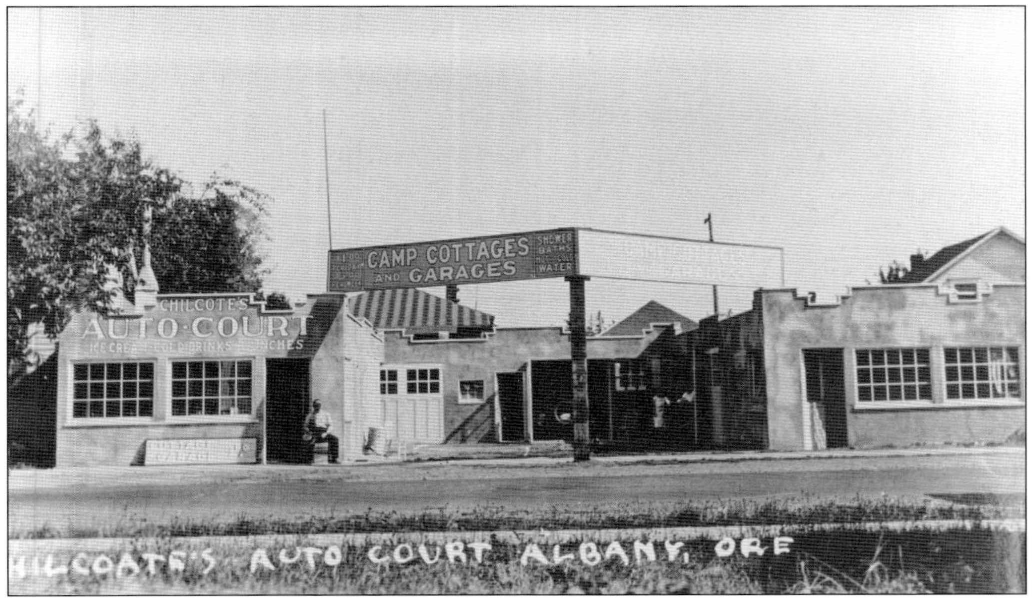

Chilcote's Auto Court was located at the east edge of Albany on Salem Road, the local name for the Pacific Highway. The U-shaped complex included a garage and a lunch counter; the units were contained in the rear portion of the "U" and rented for $1 a day. Owner W.P. Chilcote also operated a service station at 3rd Avenue and Washington Street on the west side of town. (ARM, 2008.260.Buildings.081A.)

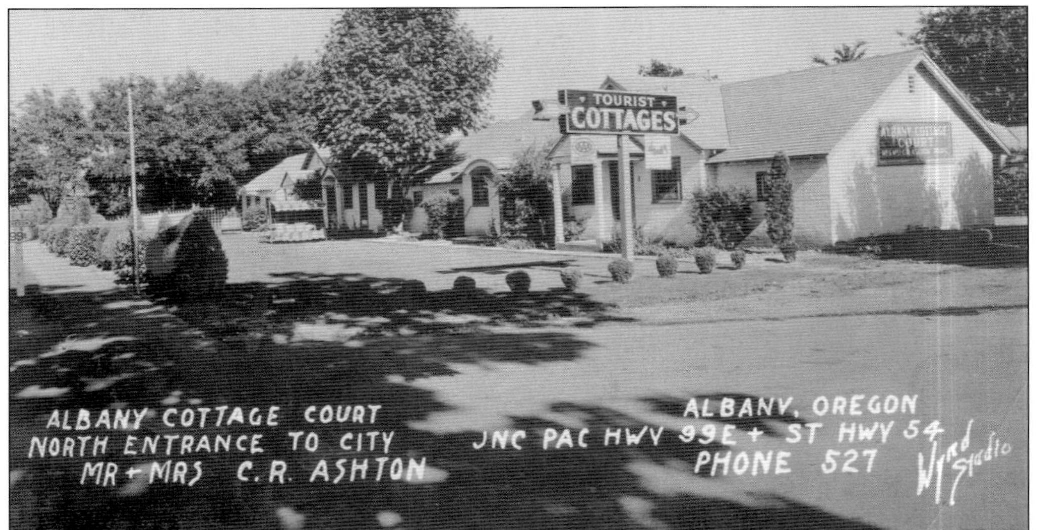

The Albany Cottage Court was across from Chilcote's on S Main Street, where the Pacific Highway jogged north for two blocks before turning toward downtown Albany. When highway realignment bypassed the motel in 1941, the "Tourist Cottages" sign was moved over to the new route to attract business. Several of the original 13 one- to three-room cottages are still standing, in use as residences.

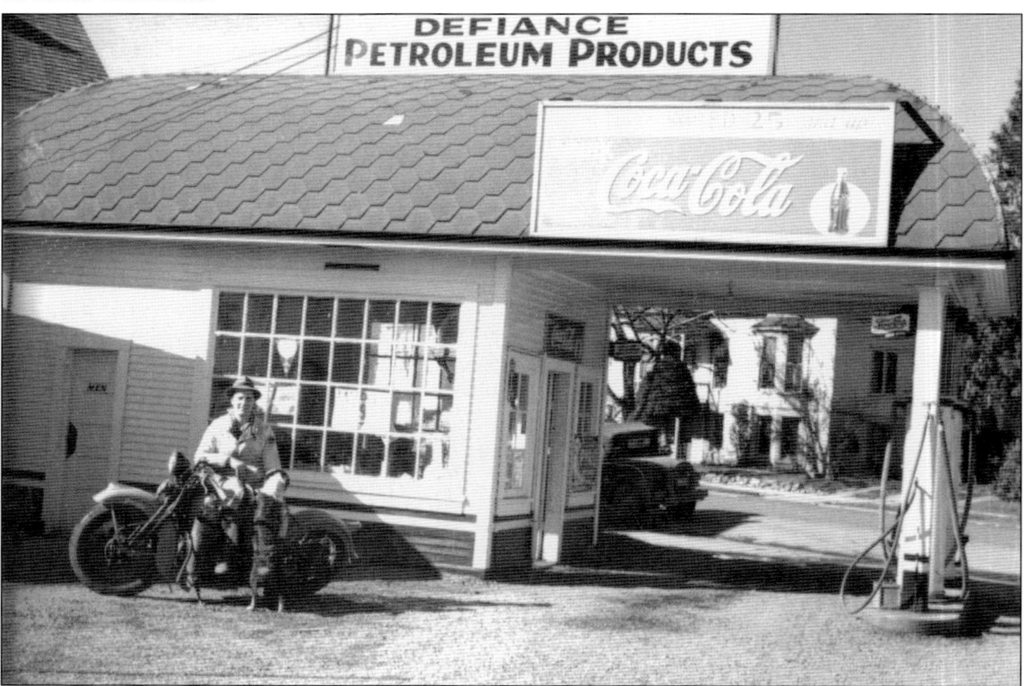

In this 1939 photograph, an unidentified motorcyclist lounges alongside the Defiance Petroleum Products station at 112 N Main Street, where the Pacific Highway turned west into downtown Albany. Clarence Feller and Rex Minard operated the station together, but Minard soon departed; later photographs portray Feller as sole owner. The station fixed flat tires in addition to dispensing gasoline and Coca-Cola. The site is an empty lot today. (ARM, 2008.26C.Transport.0017.)

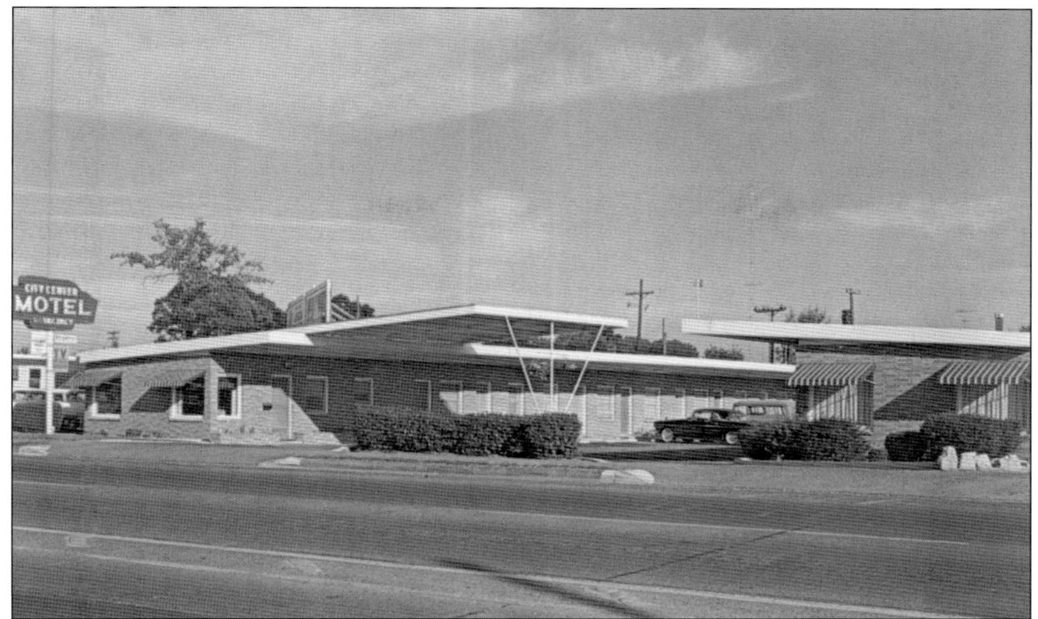

The 1941 realignment passed through the sparsely settled east edge of Albany. Roadside businesses appeared along the new highway as developers took advantage of inexpensive land. The City Center Motel, an example of contemporary modernistic style with multicolored brick and cantilevered awnings, seems a world removed (though only 20 years in time) from the homier lines of the Cottage Courts. The location, 1730 E Pacific Boulevard, is a Walgreen's today.

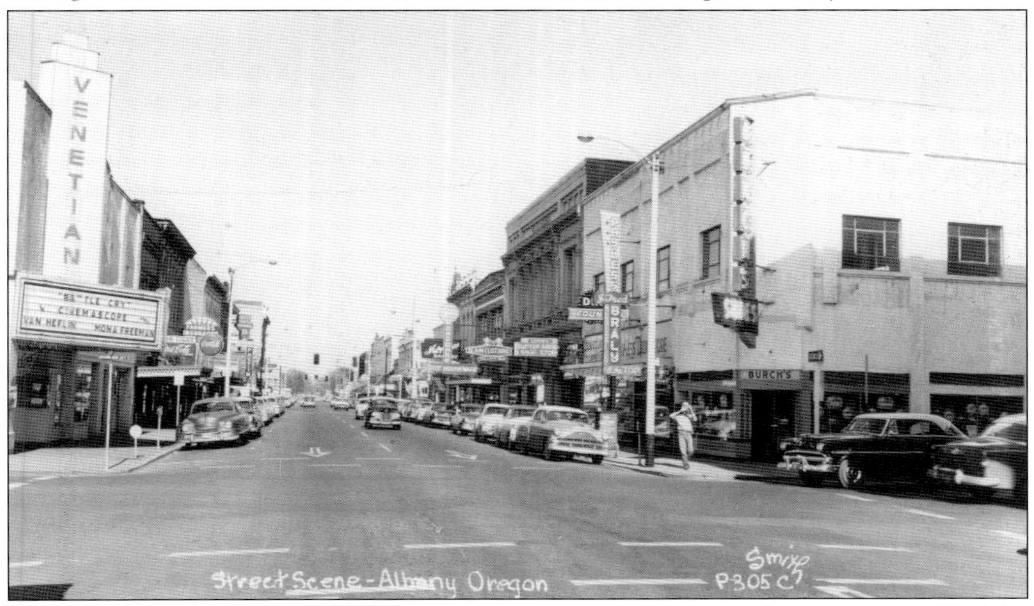

This 1955 scene shows bustling downtown Albany on a sunny summer afternoon. Autos filled the curbside parking; *Battle Cry*, starring Van Heflin and Mona Freeman, was playing at the Venetian Theatre. Signs advertised Coca-Cola, the Pastime Tavern, Farmers Insurance, Payless Drugs and Fountain, J. Fred Braly Realtor, and two shoe stores—Burch's and Long's Buster Brown Shoes. The view looks east on 1st Avenue from Broadalbin Street. (JCO'D.)

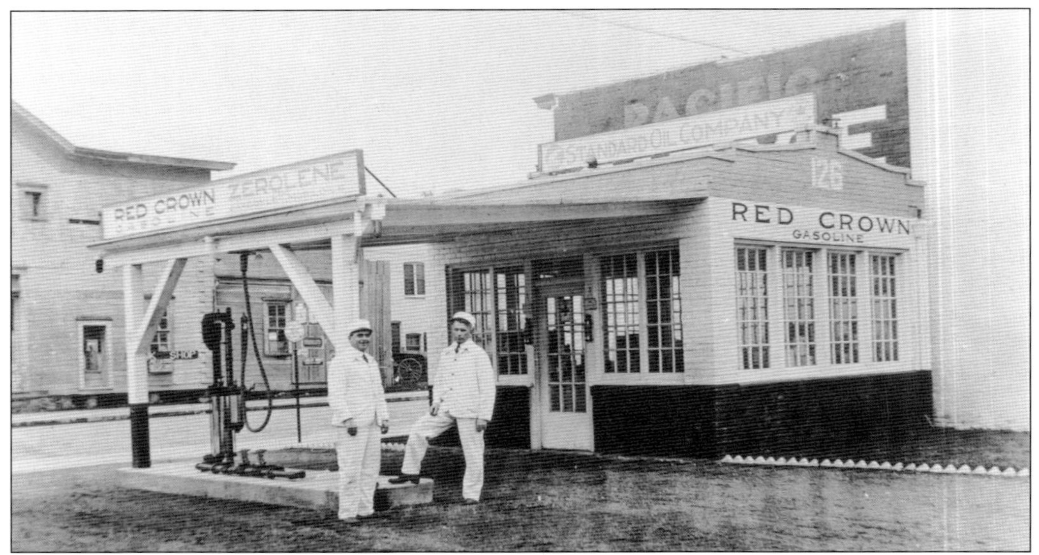

Two attendants dressed in snappy white uniforms stand waiting for customers at a Red Crown gas station in downtown Albany. Brick-built with a wooden canopy sheltering the single gravity-feed gas pump, the building represents the earliest style of service station architecture, dating the photograph to the early 1920s. The Albany Livery Stables, last gasp of the horse-and-buggy era, can be seen across Ellsworth Street from the station. (ARM, 2007.015.0C42.)

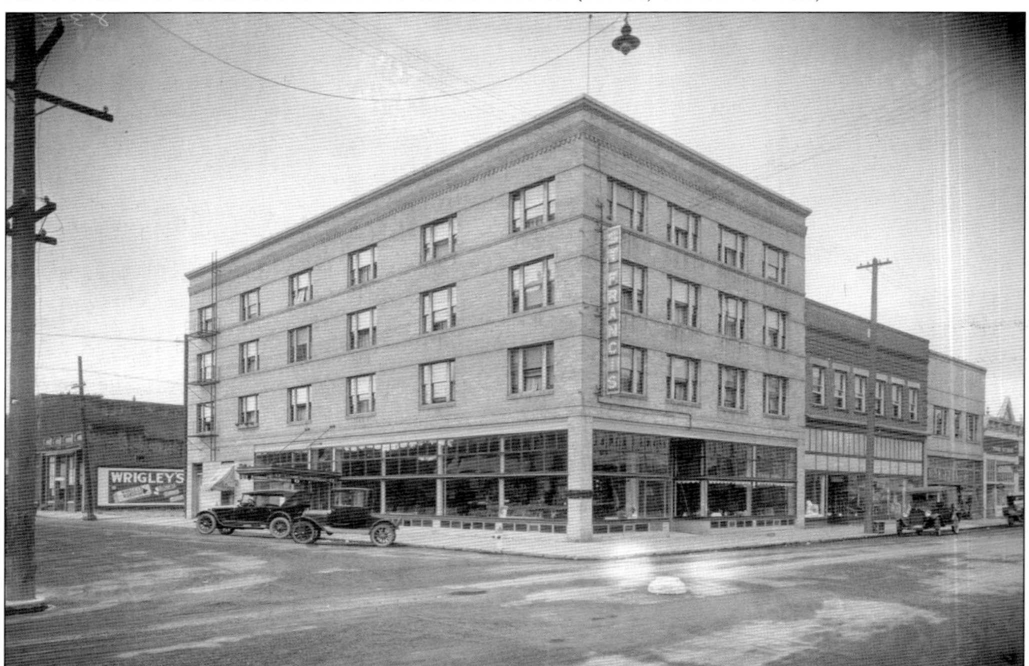

The St. Francis Hotel, at 1st Avenue and Ferry Street, was designed by architect Charles Burggraf and constructed in 1912. Its 60 rooms, each with hot and cold water, steam heat, and telephones, originally rented for 50¢ a night. The hotel's "popularly priced" dining room was open for luncheon and dinner. Plans are afoot for a full restoration of the building, which is the only survivor of Albany's nine downtown hotels. (OSL, 21290.)

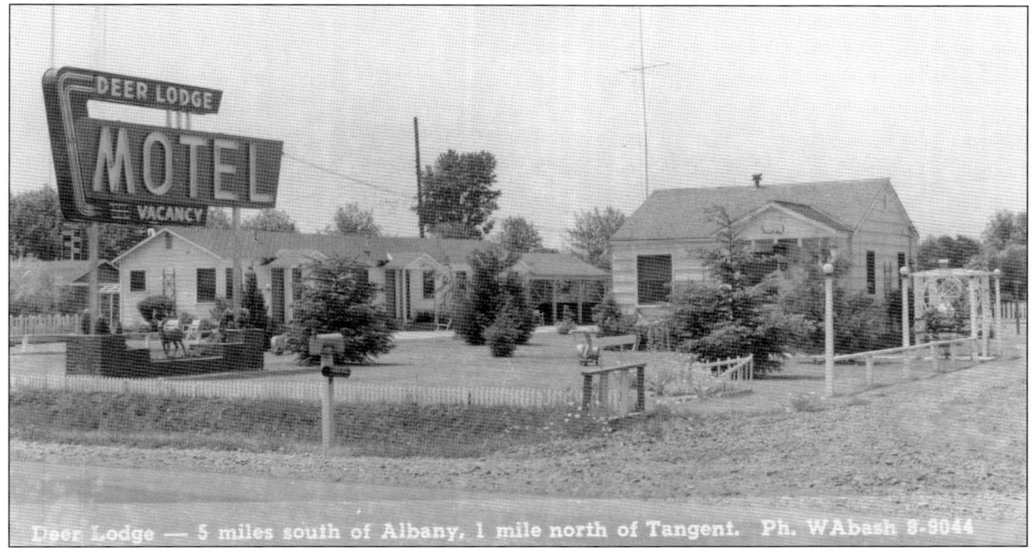

Deer Lodge — 5 miles south of Albany, 1 mile north of Tangent. Ph. WAbash 8-9044

Five miles south of Albany, Highway 99E intersected busy State Highway 34. The motorist had choices: west to Corvallis, Oregon State College, and the Pacific Ocean; east to Lebanon and the Cascade Mountains; or south through the broad Willamette Valley to Eugene. Here sat the three-unit Deer Lodge Motel. In 1954, proprietor Sanborn McMahon was elected president of the Linn-Benton Motor Court Association. The motel has disappeared under new development.

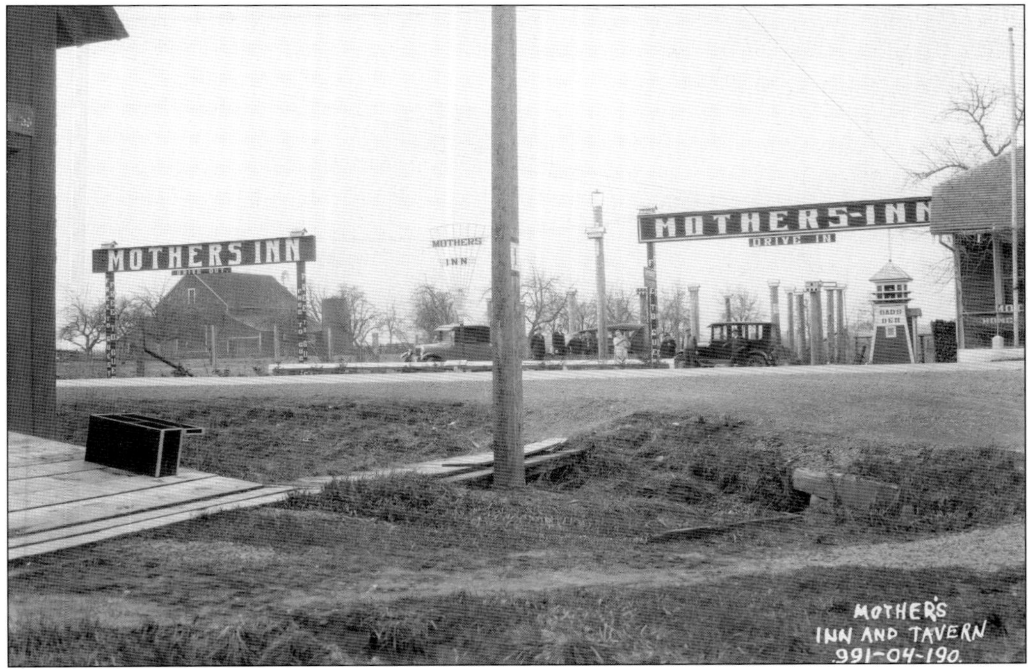

MOTHER'S INN AND TAVERN 991-04-190.

D.C. and Mamie "Mother" McClure opened Mother's Inn in 1921 at Tangent as a simple wayside eatery, expanding the following year with a larger dining room and an ice cream parlor. Within three years, Mother's was the most popular dining destination in the central Willamette Valley; folks from Albany to Eugene flocked to Mother's for 50¢ Sunday chicken dinners. The purpose of the lighthouse-shaped Dad's Den is not known. (ARM, 1991-004-190.)

MOTHER'S INN

TANGENT, OREGON

(On Main Pacific Highway No. 1, South of Albany)

Meals Like Mother Cooked and Served as Mother Served Them

SUNDAY DINNERS A SPECIALTY

WE CATER TO TRAVELING MEN—TOURISTS—PARTIES AND FAMILIES

(NO ROUGH STUFF TOLERATED)

Our Price Is Always 50c — D. C. McCLURE, Prop.

(THIS IS **NOT** A ROADHOUSE)

Roadhouses, with their drinking and carrying-on, were the scourge of early highways. The McClures wanted it understood that theirs was not that kind of place. They attributed their success to home cooking, courteous service, and a friendly, family-oriented atmosphere. Mamie McClure became locally famous for her prune conserve, which she marketed to restaurants and highway travelers. After D.C. died in 1932, Mamie continued to operate Mother's Inn for several years.

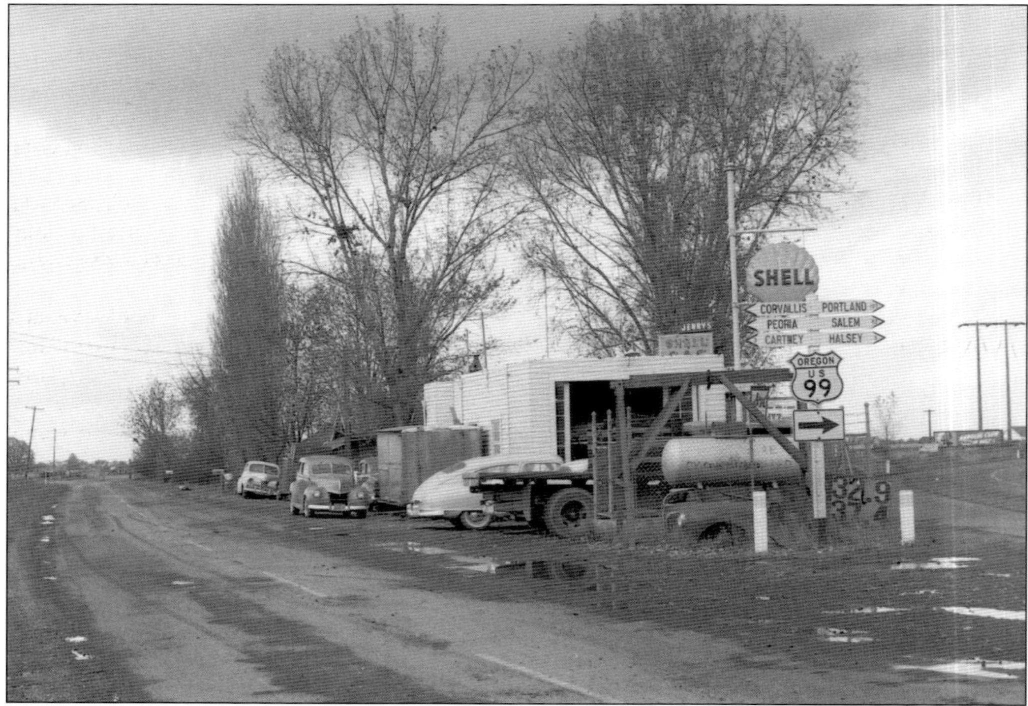

Even in its heyday, the 30-mile stretch of Highway 99E between Albany and Junction City hosted scant roadside services. Jerry's Shell gas station was one of the few. It was located just north of Harrisburg at the point where a back road to Corvallis (and Highway 99W) forked off from 99E. At the bend of the highway heading toward Albany is a billboard advertising Harold's Club in Reno, Nevada.

Two

Highway 99W
Portland to Junction City

The Pacific Highway was but a few years old when cities west of the Willamette River began clamoring for a modern highway. First was the Capitol Highway, connecting Portland with Salem via Dayton. The West Side Pacific Highway came along a few years later, running through Tigard to Newberg and McMinnville, then south to Monmouth, Corvallis, Monroe, and Junction City. It became Highway 99W in 1937.

South of Portland, 99W has maintained a stable alignment except for bypasses at McMinnville, Monmouth, and Corvallis. The major route changes have occurred in the immediate Portland area. Earliest to happen was the upgrade of Interstate Avenue as a major connector between downtown Portland and the Interstate Bridge.

Interstate Avenue predates the bridge and was planned as a major thoroughfare, but for years it ended at Kenton on the highlands above the Columbia Slough. When the Interstate Bridge opened in 1917, the main highway was routed southeast to Union Avenue. Interstate Avenue was recognized as the more direct route into Portland, but the slough and bluff precluded easy access.

The 1920s saw major improvements to Interstate Avenue, culminating with the Denver Avenue Viaduct approach to the Interstate Bridge in 1929. Now motorists had a choice. Half a mile south of the bridge, the highway forked. The east fork followed the original East Side Pacific Highway route via Union Avenue. The west fork took them up the viaduct to Kenton and down Interstate to Broadway, then west on the Broadway Bridge into downtown.

The second major upgrade was the 4th Avenue S extension to Barbur Boulevard in 1934. Along with major upgrades to Barbur, it avoided the twisty Terwilliger Boulevard. By 1946, the Broadway Bridge–Broadway route into and through downtown had been supplanted by a new riverside bypass. Harbor Drive became Highway 99's route, and the Steel Bridge took the role of carrying traffic across the Willamette River. Harbor Drive was vacated in 1972 and turned into a waterfront park, and Front Street, a block west, became the new Highway 99W. Front Street is now known as Naito Parkway.

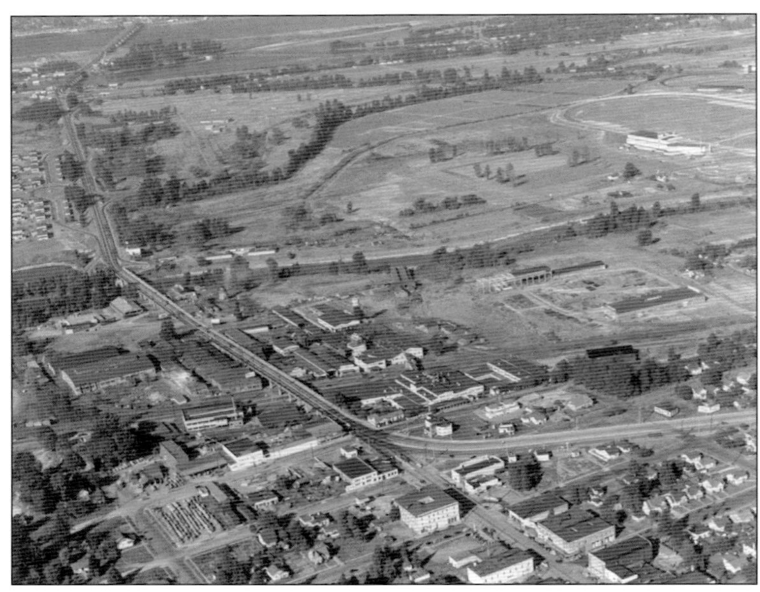

By the late 1920s, it was obvious that the route from Kenton north to the Interstate Bridge was inadequate for the traffic volume it handled. The old structure was replaced by a concrete viaduct and bridge, seen in this aerial view looking north toward the Columbia River. Known as the Denver Avenue Viaduct, the new route was dedicated with great fanfare on June 22, 1929. (CPA, A2005-001.752.)

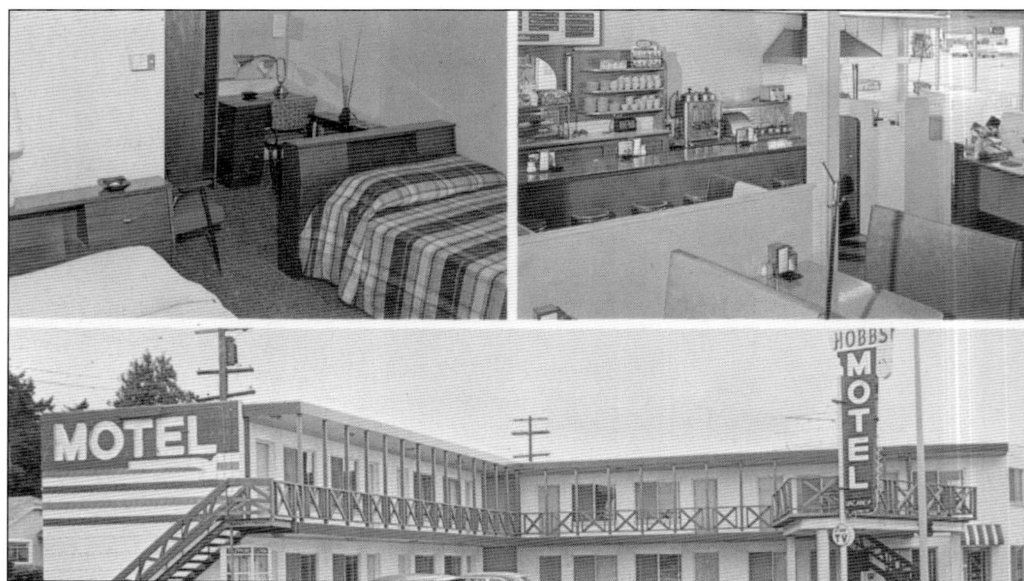

Building contractor Preston T. Hobbs constructed this 16-unit motel and restaurant, possibly as an investment; it was offered for sale almost immediately upon opening but was still called the Hobbs Motel in 1964. That year, the motel and an adjacent bowling alley, also owned by Hobbs, suffered an arson fire. Later known as the Bel Air Motel and most recently the Comfy Inn, it was located at 8355 N Interstate Avenue.

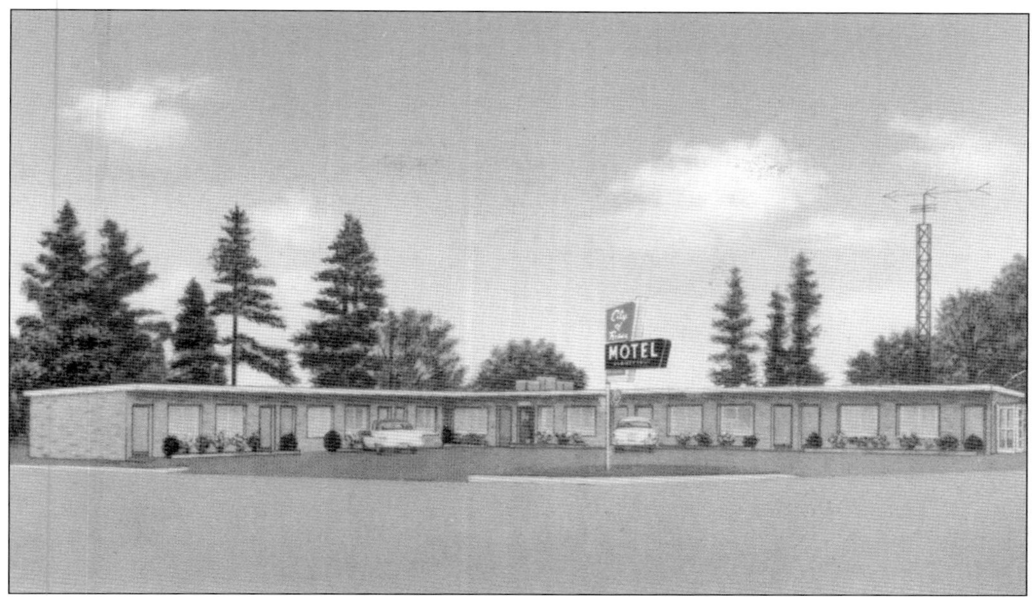

The City of Roses Motel was found at 8310 N Interstate Avenue. Its 12 units provided the standard amenities—Beautyrest mattresses, electric heat and air conditioning, and TV. Early in the morning of May 22, 1962, owners Mr. and Mrs. James R. Gates were robbed of $50 by an apologetic well-dressed gunman who said he had recently been released from a mental institution. The site is a vacant lot today.

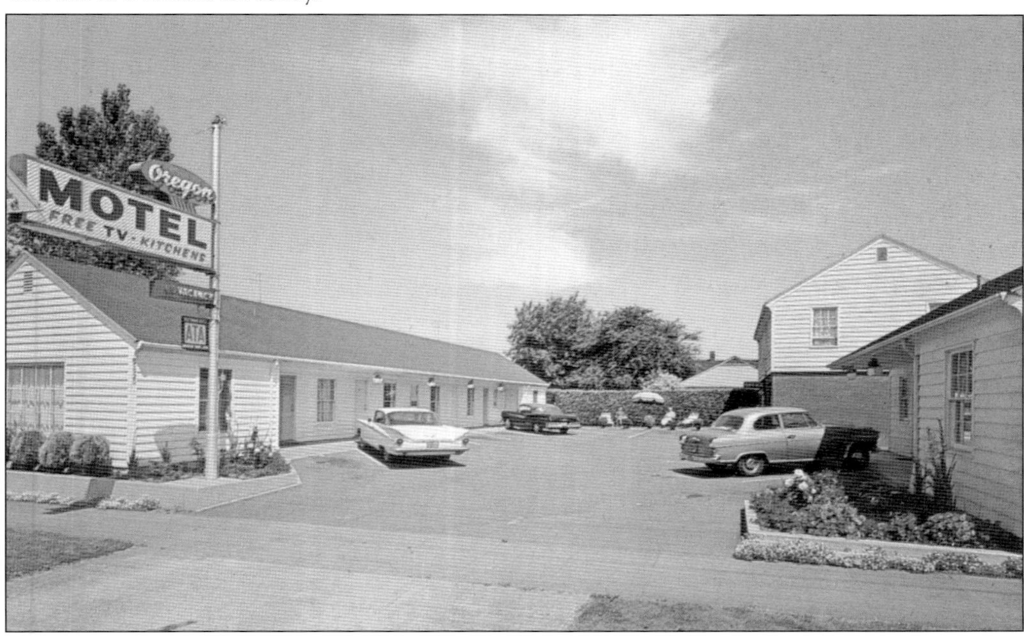

Neat and trim, the Oregon Motel offered 10 modern "spic-and-span comfortable" units with kitchens, TV, and free coffee. Guests could enjoy a green, beach umbrella–shaded lawn at the far end of the parking area. Ownership changed frequently over the years. The motel was sold in 1963 due to the owner being homesick—and again in 1967—but is still in business at 7920 NE Interstate Avenue.

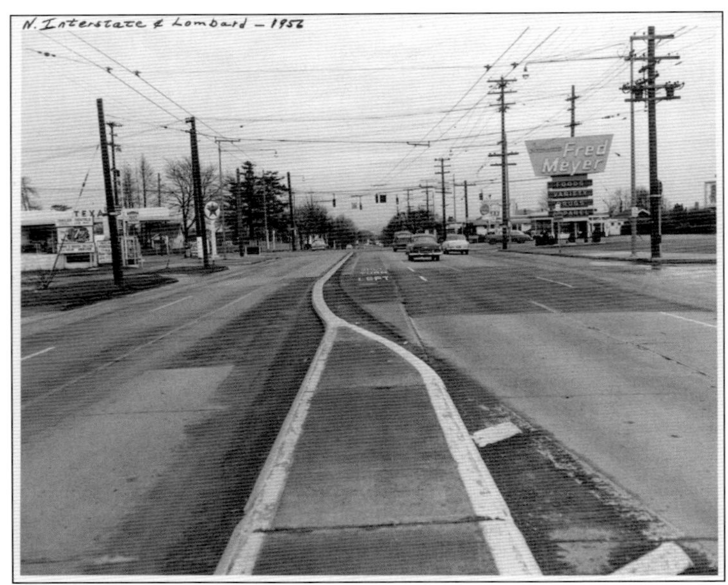

The intersection of N Interstate Avenue and Lombard Street has certainly changed since this photograph was taken in 1956. The 76 Union service station on the northeast corner is now an Astro convenience store; the Texaco station, with its classic overhanging canopy, has been replaced by a Shell; Fred Meyer now occupies the entire block; and a branch of Portland's light rail system bisects Interstate. (CPA, A2005-001.378.)

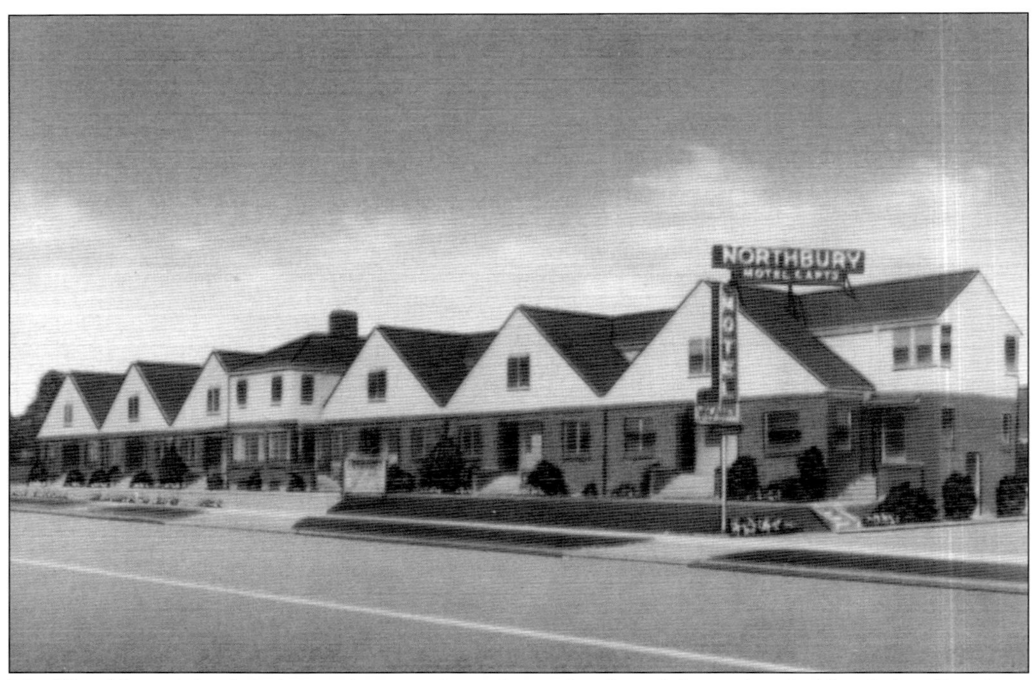

The Northbury Motel & Apartments, with its elegant brick-and-frame facade, blended well with its residential neighbors. Opened in 1950 by Mr. and Mrs. Garnet Alvers at 7319 N Interstate Boulevard, the Northbury was located a half block south of the strategic intersection of Interstate and Lombard Street. At that point, southbound Highway 99 travelers could turn onto Lombard to connect with east-west Highway 30, bypassing downtown Portland. Today, the site is a medical facility.

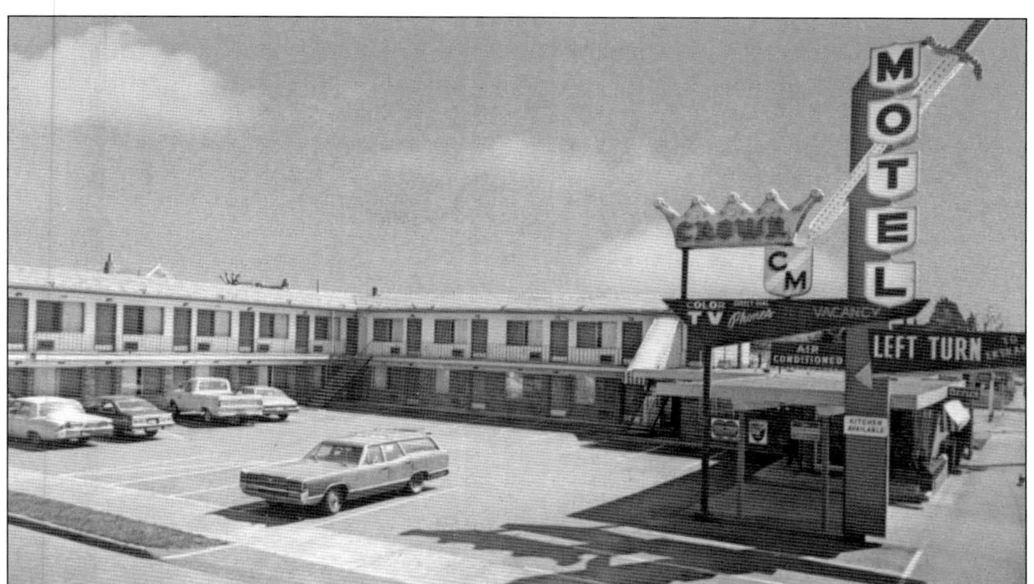

In 1958, Jacobson and Severson, former owners of the City of Roses Motel, constructed the Crown Motel at 5226 N Interstate Avenue. The two-story structure, with 22 units faced with brick on the main floor and wood veneer on the upper floor, was up-to-date with color TV, direct-dial phones, and air conditioning. The motel fell on hard times; declared a public nuisance in 1982, it was demolished in 2008.

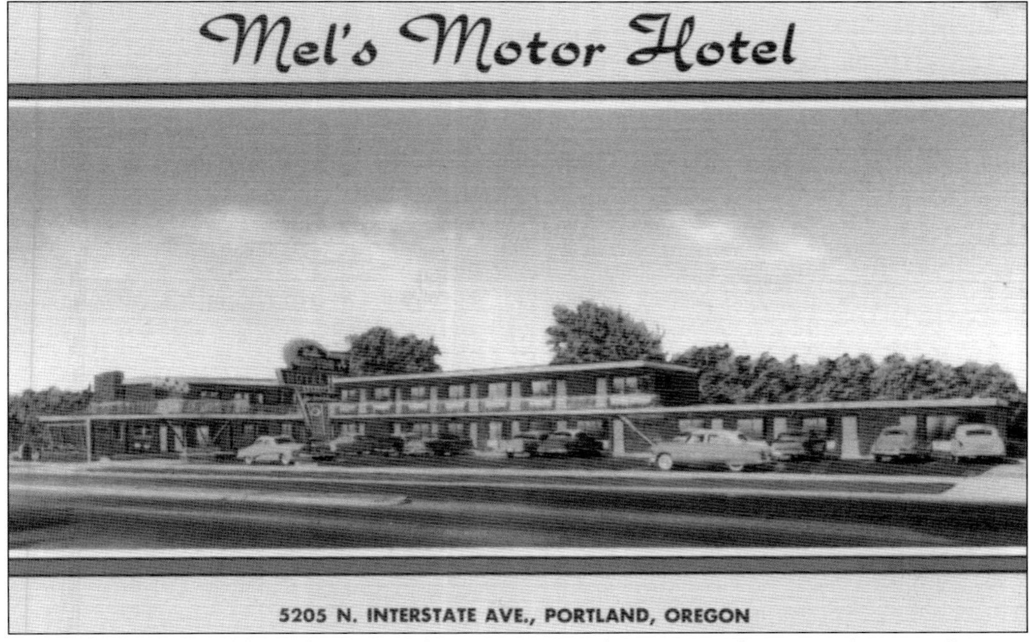

Mel's Motor Hotel celebrated its September 3, 1955, grand opening with an open house and square dancing (music provided by Eddie K's orchestra). Mel's L-shaped, two-story structure contained 24 units, all with king-sized beds, TVs, phones, tubs, and showers. In 1958, owners Mel and Beth Stricklett added 16 more units plus a restaurant—Mel's Top Deck. Located at 5205 N Interstate, the building is now a Super Value Inn.

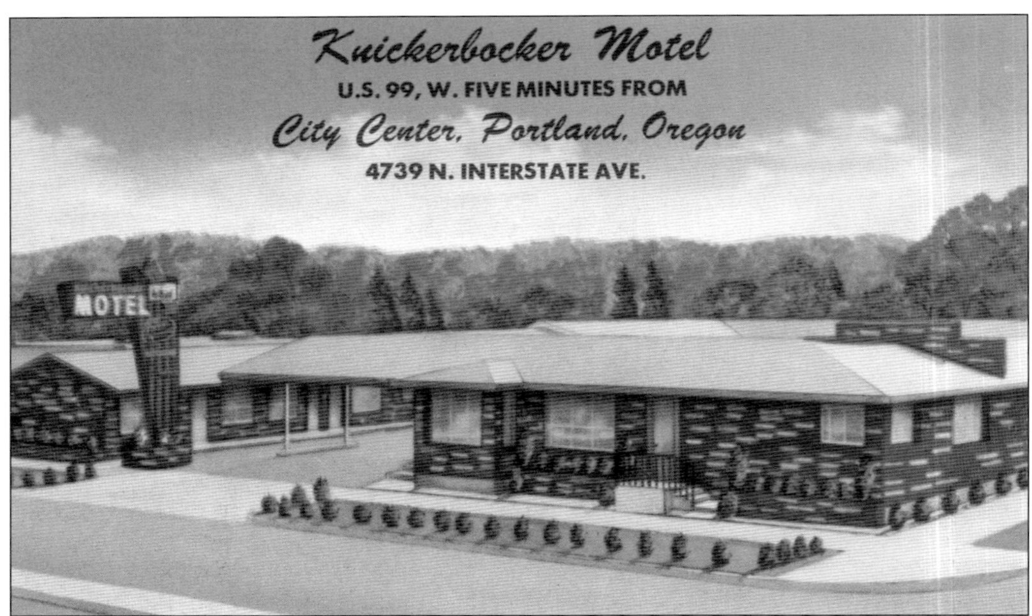

The Knickerbocker Motel, at 4739 N Interstate Avenue, also threw a party when it opened on April 1, 1955. Owners were Mr. and Mrs. M.R. Ketola. The 24-unit, U-shaped, single-story building featured Roman brick exterior. Units had telephones, television and radios, Pullman kitchens, and tiled showers—some with tinted bath fixtures. In 1961, an on-site restaurant was serving breakfast and lunch. It now operates as the Budget Motel.

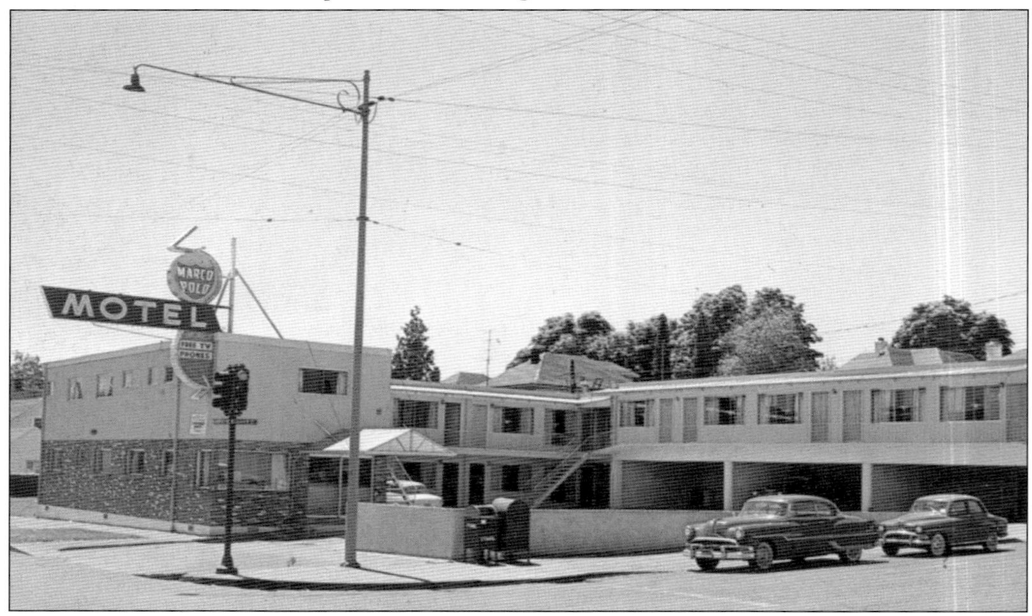

Robert and Mary Heintz owned the Marco Polo Motel until selling it to Elmo and Melva Veazey and Ruth Stark in 1958. With 20 units, the Marco Polo was among a cluster of motels along a half-mile stretch of highway north of Portland's industrial district. Each unit featured free local telephone service, television, and tub and shower bath. Located at 3971 N Interstate Avenue, today it is an Economy Inn.

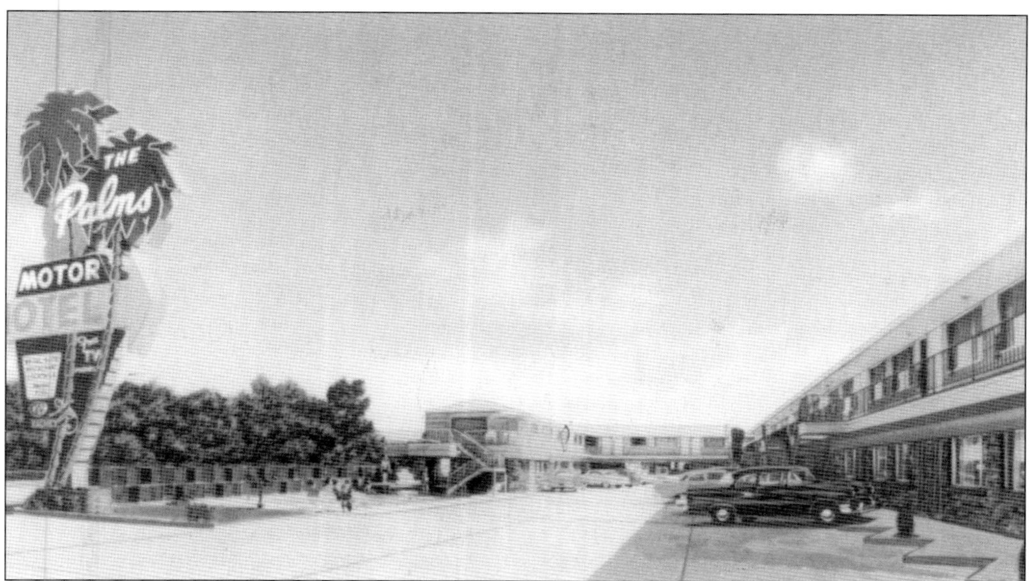

The Palms Motor Hotel opened in August 1957 at 3801 N Interstate. Constructed at a cost of $600,000 and billed as Portland's largest luxury motel, The Palms offered 52 units (each with a 21-inch television, innovative for that time), a heated pool and sundeck, and an on-site restaurant. The motel has had its ups and downs but remains in business, its magnificent, tiki-themed neon sign lighting up the night. (JCO'D)

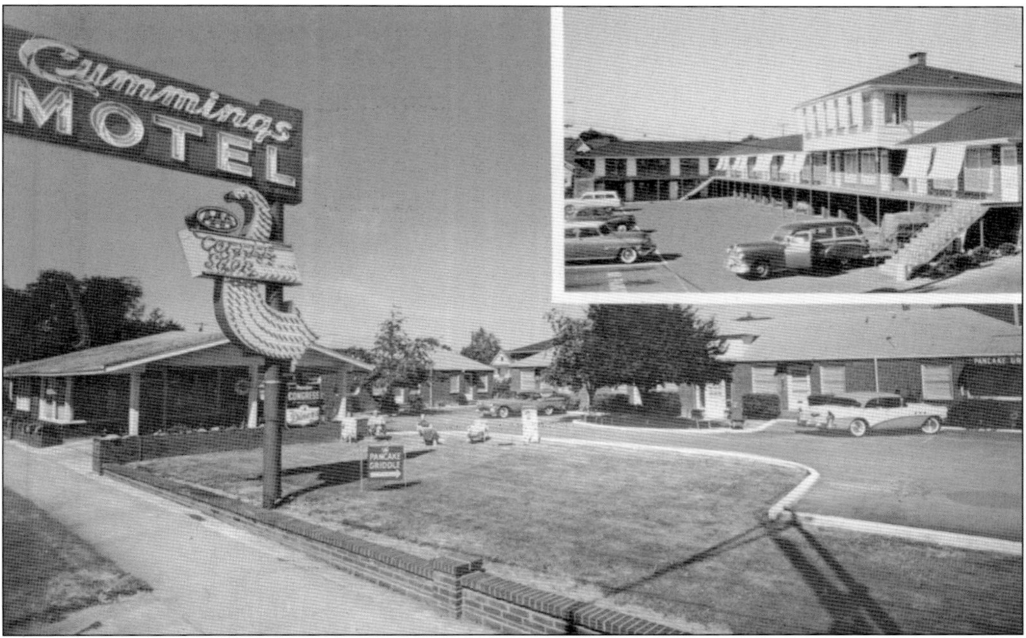

Mr. and Mrs. Harry Cummings opened the 28-unit Cummings Motel at 3620 N Interstate Avenue in 1948. By 1962, when John Goss purchased it, the motel consisted of 53 units with twin or double beds, all-electric kitchenettes, tubs and showers, and garages; a coffee shop was on-site. The southernmost of Interstate Avenue's motels, it had become the Travelers Inn by 1963. A medical building currently occupies the site.

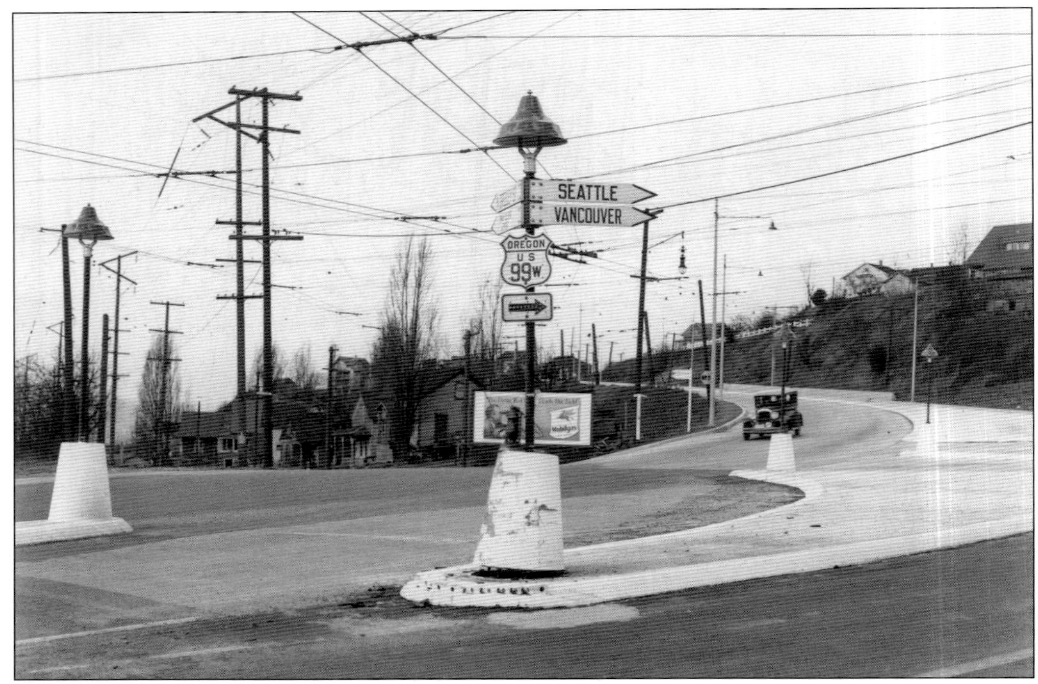

The late 1920s saw major improvements to Interstate Avenue—widening, regrading, construction of the Denver Avenue Viaduct, and a bypass around Kenton. It soon became a major arterial route and, in 1937, received designation as Highway 99W. This 1940 photograph shows one of the more confusingly signed portions of the highway—the Interstate/Greeley intersection. The concrete streetlight support in the foreground looks the worse for wear. (CPA, A2005-001.236.)

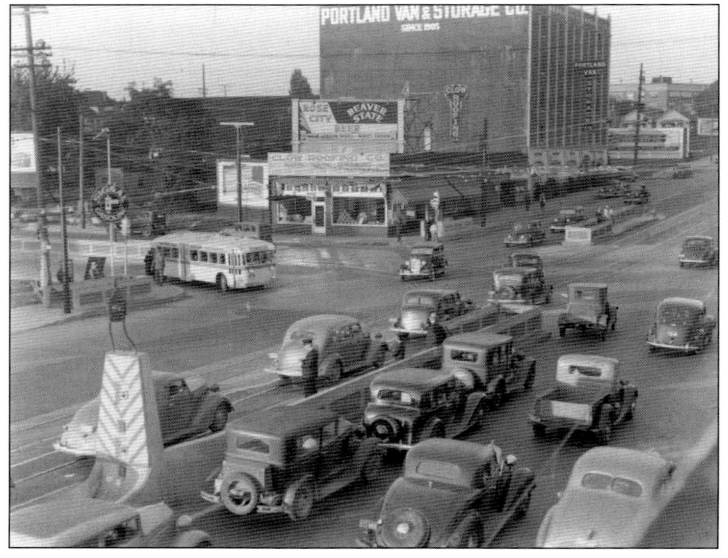

In 1937, motorists southbound on Interstate Avenue would have found themselves on Delay Street and then Larrabee Avenue once they passed the Interstate-Greeley junction—same highway, different names. At the intersection of Larrabee with Broadway—shown here crowded with autos, a bus, and streetcar tracks—a turn west would take them across the Broadway Bridge into downtown Portland, as it still does today. (CPA, A2005-001.78.)

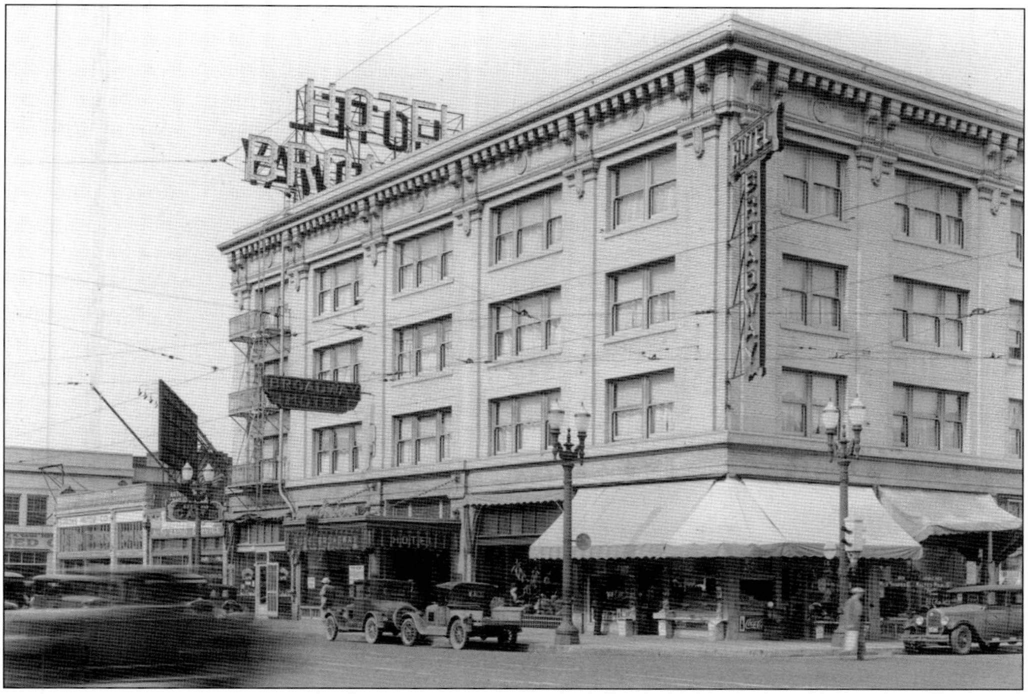

The Broadway Hotel opened in 1913 on the northeast corner of Broadway and Burnside Street. The four-story building, designed by architects Bennes & Hendricks, had the lobby entrance and storefronts on the ground floor and 105 rooms occupying the top three floors. Each room had hot and cold running water and rented for 50¢ a night. Restored in the 2000s, it is now the Helen M. Swindell Apartments. (CPA, A2001-062.12.)

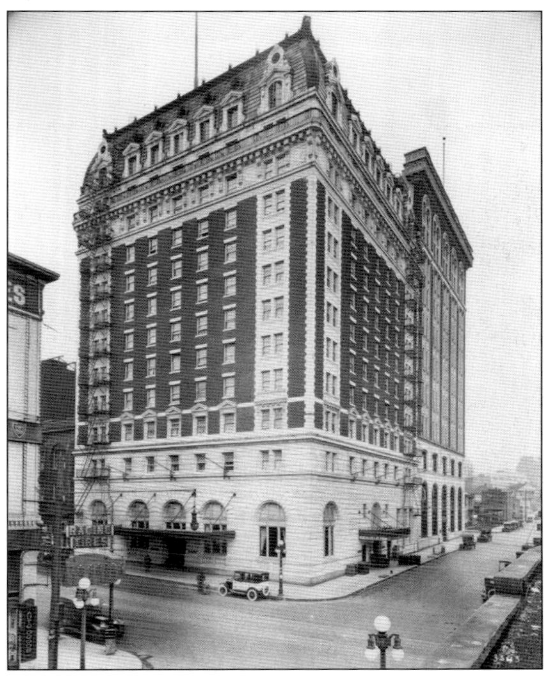

Considered Portland's most elegant hotel, the Benson opened in 1913 as the New Oregon Hotel, an annex to its next-door neighbor the Hotel Oregon. When timber magnate Simon Benson assumed control the following year, the hotel took his name. The Second Empire–style building was designed by Portland architects Doyle, Patterson & Beach. The Benson, at 309 SW Broadway, entered its second century as part of the Coast Hotels chain.

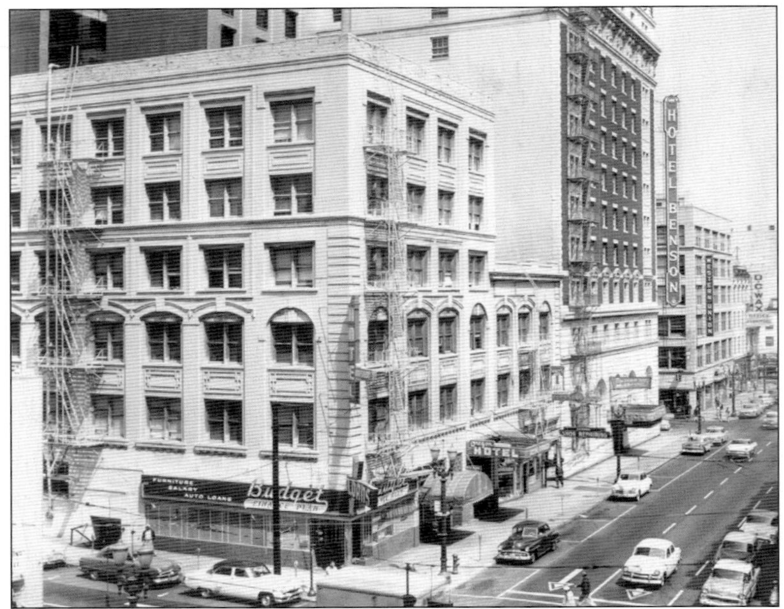

The Hotel Oregon originally occupied the south half of the block between Oak and Stark Streets. In 1906, its rooms rented for $1 per day and up on the European plan. It boasted "the handsomest grill in the West." For many years, it hosted Trader Vic's tiki bar adjacent to its ground-floor lobby. The building was demolished in 1959 for construction of a 175-room annex to the Benson Hotel.

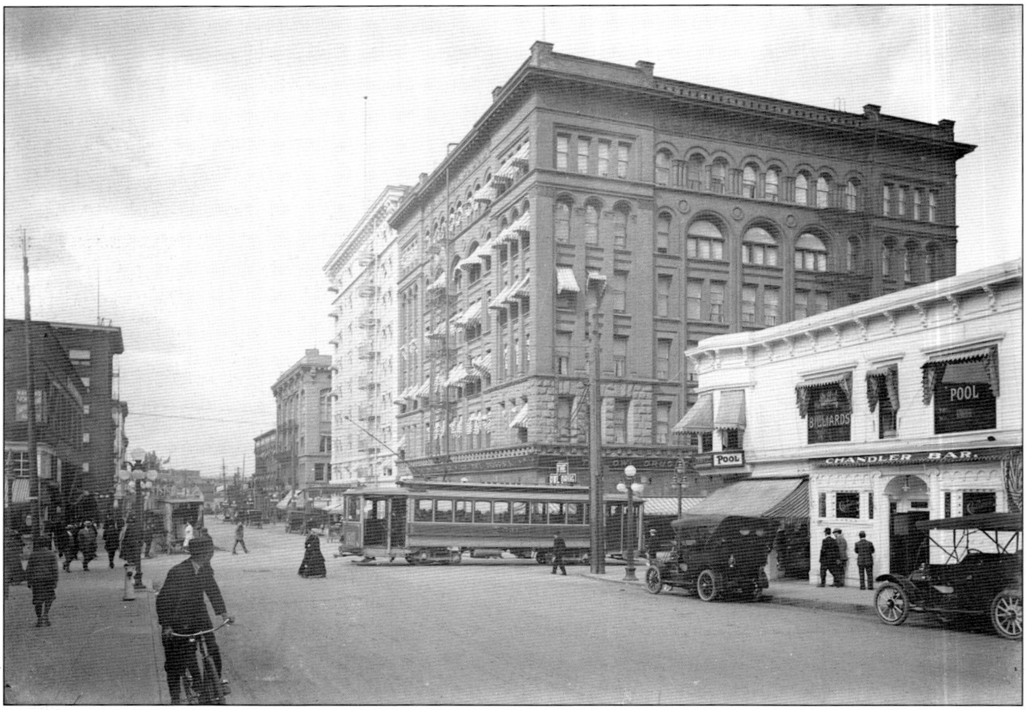

The 1890s-era Imperial Hotel looms at the corner of Broadway and Washington Street; just north on Broadway rises the nine-story, 350-room New Imperial Hotel, opened in 1909. For years, the new building was considered merely an addition to the original. In 1949, they were finally divided into separate businesses. Both are still hotels—the original is the Hotel Vintage Plaza, while the "addition" is the Hotel Lucia. (OD, P218.SG1.21.11.)

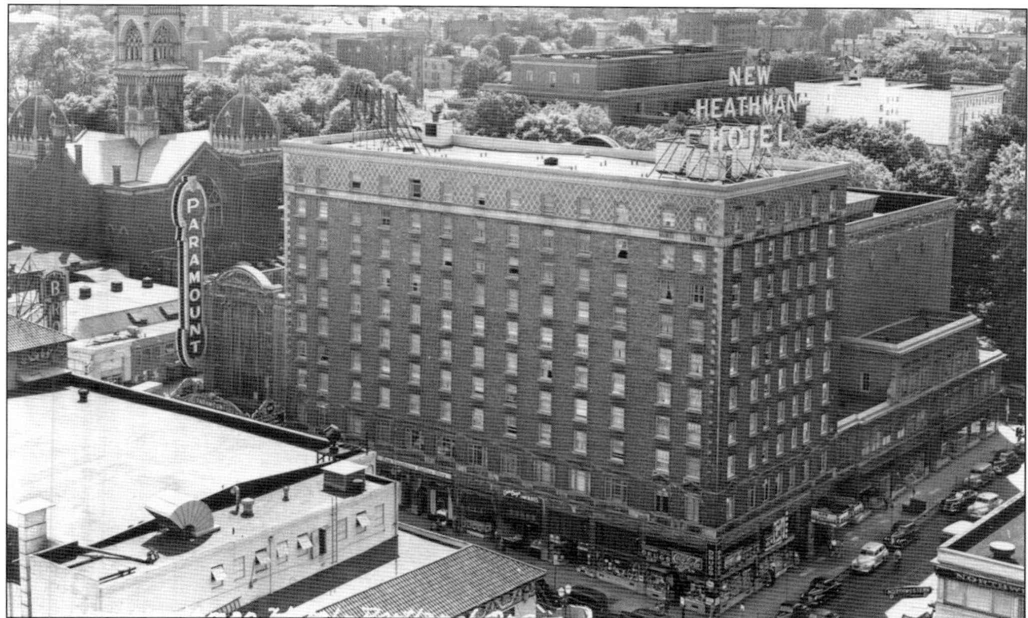

In 1926, George Heathman opened a hotel on Salmon Street at Park Avenue. A year later, he invested in another hotel under construction a block away on Broadway. Appropriately, it became known as the New Heathman Hotel. From 1927 to 1944, radio station KOIN broadcast from the hotel. Renovated and reopened in 1984 (dropping "New" from its name), the Heathman is regarded as one of Portland's most upscale hotels. (CPA, A2004-002.2789.)

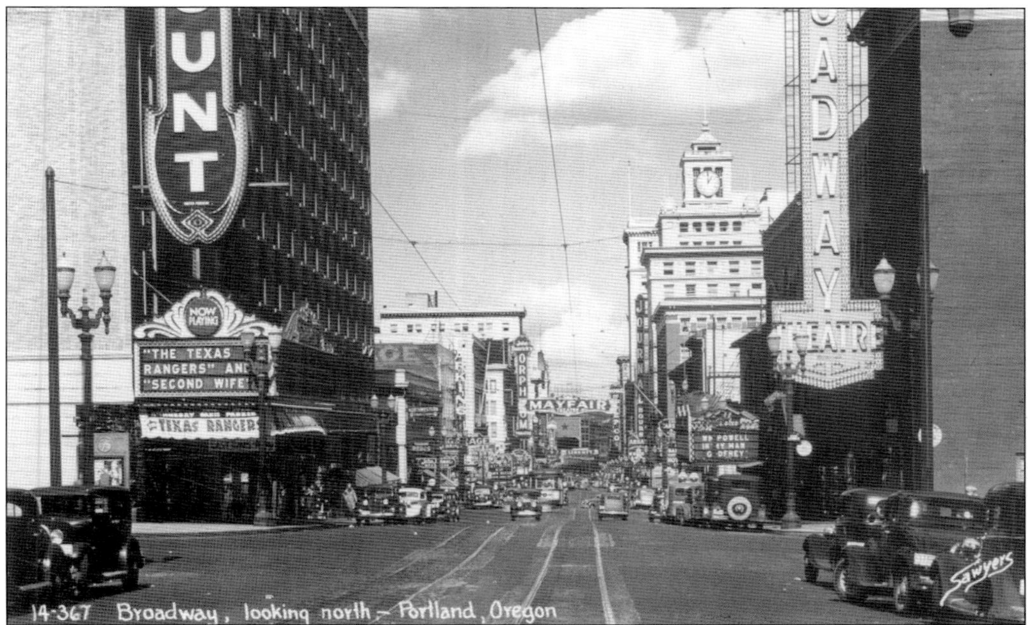

This c. 1936 view looks north on Broadway into the heart of Portland's theater district. At left is the Paramount; across the street is the Broadway Theatre; and further up were the Orpheum, Mayfair, and Liberty Theatres. Only the Paramount survives—purchased by the City of Portland in the 1980s, it was completely restored and reopened as the Arlene Schnitzer Concert Hall.

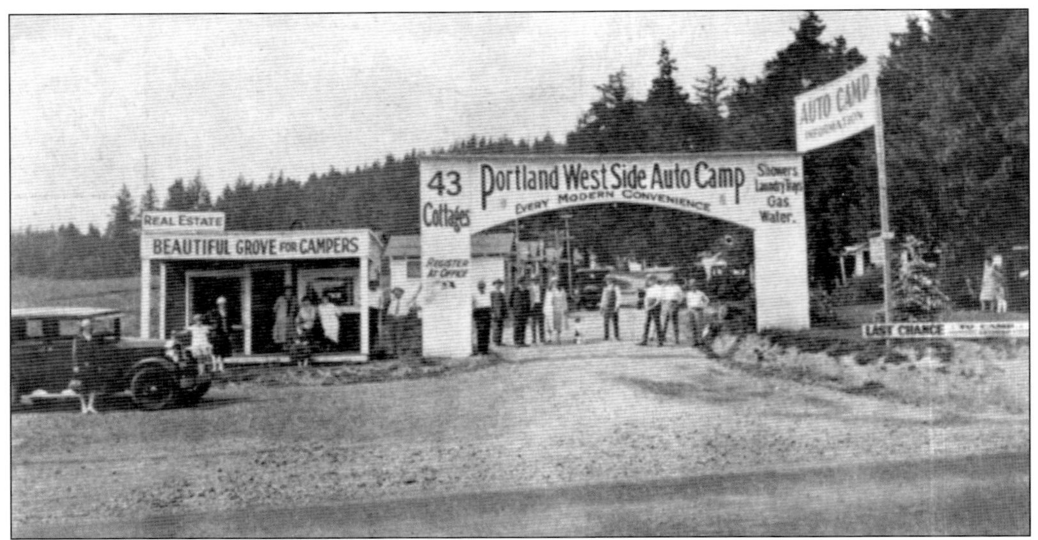

The Portland West Side Auto Camp took its name from the West Side Pacific Highway, which in early days turned from Terwilliger Boulevard onto Capitol Highway a few miles south of Portland. In 1928, the camp, operated by George and Elsie Battey, offered 43 cottages "with every modern convenience." Located at the intersection of Capitol Highway and Sunset Boulevard, it was still in business in 1952. (CPA, A2004-002.877.)

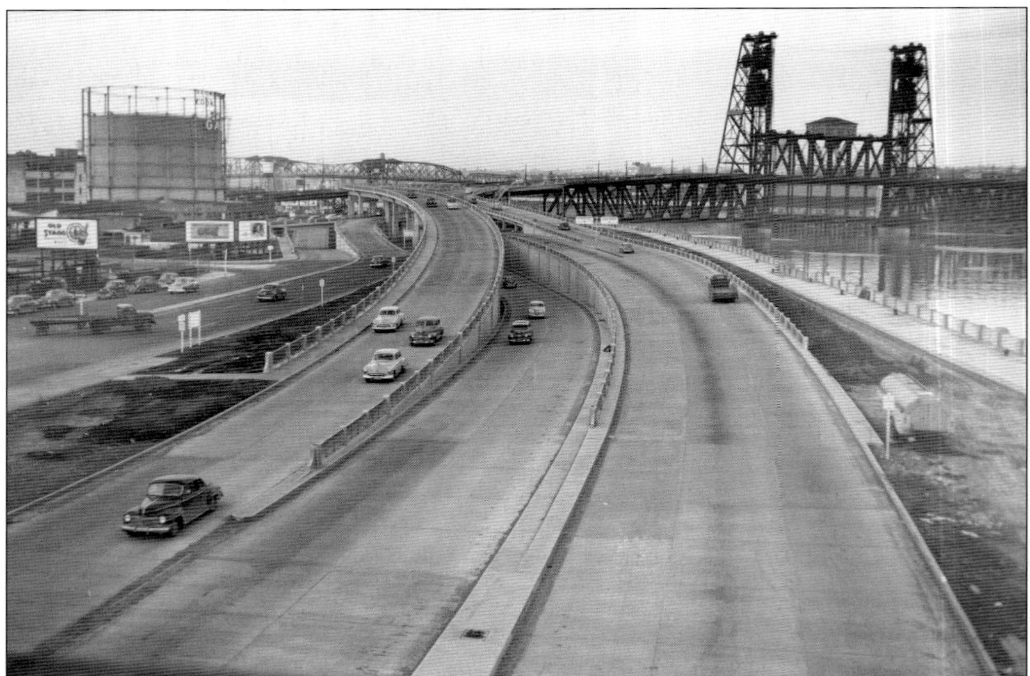

By 1935, proposals were floated for highway traffic to avoid downtown completely via a new connection between the Steel Bridge and Barbur Boulevard along Front Street. By 1950, new approaches to the venerable Steel Bridge had been constructed (the east side ramps are shown here) and the proposed route had shifted from Front to Harbor Drive. This became the Highway 99W alignment of the 1950s. (OSA, OHD4730.)

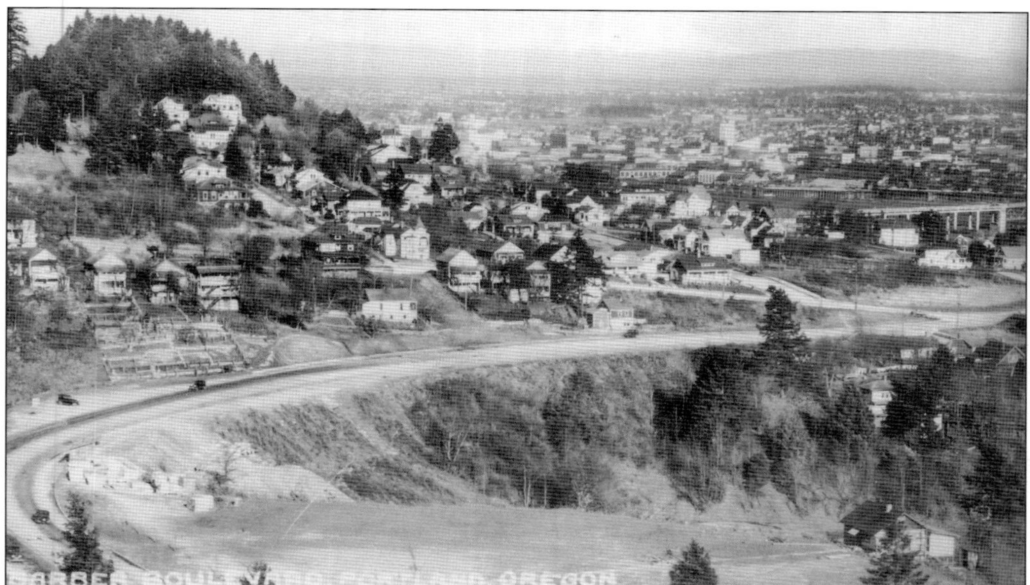

In 1932, work began on the Fourth Street Extension south from downtown Portland. Described as the city's most modern highway, the new road cut off two miles between Portland and Tigard. It also bypassed the earlier Capitol Highway–Terwilliger Boulevard route, which was proving too narrow and curvy for modern traffic. When completed in 1934, the road was named Barbur Boulevard. By 1945, it had been designated Highway 99W.

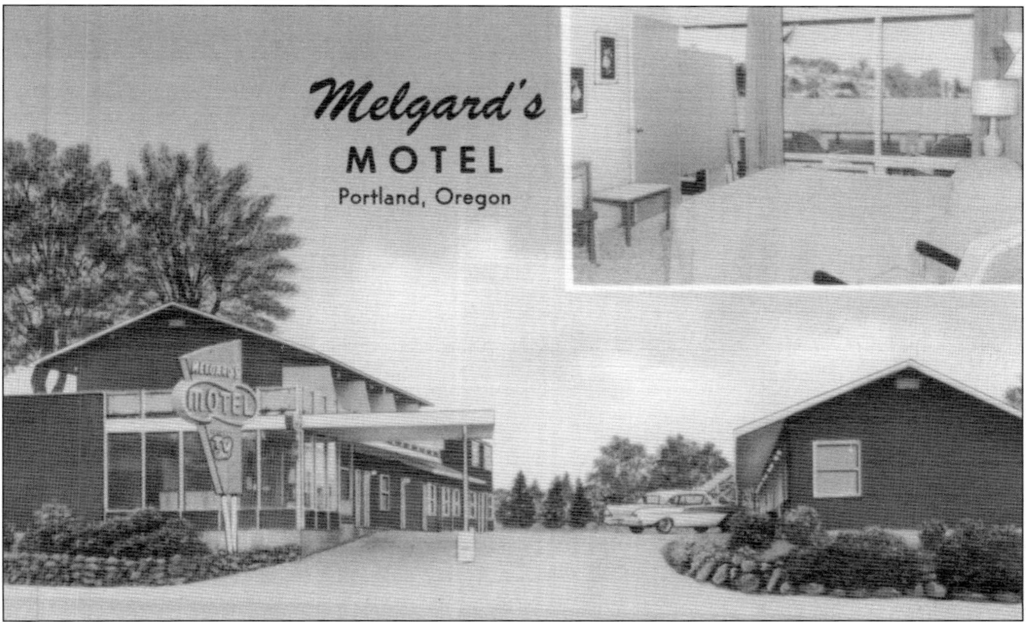

Melgard's opened in 1940 with 8 units, and the count was up to 19 by 1948. A complete top-to-bottom remodel grew the number to 36 motel and apartment rooms in 1957. Units offered kitchenettes with dishes and utensils provided, Beautyrest mattresses, free radio and television, and tiled tub/shower combinations. Alexander and Ada Melgard owned the property at 8255 SW Barbur Boulevard. A medical facility occupies the site today.

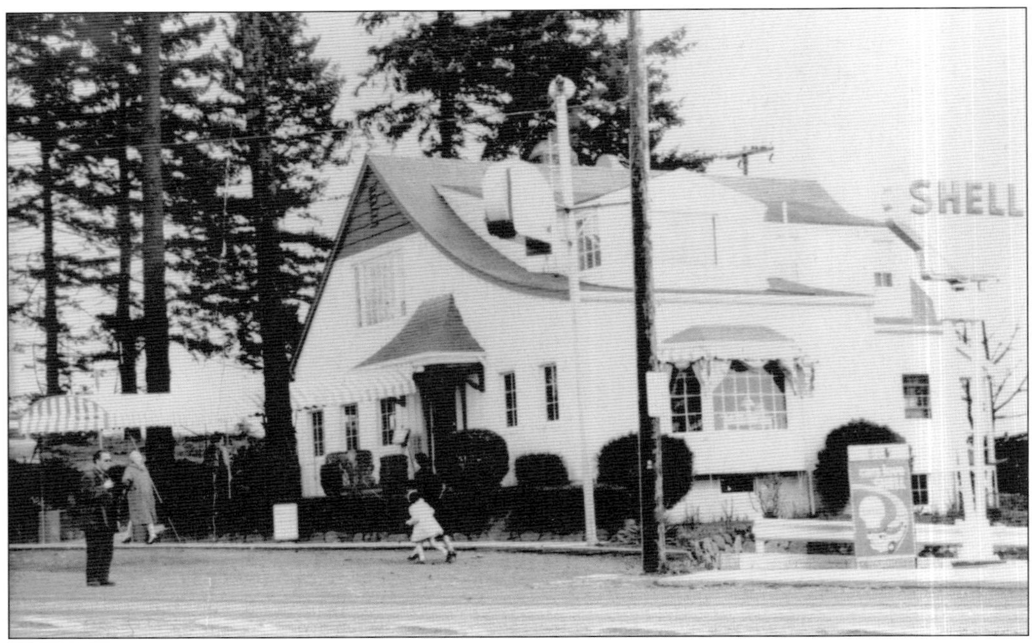

When Les Highet and Erma Hueneke took over management of the Pancake House in 1953, it had already been in business for 14 years. Newspaper advertisements for "pancakes mornin', noon and night" quickly grew the restaurant's popularity, and in 1958 it was rechristened the Original Pancake House. The original Original is at 8601 SW 24th Avenue, but over 100 franchises can be found across the United States and even in Japan. (OPHF.)

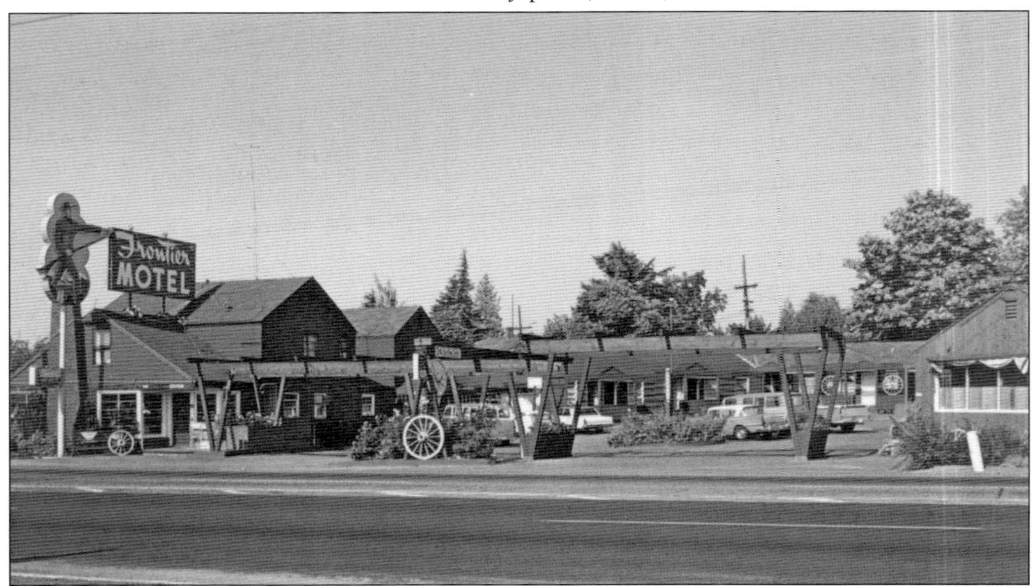

Original owner R.A. Cougher sold his Coucher's Auto Court to Garland Allen in 1954, who renamed it Allen's Motel. By 1957, it was the Frontier Motel, adopting a Western theme with wagon wheels and a neon sign of a frontiersman pointing to the U-shaped motel. The Frontier comprised 14 one- and two- bedroom units. Located at 8715 SW Barbur Boulevard, it is in business today as the Budget Lodge.

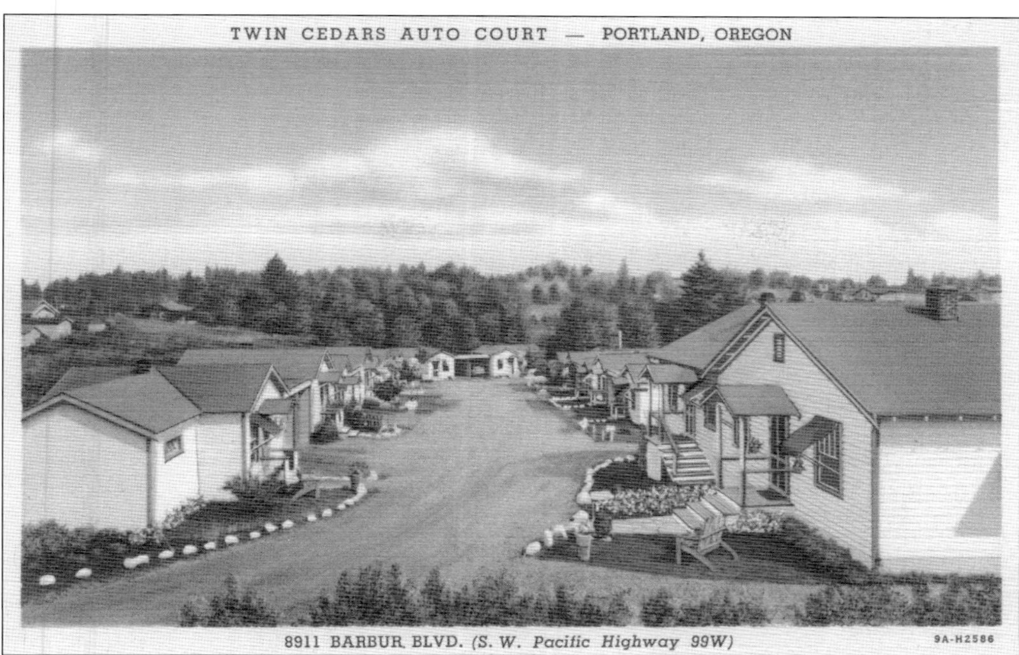

C.E. and Grace Throne purchased the Twin Cedars in 1936 and ran it for the next 30 years. The auto court evinces an early style of roadside architecture—18 semidetached cabins with gables and awnings, separated by carports and set in rows on parklike grounds away from the highway. Located at 8911 SW Barbur Boulevard, the Twin Cedars was still in business in 1982 but has since vanished.

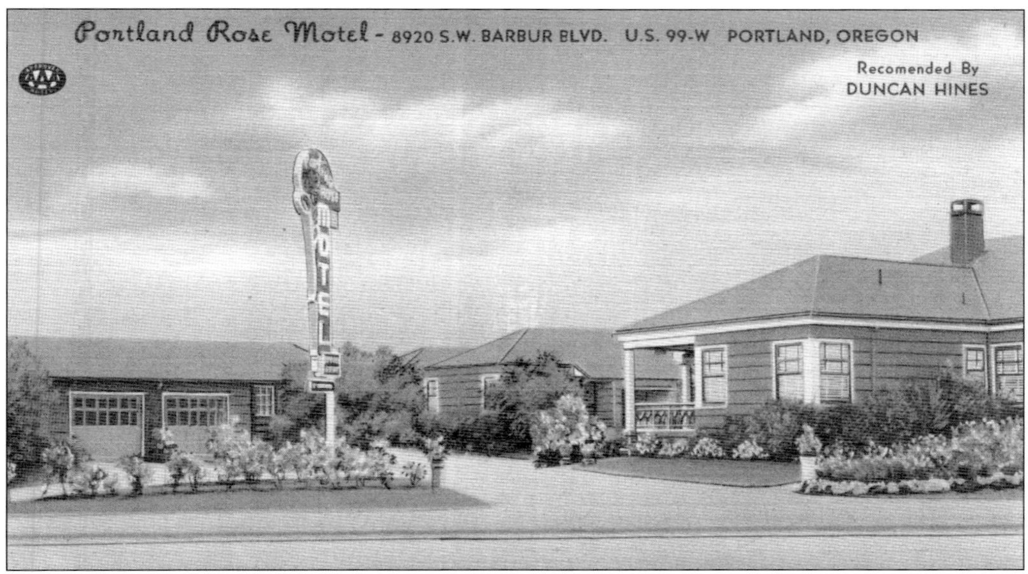

The Portland Rose Motel, at 8920 SW Barbur Boulevard, was in business by 1944. The motel offered 24 units (half with kitchenettes), radios, tile showers, and private garages. In 1948, when owned by Mr. and Mrs. Leonard E. Cornelius, a single room was $3.50 to $6 nightly; a double, $5 to $8.50. The Corneliuses sold to T.H. and Clara Gray in 1952. Still operating in 1987, there is a Les Schwab Tire Center there today.

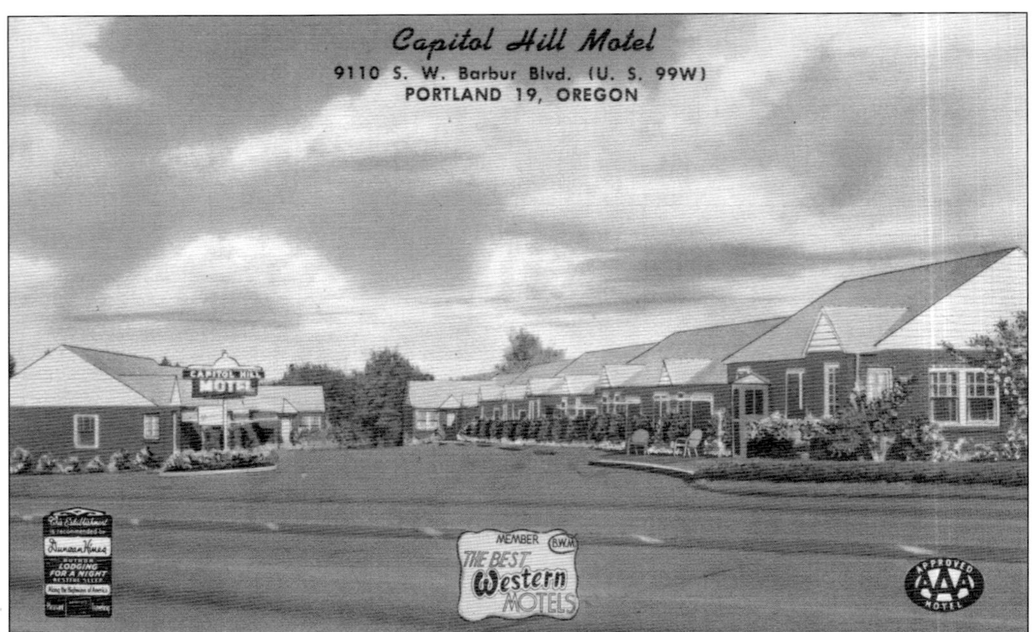

The Capitol Hill Motel's magnificent neon signs still shine brightly above Barbur Boulevard. Dating from 1939, the Capitol Hill and its 14 two- and three-room deluxe brick cottages received the Duncan Hines Signet Club designation in 1955; it was also AAA-approved and a member of United Motor Courts and Best Western. Nine of the units were equipped with kitchenettes; all had Simmons mattresses, tile showers, and locking garages.

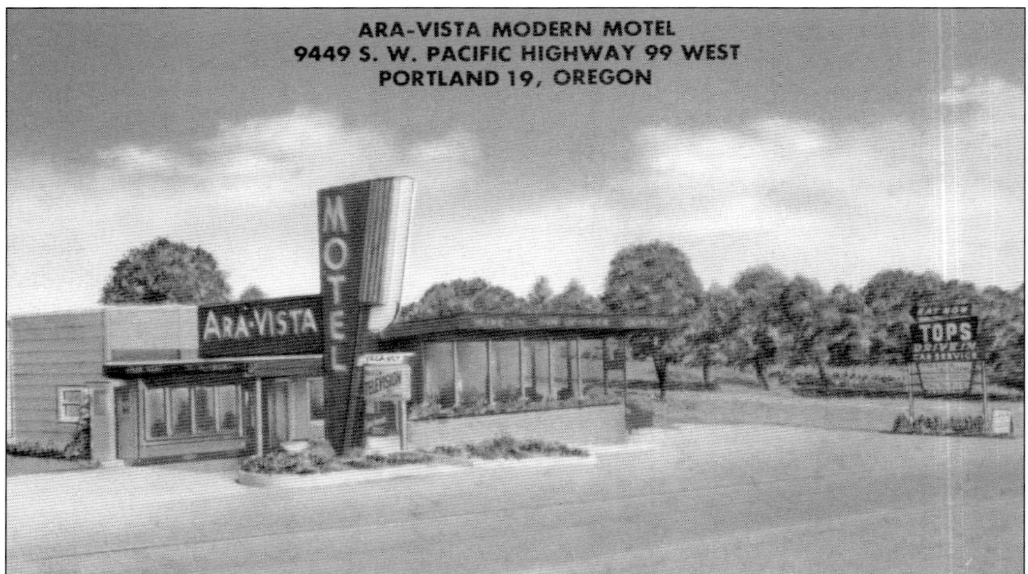

The Ara Vista began life as Craig's Auto Court; construction of the nearby Ara Vista subdivision probably prompted the name change. The motel, at 9449 SW Barbur Boulevard, had 12 modern two- or three-room cottages with the usual amenities. Recommended by Duncan Hines for overnight accommodations, by 1955, the Ara Vista advertised fully furnished apartments for $12.50/week. Next door, Tops Drive-In served up beefburgers, fish and chips, and homemade pies.

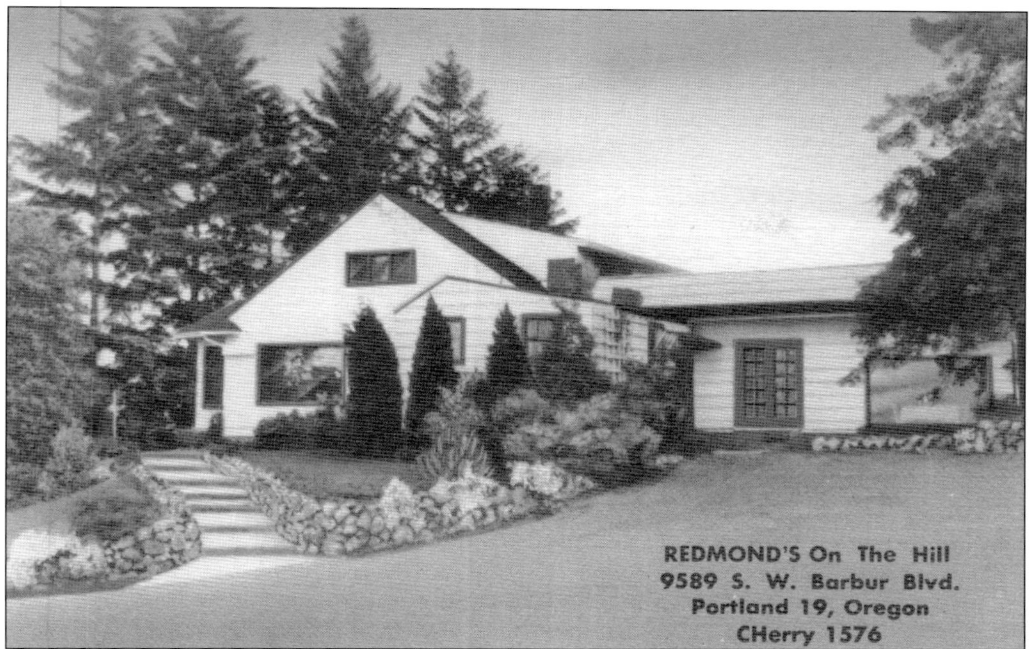

Redmond's on the Hill was serving sizzling steak and chicken dinners as long ago as 1938. After owner Martha Redmond sold out to Henry and Jeanne Ford in 1957, the name was modified to Ford's at Redmond's on the Hill; it became Henry Ford's in 1961. Located at 9589 SW Barbur Boulevard, Redmond's featured family-style dinners in a setting of lace tablecloths, silver, and candlelight. Their dessert specialty was rum pie.

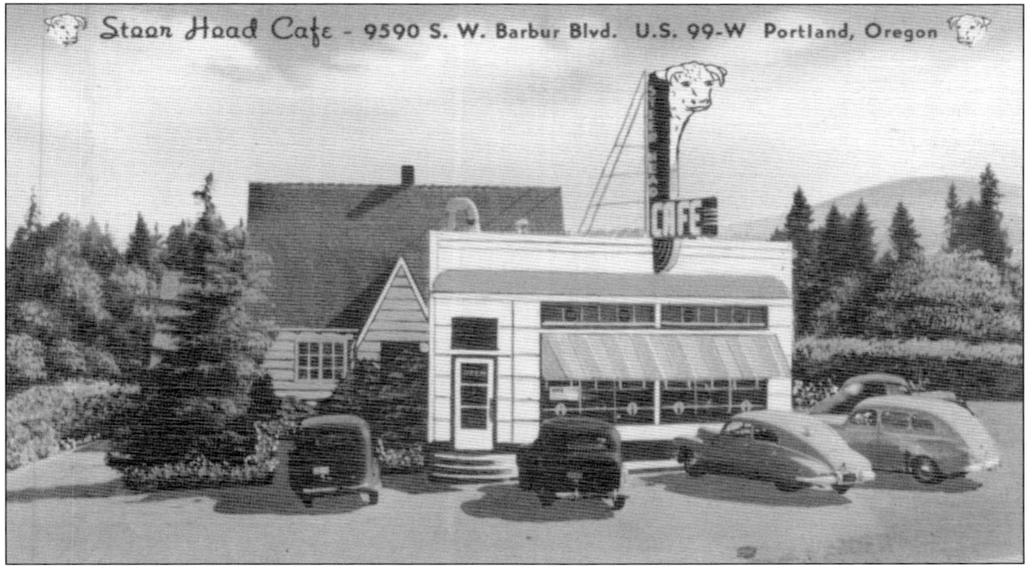

Opposite Redmond's was the Steer Head Cafe, at 9590 SW Barbur Boulevard. John and Mary Davis opened the café in 1941 and ran it until their retirement, when their son Maurice took over. The Steer Head offered table and counter service at prices lower than their competition across the street—in 1947, a complete home-style fried chicken dinner cost $1.50. It became Amelia's Patio, a Mexican restaurant, in 1960.

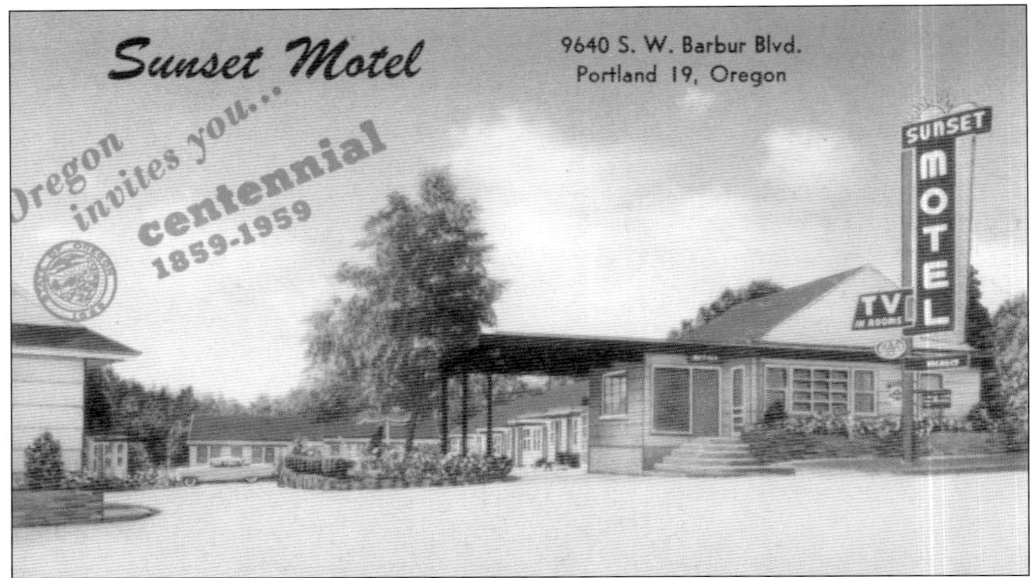

Next door to the Steer Head Cafe was the Sunset Motel at 9640 SW Barbur Boulevard. Its 25 one- and two-bedroom units were arranged in a U-shape with a modern convenience: an office entrance canopy to keep rain off customers when checking in. Fred and Ida Chapman were the owners; AAA and Duncan Hines recommended it. The motel was demolished in 1986 to make way for an office building.

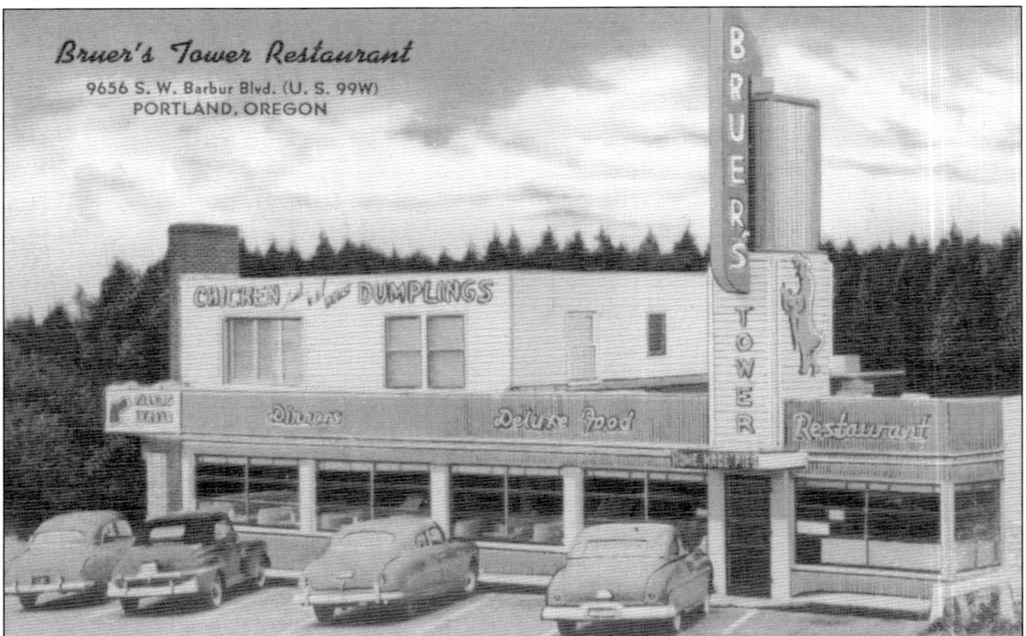

In 1951, George and Rosalie Bruer purchased the Tower Cafe at 9656 SW Barbur Boulevard and renamed it Bruer's Tower. Having managed Tad's Chicken n' Dumplings on the Columbia River Highway outside Troutdale, they adopted the same specialty at their new restaurant and also served steak dinners and homemade pies. Known in 1961 as Francisco's Tower, it was a Chinese restaurant in 1975. Today, it is called The Old Barn.

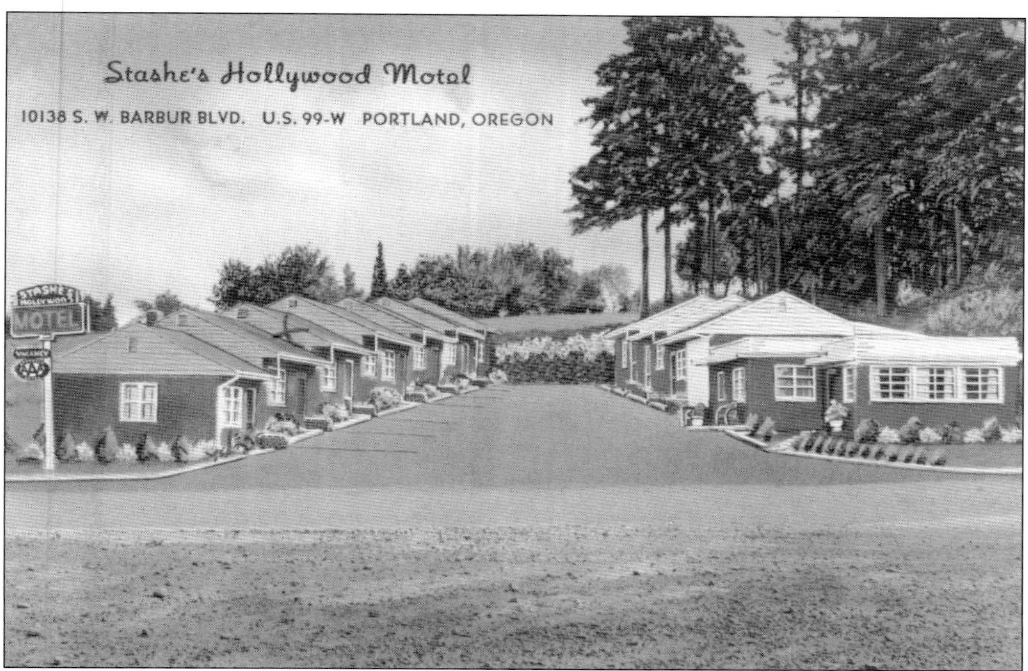

Stanley "Stashe" Bant owned the brick 10-unit Hollywood Motel in 1948, selling it to William and Opal Poplar in 1952. Two years later, it was renamed the Antler Motel and had grown to 22 units, some with kitchens, all with Beautyrest mattresses, carpeted floors, and televisions. Renamed yet again as the Ranch Inn in 1958, it is still in business at 10138 SW Barbur Boulevard.

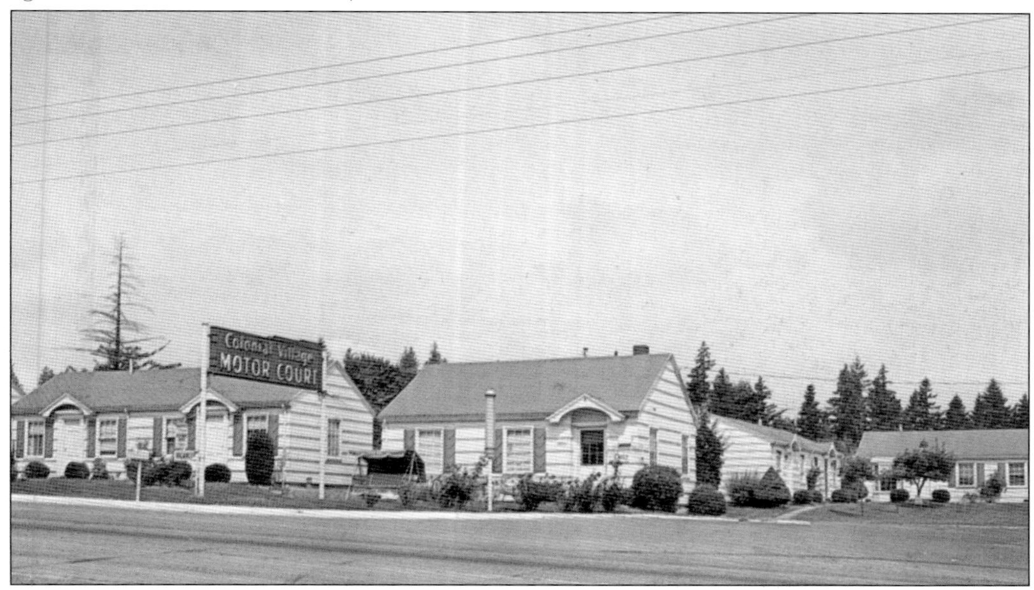

The trim white cottages of the Colonial Village Motor Court created a homey atmosphere of spacious lawns and tall trees. In 1941, the nightly rates for its 20 units—some with optional kitchenettes and refrigerators—were \$2 to \$3 single, \$2.50 to \$4 double. Garages without doors were provided for guests' use, and there was a restaurant on the premises. Regency Home Care now occupies the site at 10211 SW Barbur Boulevard.

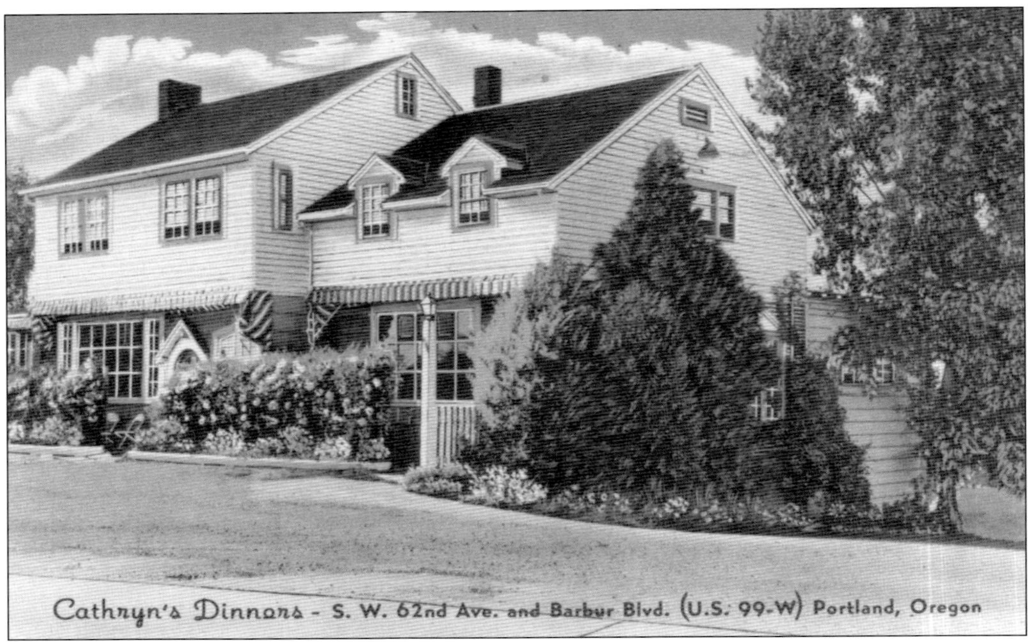

Kathryn (with a "K") Pettigrew was operating Cathryn's (with a "C") Dinners as early as 1940, specializing in pan-fried chicken and steak dinners. Though she sold the restaurant in 1946, the new owners, Virta and LaVell Des Bouillons, retained the name and invested $40,000 remodeling the place. By 1956, Cathryn's had been replaced by the Hi-Hat Chinese restaurant. The location, at 11311 SW Barbur Boulevard, is buried under Interstate 5.

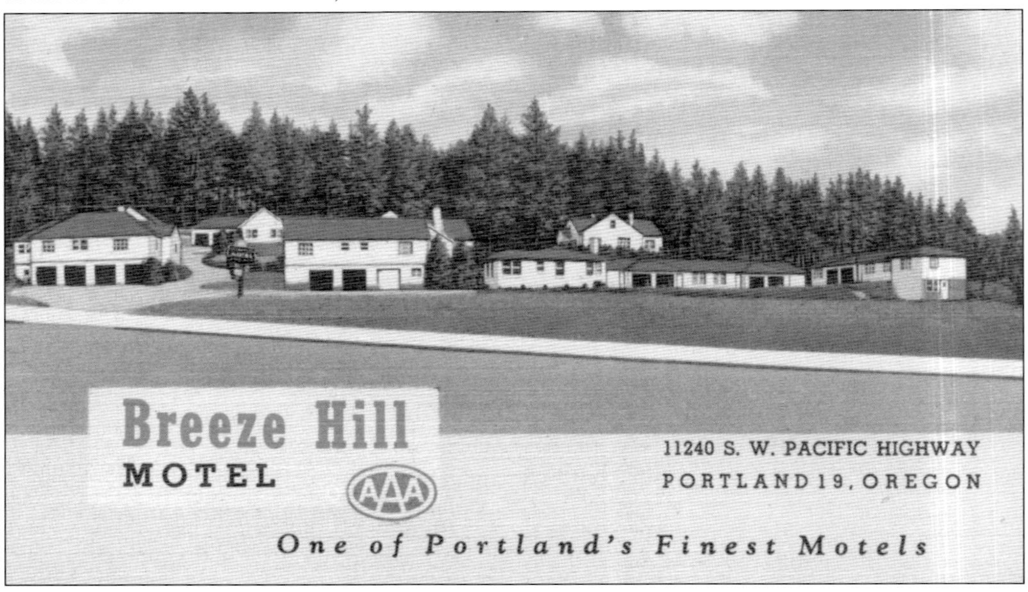

The first three units of the Breeze Hill Motel, owned by G.W. and Cleo Faulkner, opened in 1938. By 1949, the motel had grown to 25 units with the ubiquitous Beautyrest mattresses, electric kitchens, and tiled baths. Set on quiet, beautiful grounds against a backdrop of tall trees, the Breeze Hill was located at 11240 SW Barbur Boulevard. Like Cathryn's, it was a victim of freeway construction.

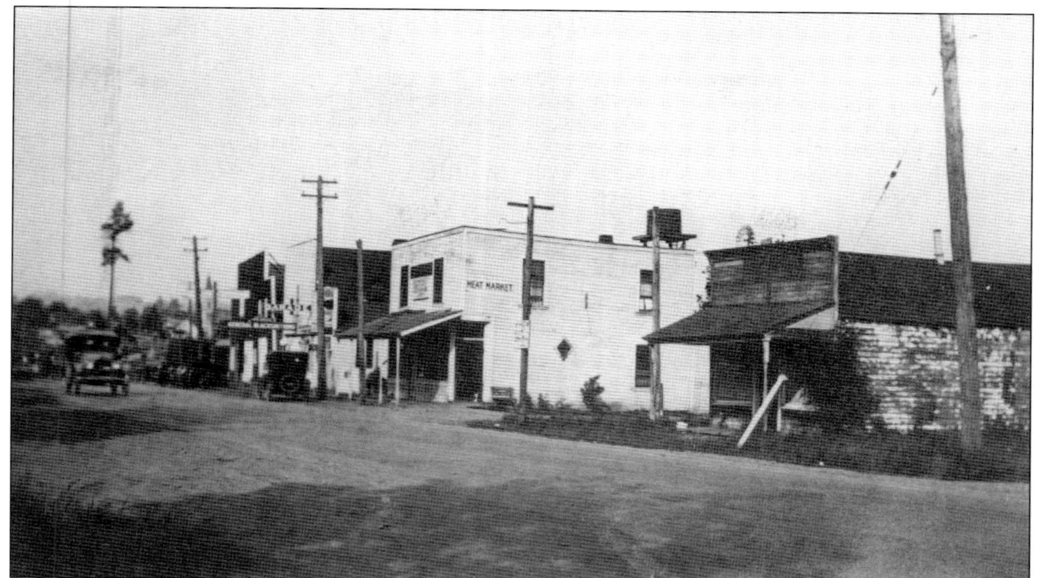

Tigard was a quiet country town when this photograph was taken around 1920; today, it is a satellite of Portland with a population of nearly 50,000. Main Street (originally Taylor's Ferry Road, one of the oldest in Oregon) carried the Pacific Highway through town. Four commercial buildings line the right side of the street. Next to the meat market was the blacksmith shop/garage of William Ariss. (TPL, TPLpic_0023.)

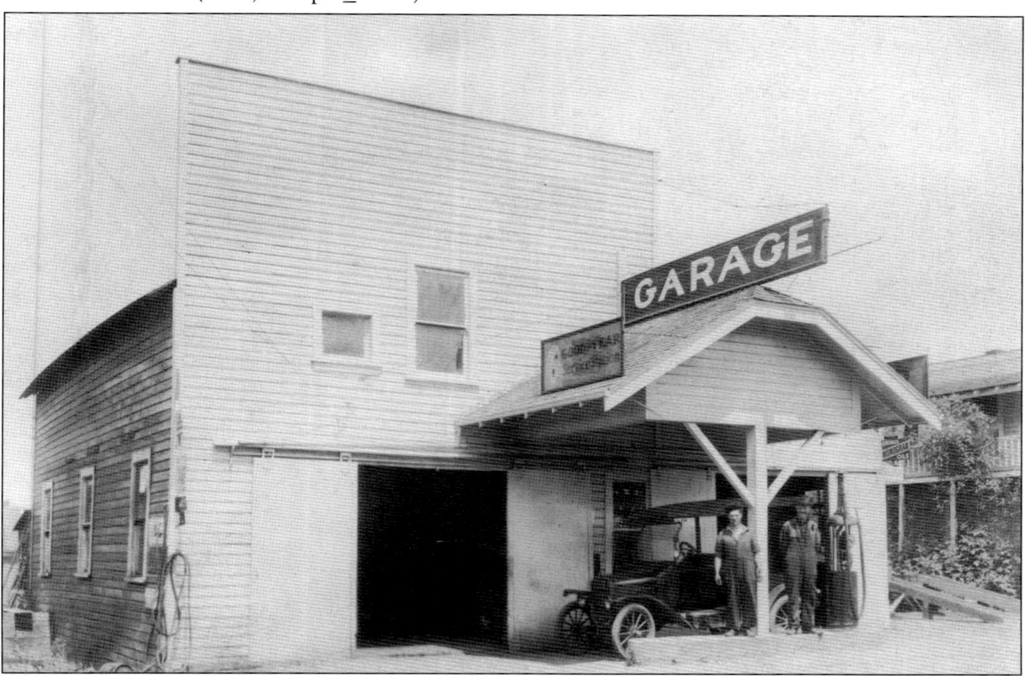

When William Ariss opened his blacksmith shop on Tigard's Main Street in 1911, automobiles were still considered playthings of the rich and adventurous. Autos proved to be more than a passing fad, however, and this view shows that by 1918, Ariss had given in to the inevitable and converted his shop to a Goodyear service station and garage. (WCM, WCMpic_002861.)

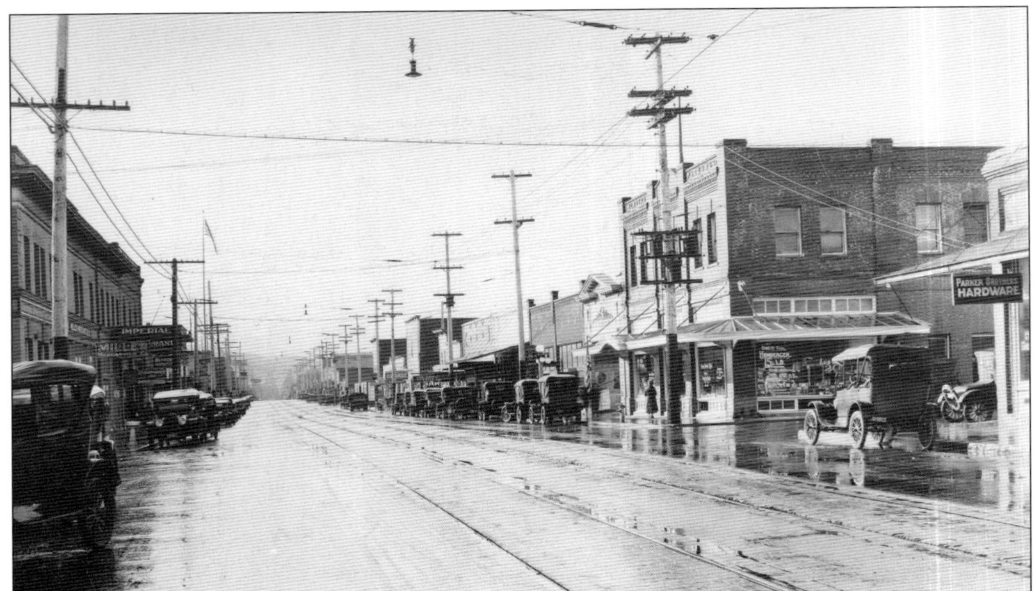

Downtown Newberg shimmers in the rain in this 1926 view. Autos line the street, but there is no traffic. Only one pedestrian is visible: a woman gazing into the window of a grocery store ("Hamburger 15¢ Lb."). Newberg was the first large town on the West Side Pacific Highway out of Portland, with a population of about 2,600 when this photograph was taken; today, it is home to 22,000. (OSL, 23984.)

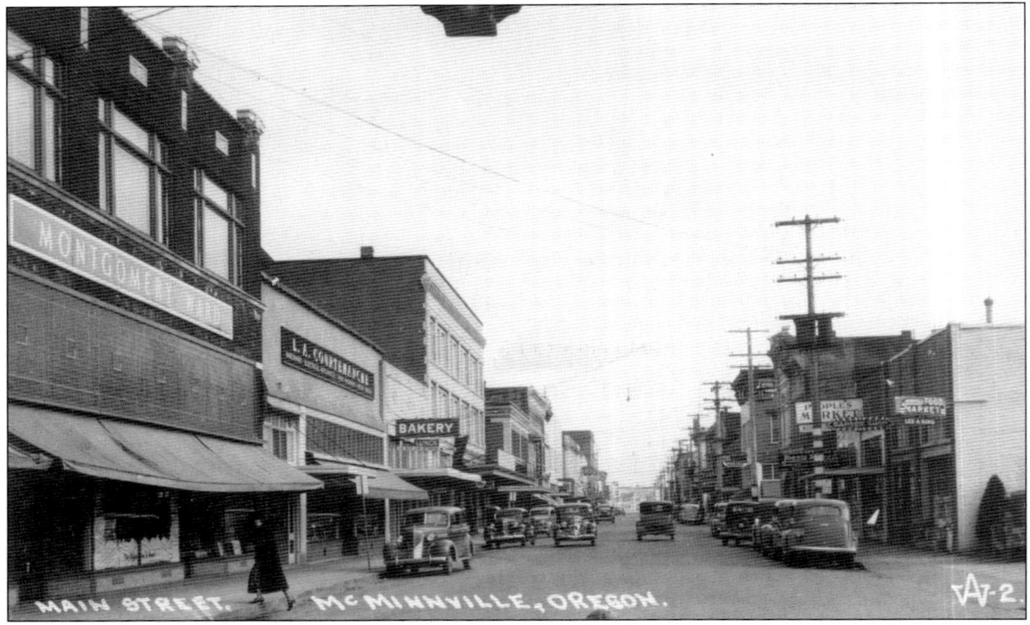

Before Highway 99W bypassed downtown, southbound traffic flowed through McMinnville on Main Street via Lafayette Avenue. This view of the business district shows signs for Montgomery Ward, L.A. Courtenance's Hardware, the McMinnville Food Market, and a bakery/lunch advertising "the best cup of coffee in town." At a junction outside of town, travelers could take State Route 18 to the Oregon Coast or continue south on 99 toward Monmouth and Corvallis.

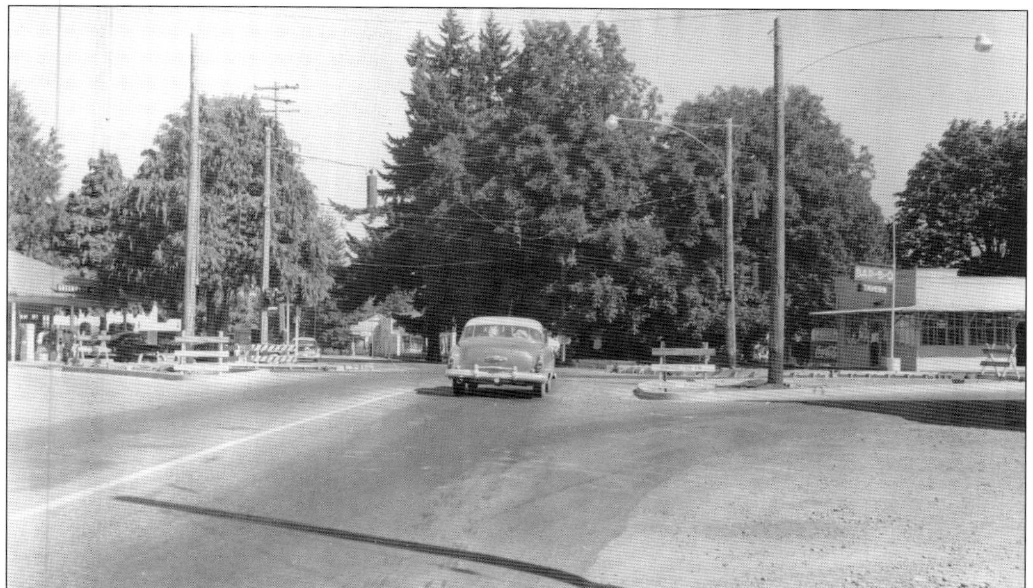

At Rickreall, Highway 99W crossed paths with the main road running east to Salem and west to the Oregon Coast. The Bar-B-Q Cafe, pictured on the right, was the scene of a Wild West–type shootout in November 1955. Two gun-toting robbers held the place up, but their escape was foiled when their car stalled. A gunfight followed, leaving one of the robbers dead and a state patrol officer wounded. (PCHS.)

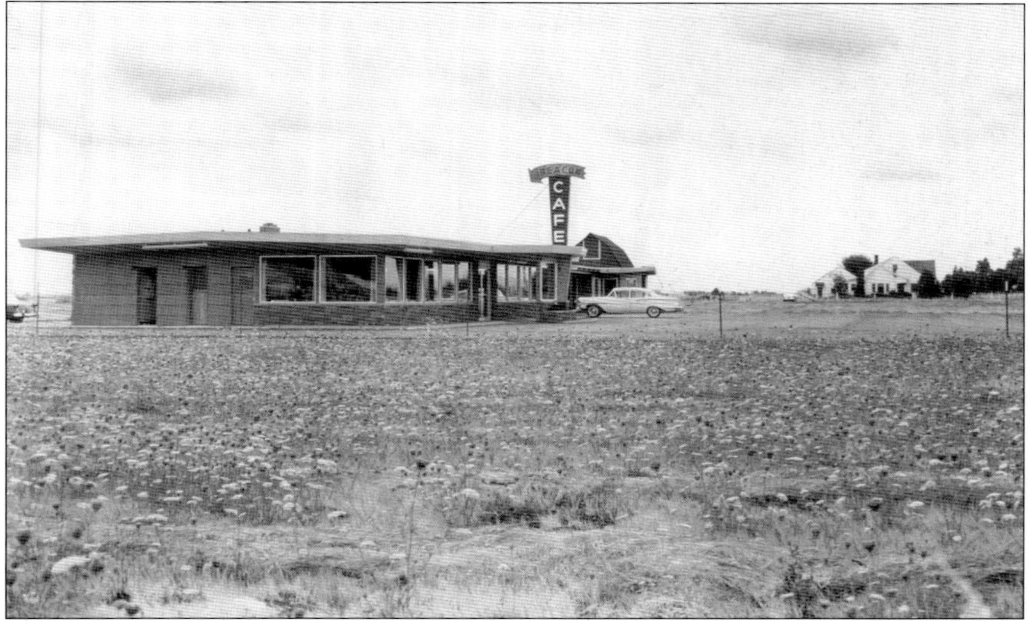

In 1950, Polk County chose a site along Highway 99 south of Rickreall as the county fair's permanent home. George Esau, whose farm bordered the site, saw a business opportunity and in 1959 constructed the Beacon Cafe and adjacent 16-unit motel. Each of the café's booths offered a view of the highway. Known today as Farrol's, it is part of the local Rock-N-Rogers chain. The motel is out of business. (PCHS.)

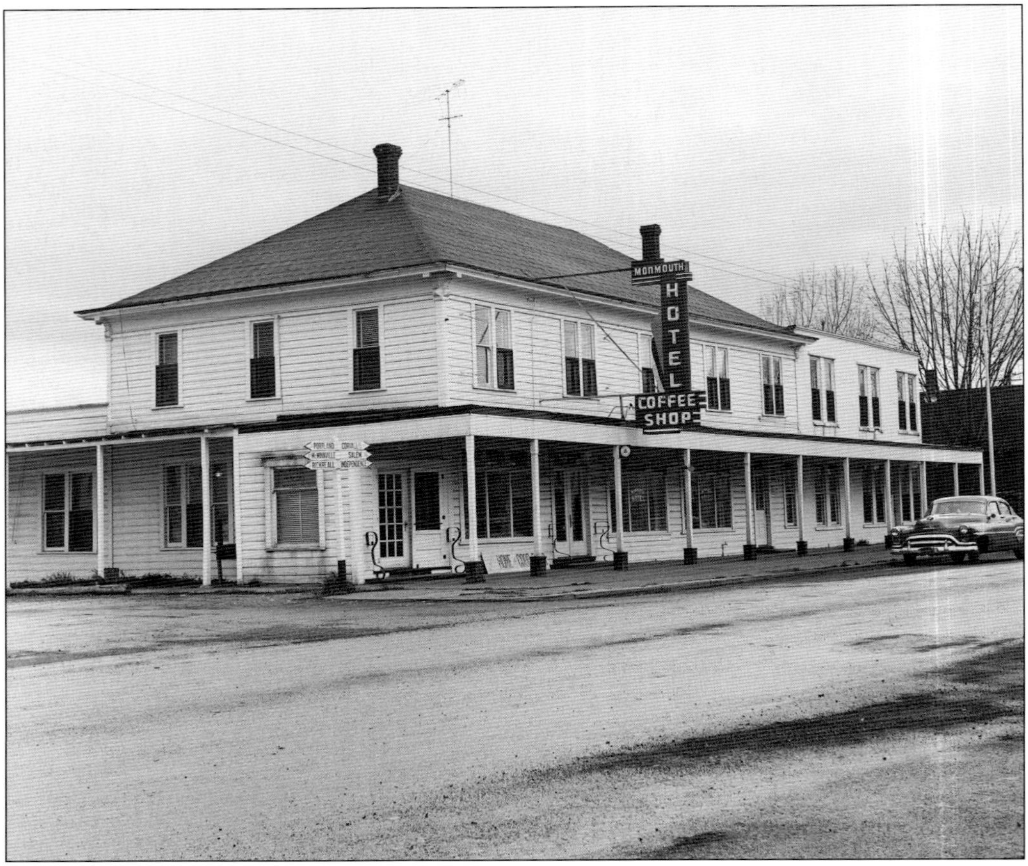

The Monmouth Hotel opened around 1921 and was operated for 20 years by E.J. and Anna Sivier. He ran the hotel, and the dining room was her domain. The 22-room hotel was the social center of town, with local organizations such as the Kill Kare Club meeting there for monthly lunches. Still in business in 1964, it is now gone. This is how it looked in 1958. (OHPC, 6497.)

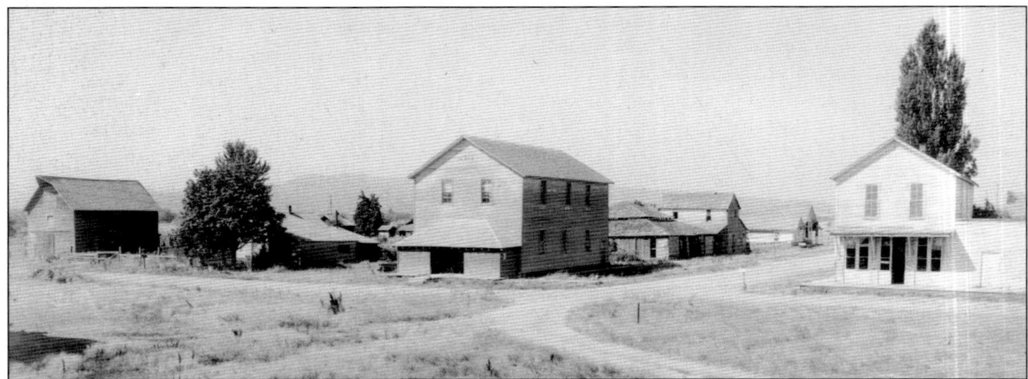

Seven miles south of Monmouth, the few remnants of Suver Junction sit astride Highway 99W. The original site of Suver was along the railroad a mile east. In the 1890s, Suver had a store, blacksmith, shoe shop, dance hall, depot, and grain elevators. When the highway passed the town by, businesses moved to take advantage of motor traffic. The old town gradually withered; all these buildings have vanished. (OSL, 27981.)

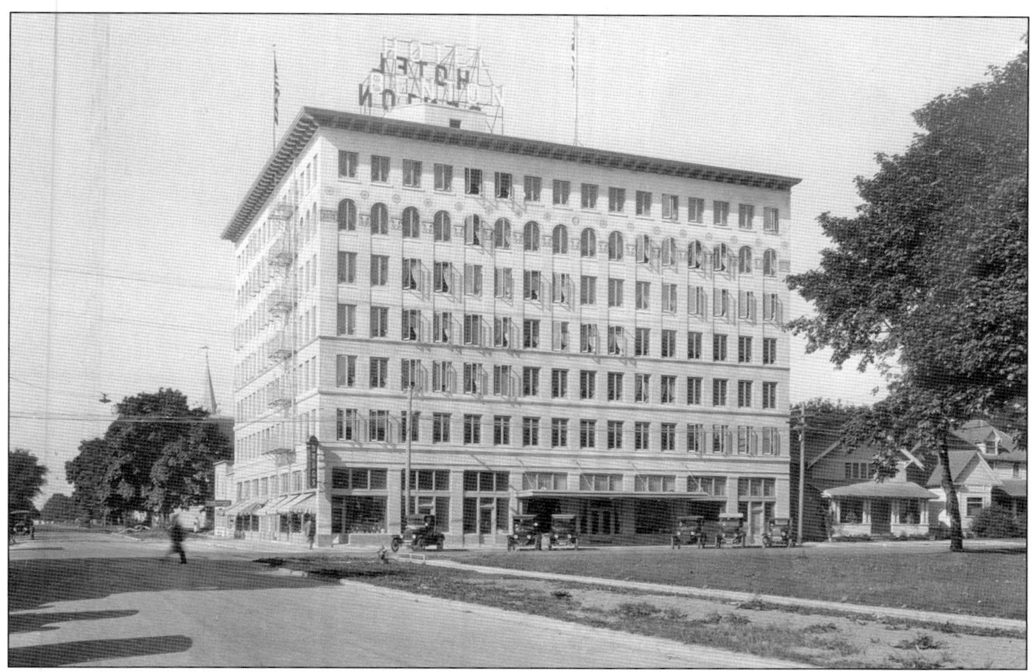

The Hotel Benton, at 408 Monroe Avenue, marked the Pacific Highway's grand entrance into Corvallis. Its seven stories held 110 rooms, 70 with baths; a ballroom and mezzanine; dining/banquet rooms; and a coffee shop that served "well cooked meals." Opened in July 1925, it immediately became the prestigious meeting place in town. The hotel fell on hard times in the 1970s; refurbished, it serves as low-income housing today. (BCM, 1999-125.00010001.)

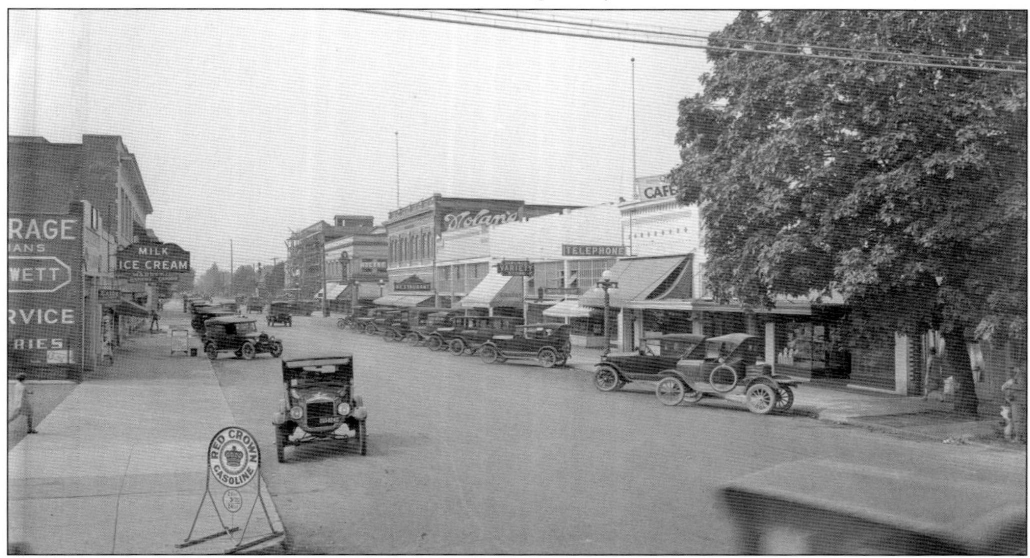

The Pacific Highway was carried through the heart of Corvallis on 3rd Street. Seat of Benton County and home to Oregon Agricultural College (Oregon State University today), the city dates its settlement to 1845. Its population is currently about 56,000, a tenfold increase from 1926 when this photograph was taken. The view is south on 3rd from Monroe Avenue. Some of these buildings still stand, hidden behind modern facades. (BCM, 1990-068.13070001.)

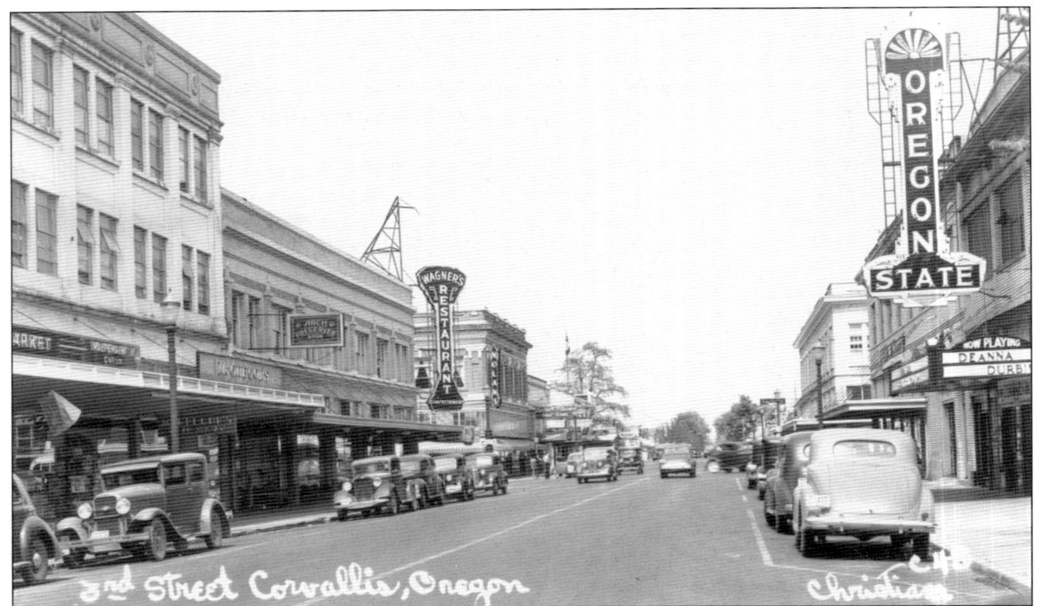

This c. 1940 view looks north on 3rd from Jefferson Avenue. Autos crowd the curb, but the sidewalks seem empty of pedestrians. Visible signs include McGregor's 5-10-25¢ store, Wagner's Restaurant, Nolan's Department Store, and the Oregon State Theatre. Most of the buildings on the left still exist; unfortunately, only a parking lot remains where the theater was. (BCM, 2003-061.0001.)

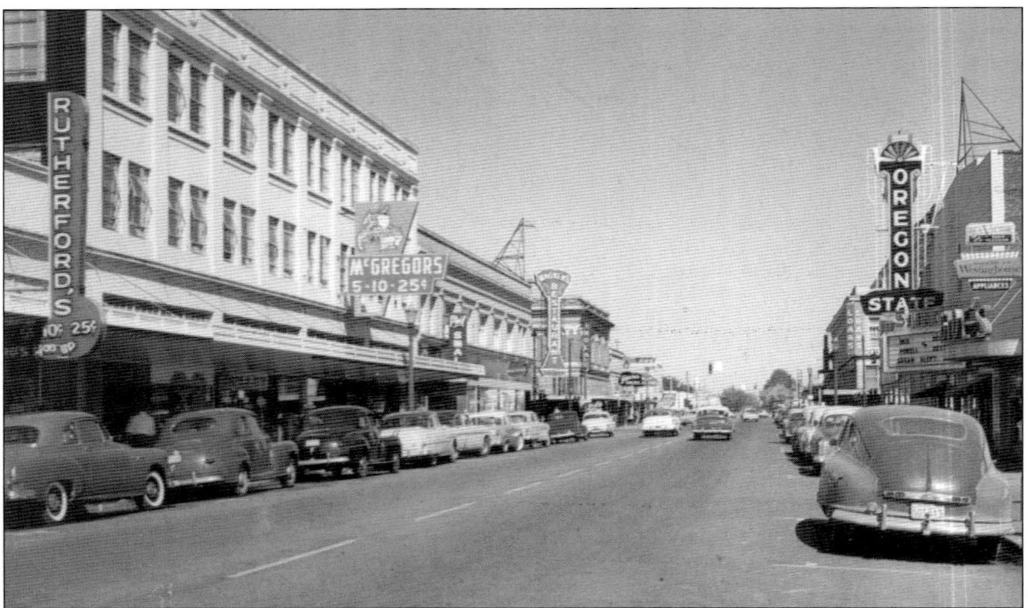

By the late 1940s, Corvallis was grappling with increased traffic volumes and narrow downtown streets. In August 1949, a one-way couplet was established: southbound traffic traveled on 4th Street, northbound on 3rd. This 1954 view of 3rd Street is from the same vantage point as the last. Other than the direction of traffic, not much had changed, though McGregor's had a larger sign. (BCM, 1981-106.0028P.)

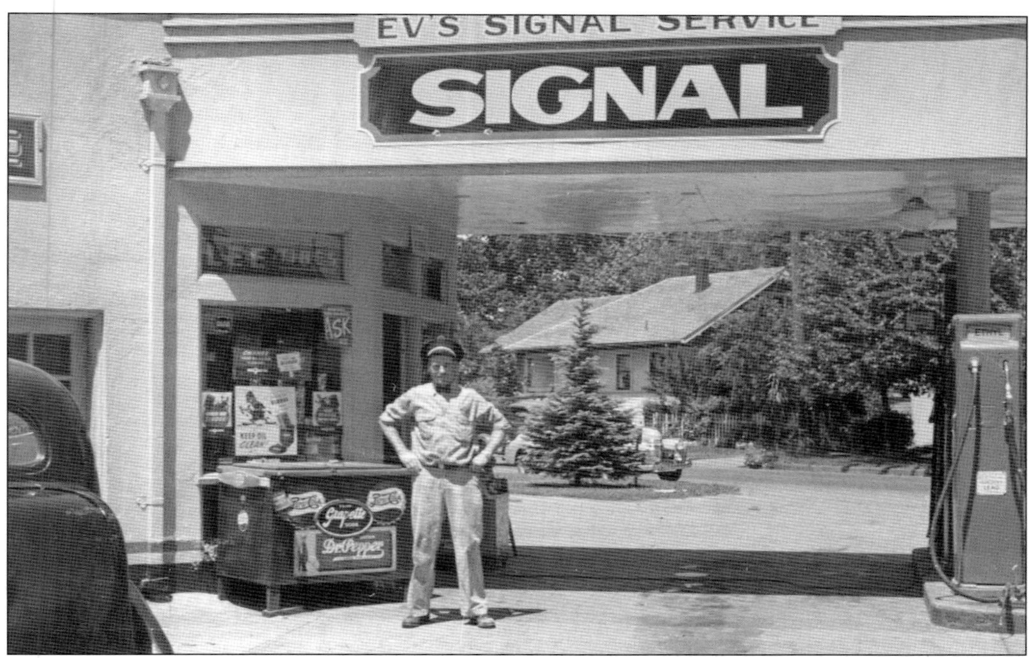

In the 1940s, Everett Miller changed careers from millworker to service station operator, opening Ev's Signal Service at 3rd Street and Western Avenue. In addition to gasoline, Ev sold Lee Tires and Pepsi, Dr. Pepper, and Grapette soda from an ice-filled cooler. After Corvallis adopted one-way traffic on 3rd and 4th in 1949, he started a new station at 4th and Western. Neither building exists today. (BCM, 2004-051.0001.)

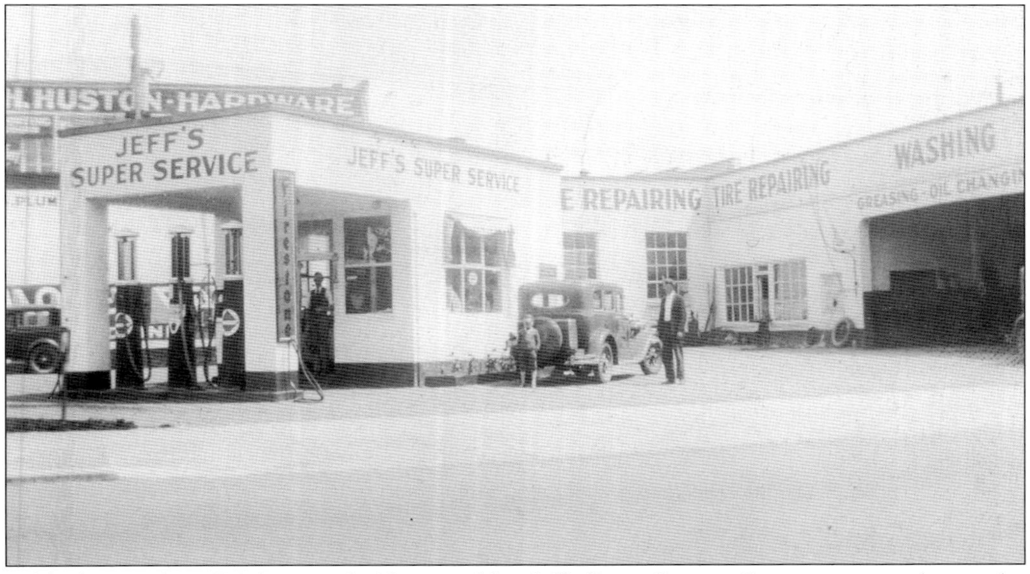

A block away from Ev's but nearly 20 years older, Jeff's Super Service Station was another in the string of gas stations lining 3rd Street on the way out of Corvallis. Jeff's was operated by brothers Jeff and Andy Ayers and prided itself on being a well-stocked station providing lubrication service and Firestone tires in addition to pumping gasoline. Jeff's was located at 636 S 3rd. (BCM, 1980-030.0065.)

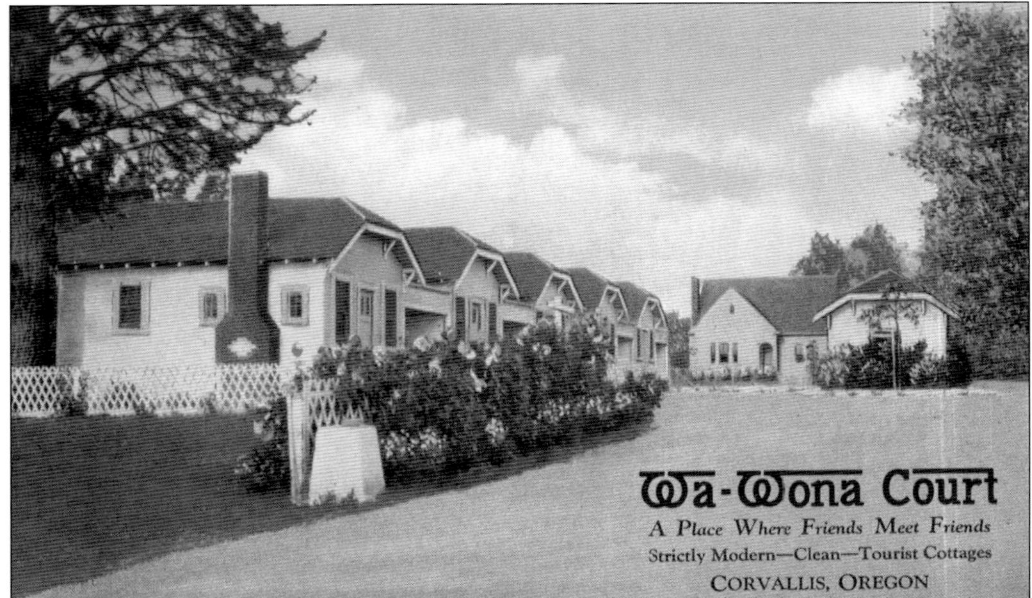

The Wa-Wona Court was beautifully situated on Mary's River at the south edge of Corvallis. Nine two-, three-, and four-room cottages connected by open carports and festooned with flowers and vines were set among attractive grounds next to Corvallis's city park. The comfy cabins were provided with Beautyrest mattresses and cooking facilities. The Wa-Wona was located at 816 S 3rd Street just north of the Mary's River Bridge. (BCM, 2002-013.0001.)

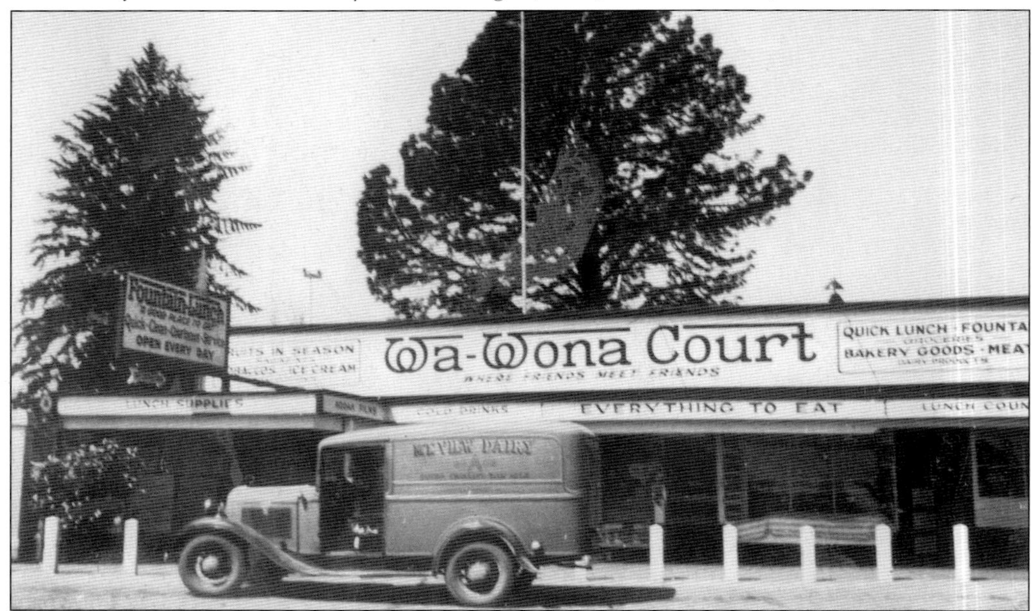

Edward Fehler opened the Wa-Wona Court in 1926 and soon built it up into a self-contained resort by adding an on-premises service station, store, and fountain lunch. Russell Morss operated the service station; Mr. and Mrs. Ted Hise ran the store, lunch counter (its slogan: "Everything to Eat"), and soda fountain. The significance of "Wa-Wona" is unknown, though there is a famous hotel by that name in Yosemite Valley. (BCM, 1999-108.)

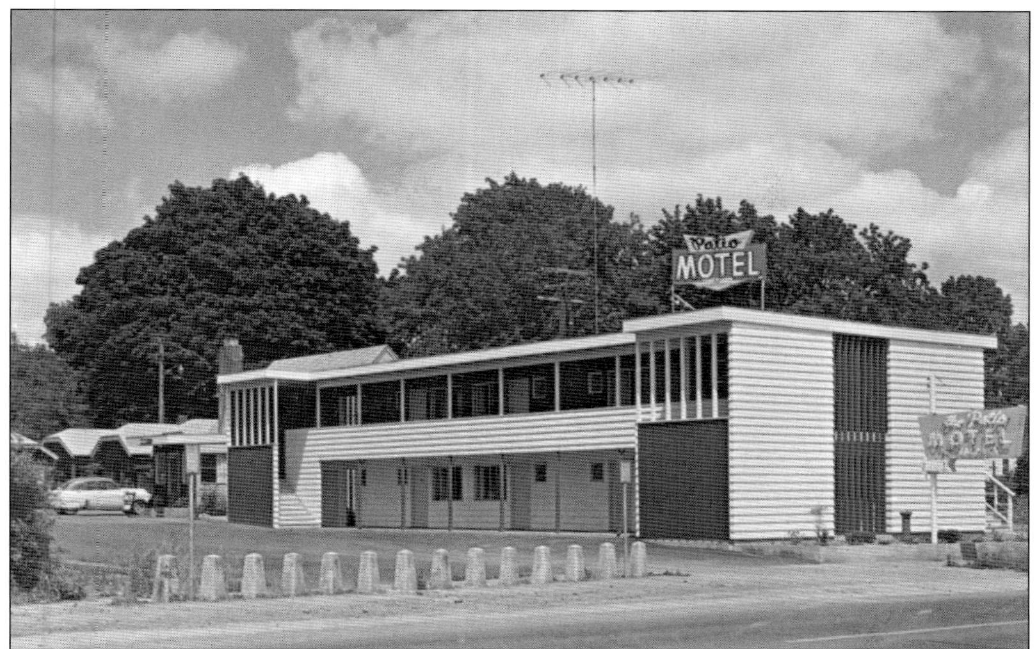

The Wa Wona became the Patio Motel a few years after Edward Fehler passed away in 1949. By the early 1960s, the old cottages had been moved to Philomath (where they are still in use as apartments) and a new Patio Motel—drastically different in style from its predecessor—had been built. It is all gone today, buried under the Highway 99 approach to the Mary's River Bridge.

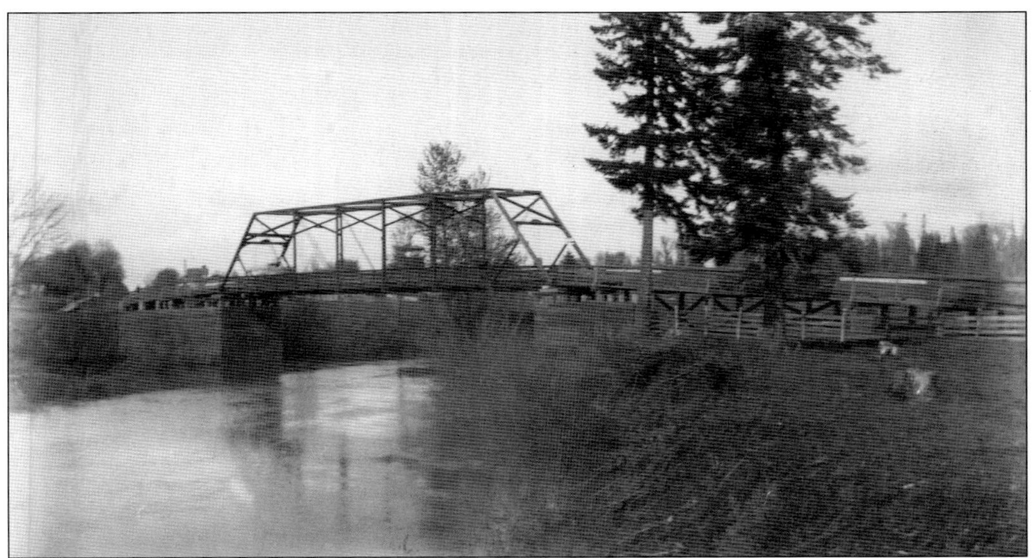

This primitive-looking structure was the original Mary's River Bridge just outside Corvallis. Built in 1910 by Benton County, the 100-foot-long steel truss bridge was later taken over by the state highway department. On August 16, 1932, an overloaded truck struck the south end-post of the span, knocking it off its foundations and sending the bridge, the truck, and an auto into the river. (DO-OSU, HC596.)

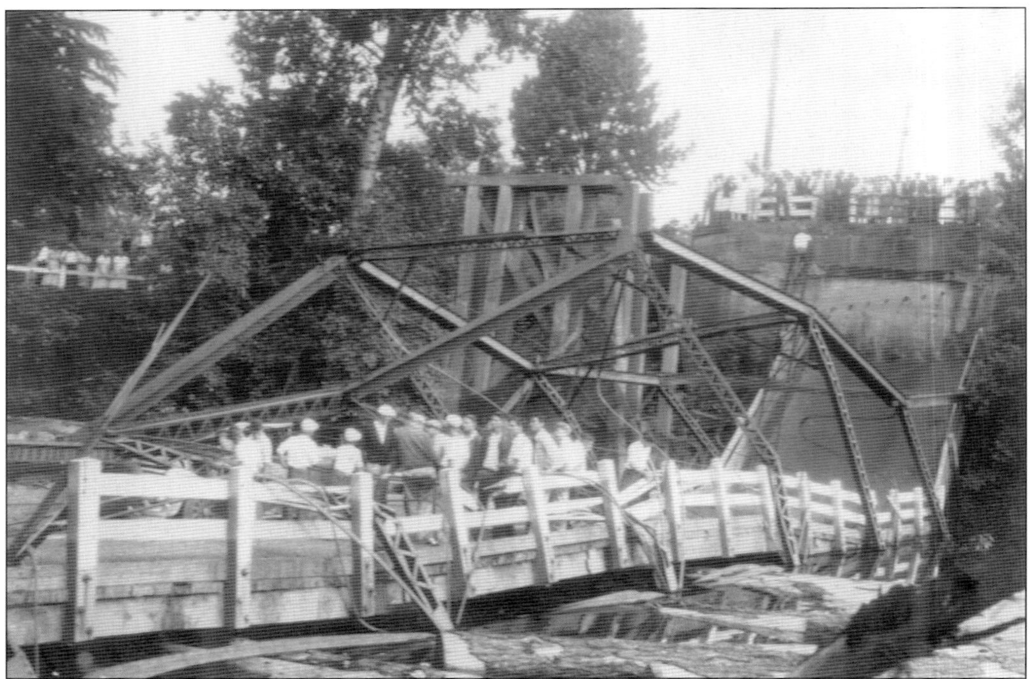

A curious crowd views the Mary's River Bridge laying in shambles after being dislodged from its supports. The driver of the automobile that plunged into the river was not seriously hurt. The span landed on a log raft, sufficiently intact that it could still carry pedestrians, but West Side Pacific Highway traffic had to be rerouted over to the East Side highway while a temporary replacement was erected. (BCM, 1998-016.0008.)

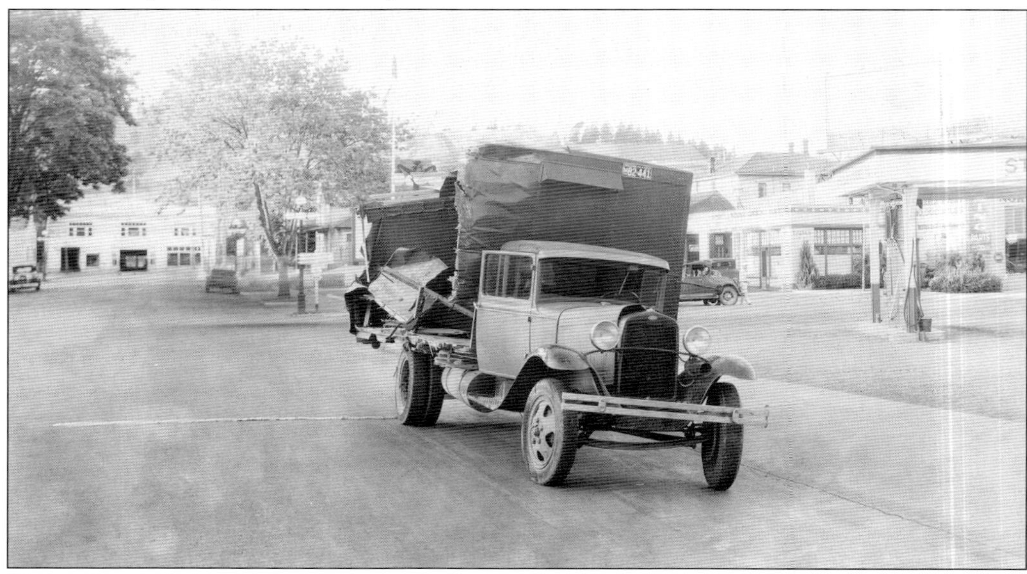

This is the truck that collapsed the Mary's River Bridge after it was towed into Corvallis. The driver claimed that he was blinded by oncoming headlights, lost control, and collided with the bridge, but the truck's load—six tons of groceries at the time—exceeded the allowable weight limit. Highway 99 runs left to right in the photograph. Note the gas stations behind the truck. (OSA.)

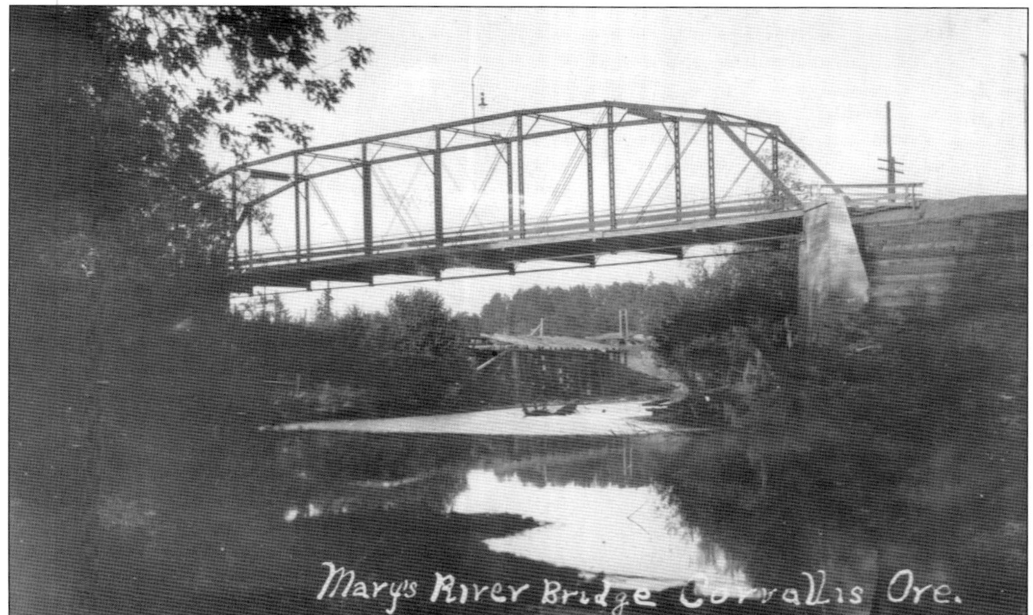

This 150-foot steel Parker through-truss structure replaced the collapsed Mary's River Bridge in 1933. It was rather plain in design, but decorative elements such as ornate lanterns, entry pylons, and concrete handrails were added later. It was sympathetically restored, and the lamps relit, by the Oregon Department of Transportation in 2011. The bridge was built for two-way traffic, but today it carries only northbound traffic into Corvallis on 3rd Street. (BCM, 1984-015.00595.)

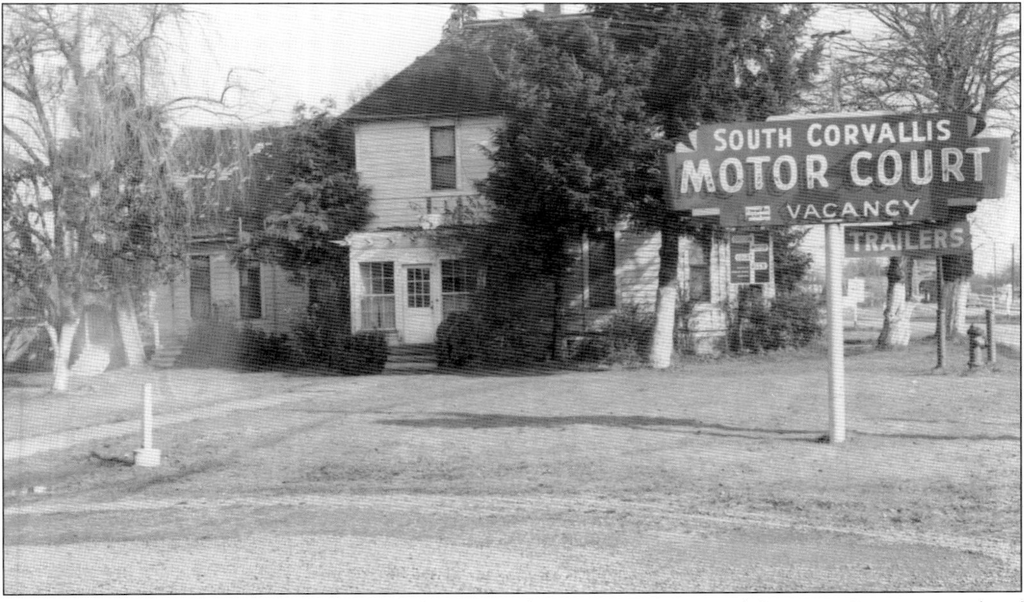

In 1934, A.E. Thomas was operating the Bungalow Auto Court and Service Station south of the Mary's River Bridge. By 1941, he had started the South Corvallis Auto Court directly across the highway. The new court consisted of two single and four double-unit cottages and spaces for 40 trailers. Later known as the South Corvallis Motor Court and Trailer Park, it was located on Highway 99W opposite Chapman Lane. (BCM, 2002-073.0005.)

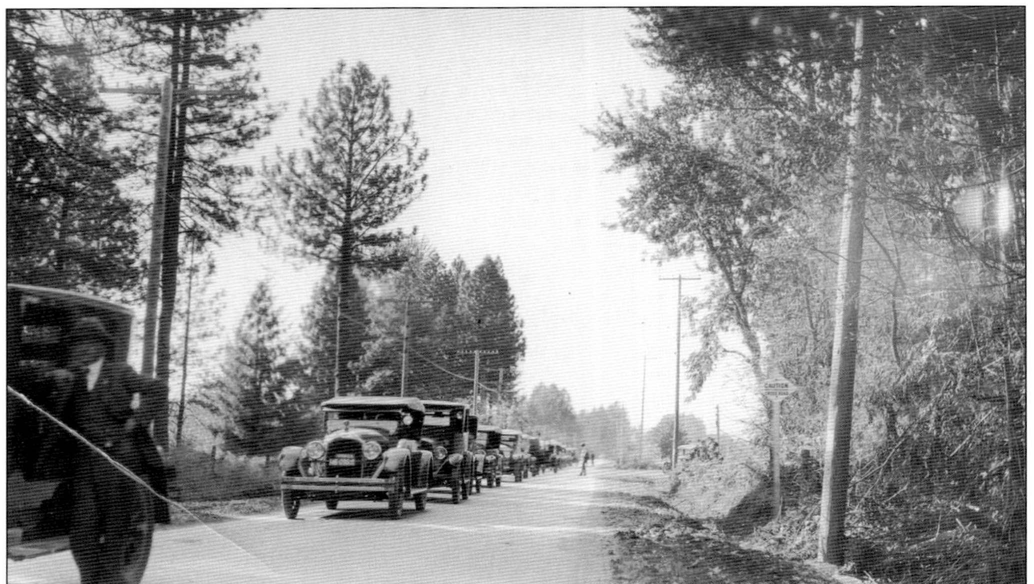

South from Corvallis, the West Side Pacific Highway overlaid the Old Territorial Road—one of the earliest routes in Oregon, dating to 1851. Grading and paving of the old road began in 1919 and was performed in sections of 10 or fewer miles at a time. When work was finally completed in September 1924, Corvallis residents used the occasion for an auto parade on the newly paved highway. (BCM, 1996-100.00520001.)

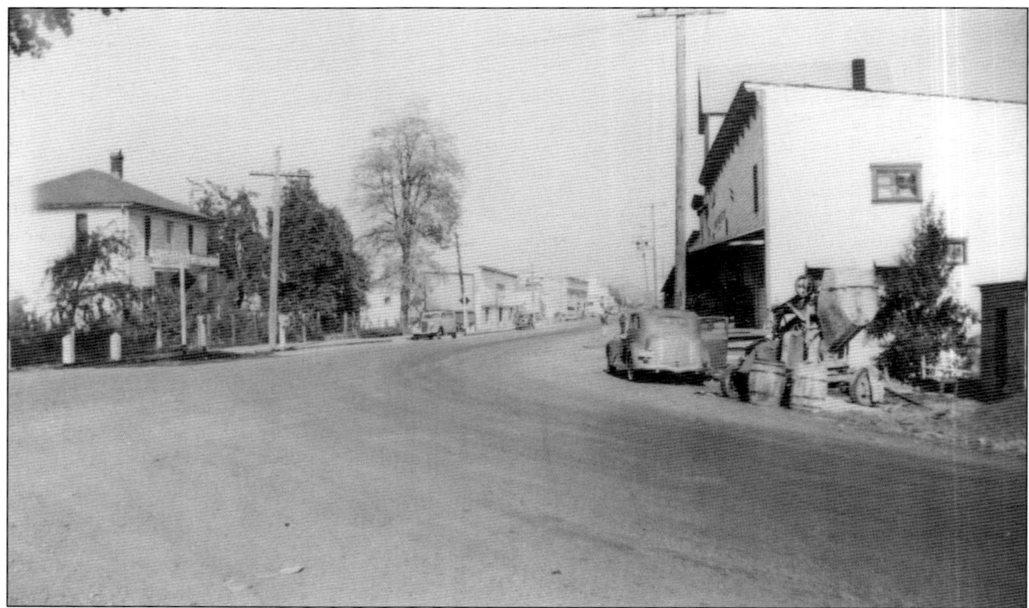

At the south end of Monroe, the Pacific Highway departed the Old Territorial Road to curve southeast toward Junction City. The view looks north; a bridge across the Long Tom River is just out of sight to the right. The shallow river often overflowed during the rainy season, flooding the highway and disrupting traffic. Most of these buildings in downtown Monroe have disappeared. (BCM, 1980-034.00050001.)

Three

Highway 99
Junction City to the State Line

After splitting north of Portland, Highways 99E and 99W reunite at Junction City, halfway down the state. In early days, the highway passed through town along 6th Avenue before turning south on River Road to Eugene. This segment was bypassed in 1938 by a more direct route.

Along 6th and 7th Avenues were Eugene's "motel row." The highway navigated surface streets through the city before heading out on Franklin Boulevard. At Glenwood, a fork in the road took eastbound vacationers over the Cascade Mountains via McKenzie Pass, while Highway 99 turned south toward Goshen and Creswell.

At Cottage Grove, the level, agricultural Willamette Valley gives way to rolling hills and tall timber, finally leaving the Willamette River behind. From this point south, the interstate freeway plays leapfrog with the old highway all the way to California. Compared to the spacious Willamette Valley, choices for highway alignments were more limited. In many places, the modern freeway overlays older alignments.

Major realignments in 1956 bypassed Drain and Yoncalla, Oakland and Sutherlin, and Winston and Dillard. Being left off the main highway left their downtowns frozen in time. Fortunately, freeway planners routed the interstate around (rather than through) Roseburg, Grants Pass, Medford, and Ashland, preserving their downtown cores.

South of Canyonville is Wolf Creek, home to Oregon's oldest operating hotel—the Wolf Creek Tavern. The interstate has obliterated much of the old highway at Smith Hill and Sexton Mountain, but between the two is Sunny Valley with its Grave Creek Covered Bridge.

Southeast of Grants Pass, Highway 99 crossed the Rogue River and entered the famous Rogue "vacation wonderland." In 1955, more than 30 motels lined a six-mile stretch of highway southeast of the city. Next up were Gold Hill, Medford, Phoenix, Talent, and Ashland.

Ten miles beyond Ashland, the highway began its climb to 4,500-foot Siskiyou Summit. The earliest highway alignment has long since been obliterated—first by 99 improvements in the 1940s, and more recently by interstate construction. It was five more miles to the California state line; from there, Los Angeles was a mere 700 miles away.

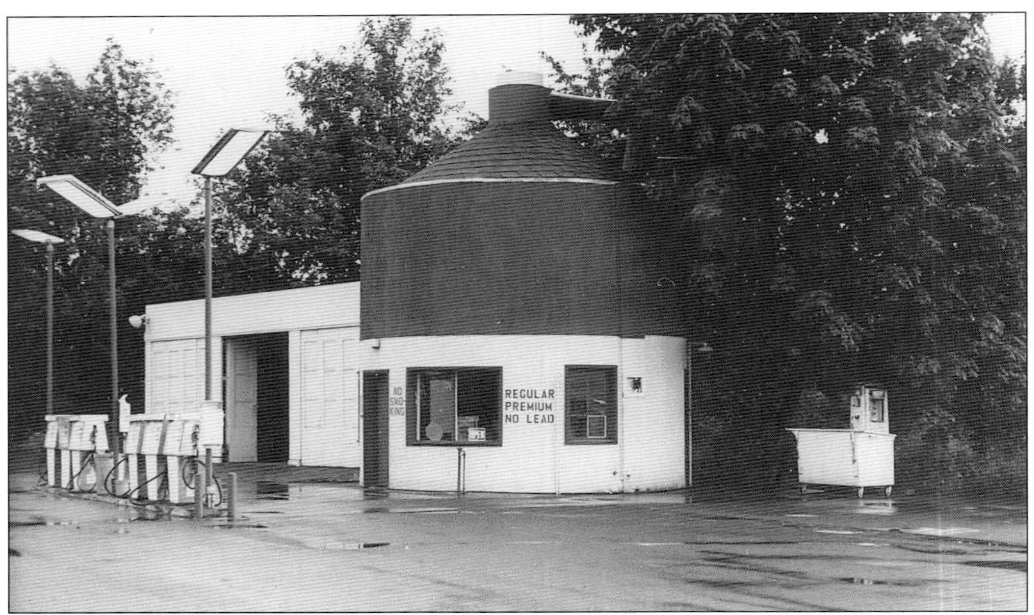

Prohibition had not ended when Fred Newman opened the Brown Jug Service Station in Junction City. Despite tongue-in-cheek speculation that it only replicated a giant vinegar jug, few doubted the real source of the builder's inspiration. Newman operated the Brown Jug until moving to Bend in 1946. The station was still pumping gas in the 1980s and today remains standing, part of a commercial glass business at 1667 Ivy Street. (OSHPO.)

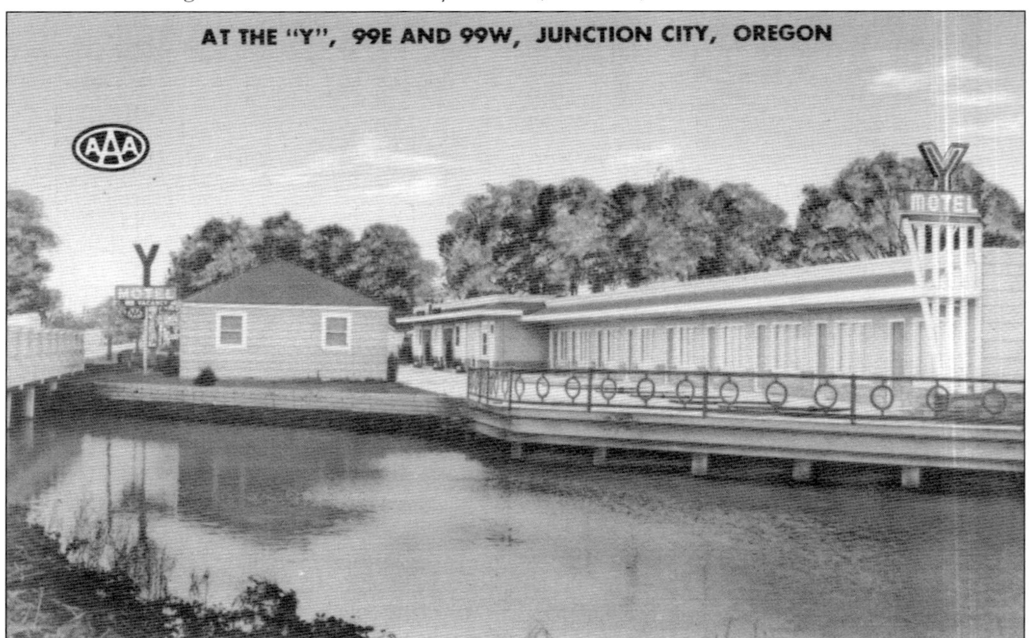

Appropriately enough, the Y Motel was located at the "Y" junction of Highways 99E and 99W at the north end of Junction City. Its units could be configured as eight single or four double rooms. All units provided tile showers, steam heat, free radios, and garages. A patio overlooking a brook provided a rustic touch. The site, at 1575 Ivy Street, is now a Regency Inn.

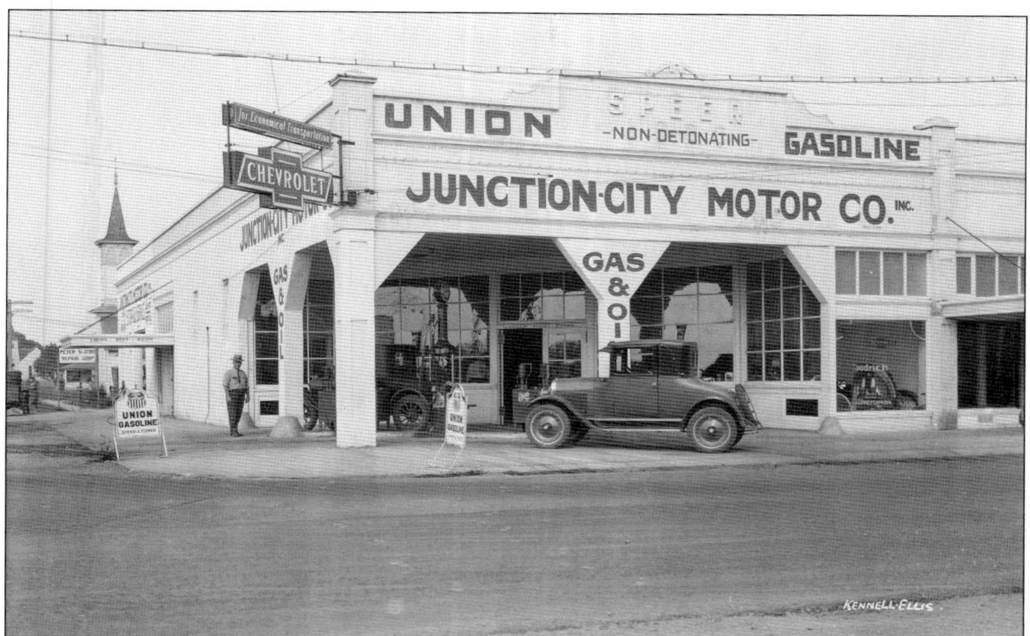

In 1927, the Junction City Motor Co. won a silver cup for selling the most Chevrolets (17) in its district. Opened by Charles Nelson and Ole Peterson in 1924, its corner service station sold Union Non-Detonating Gasoline as well as oil and tires. By the 1950s, it had become Larson-Nix Junction City Motors. Part of the building is still in use at 380 W 6th Avenue. (LCHM, KE922.)

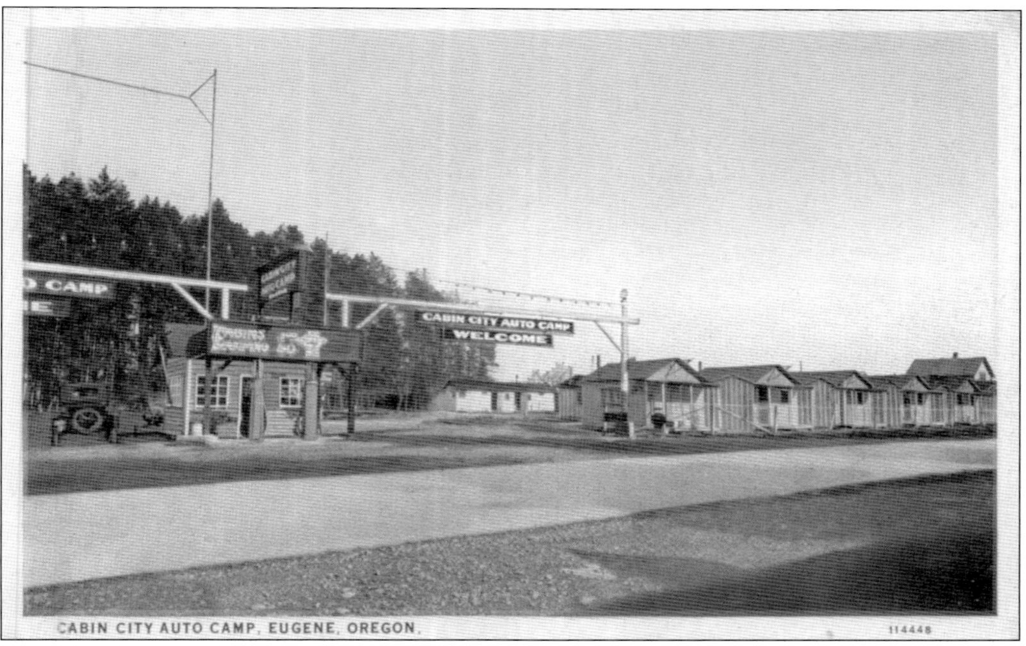

In 1925, Cabin City Auto Camp was one of three such in the Eugene area. It was located at the city's north edge on River Road, an early alignment of the Pacific Highway between Junction City and Eugene. By 1931, the camp included 48 cabins, a service station, and a large log cabin containing a store and lunchroom. Still in business in 1939, the camp has long since disappeared.

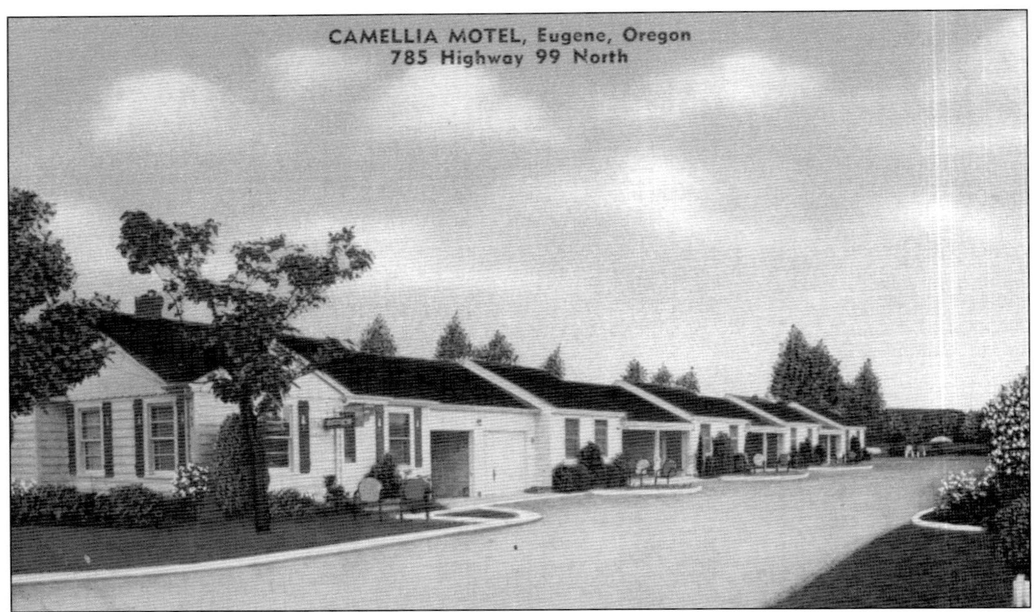

Several motels coexisted within 100 yards of each other just a mile north of Eugene. First up was the Camellia Motel at 785 Highway 99 N. Recommended by AAA and Duncan Hines, the Camellia's seven double and single rooms featured tiled showers, carpeted floors, and Beautyrest beds; some units included kitchenettes, and all provided colorful lawn chairs by the front door. It is still in use as low-rent housing.

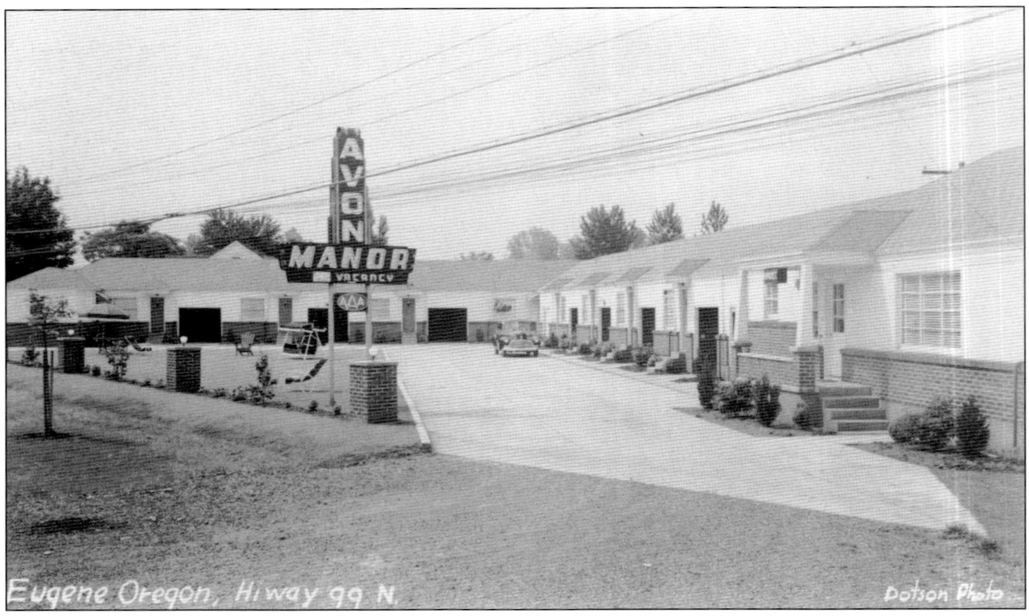

Just across from the Camellia at 780 Highway 99 N was the Avon Manor. Its nine units and office formed an "L" shape angled away from the highway. In the grassy angle of the "L" were lawn chairs, swings, and umbrellas for guests' enjoyment. The Avon Manor remained in business long after the bulk of traffic shifted to I-5. Today, the building houses Sheltercare, a private, nonprofit human services agency.

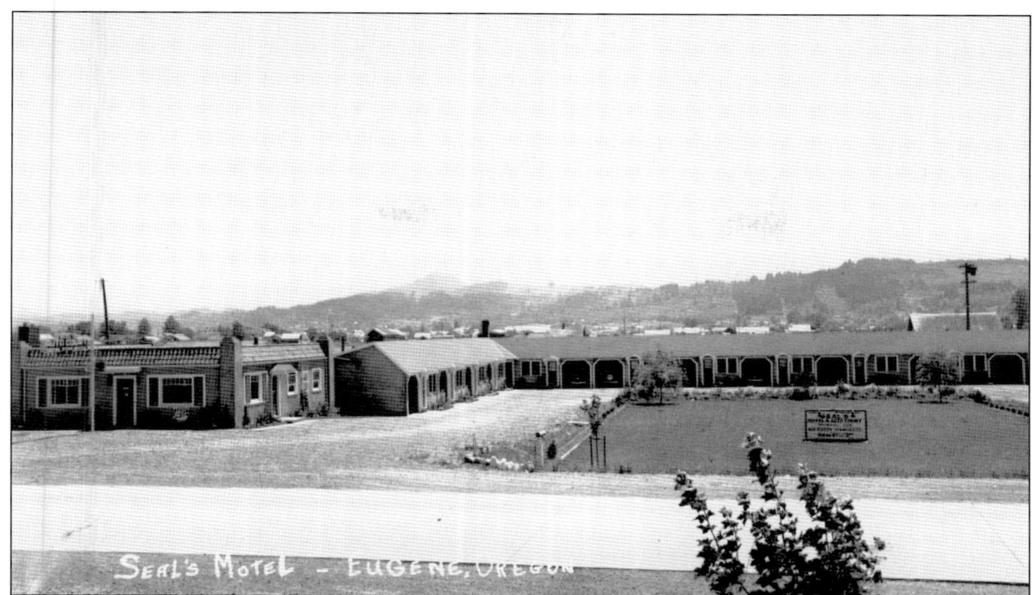

Seal's Motel was in business by 1939 under the ownership of Mr. and Mrs. Frank Seal. Its 30 units were arranged in a "U" configuration around a flower-lined, tree-shaded lawn. Some of the steam-heated units included kitchenettes; they all had Beautyrest mattresses, private baths, and attached garages. The Seals took pride in their motel's AAA and United Motor Courts memberships. Located at 1900 6th Avenue, a McDonald's occupies the site today.

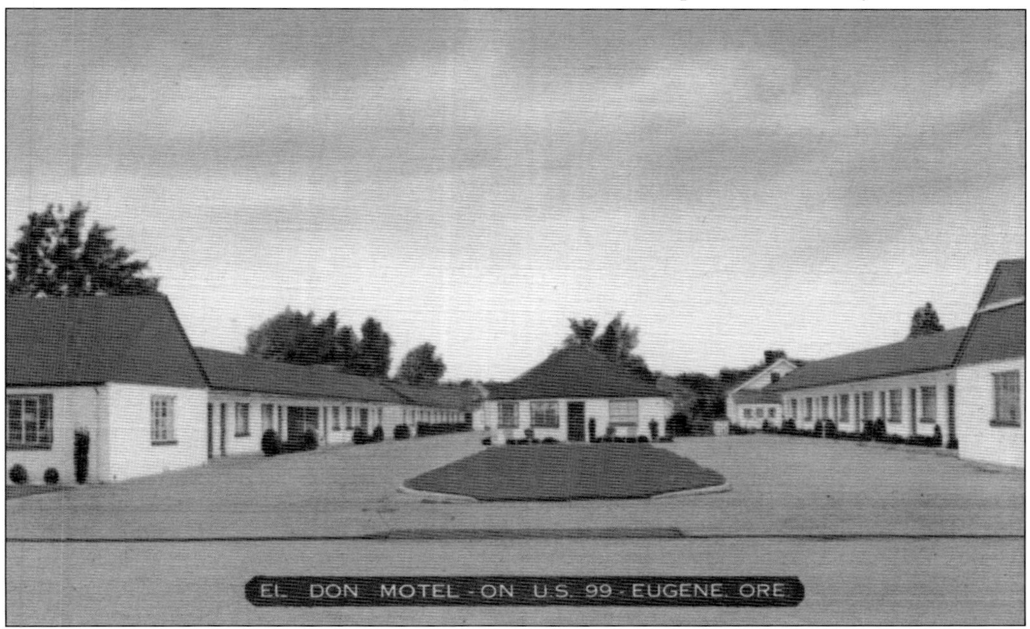

The El Don Motel, at 1140 W Sixth Avenue, opened in the late 1940s and was owned by Mark Siddall in 1954. Its deluxe units provided the customary facilities: hot water heat, carpeted floors, Beautyrest mattresses, tiled showers, and in-room phones. Today, it does business as America's Best Value Inn. The two rows of units, the central office, and even the small lawn remain largely intact.

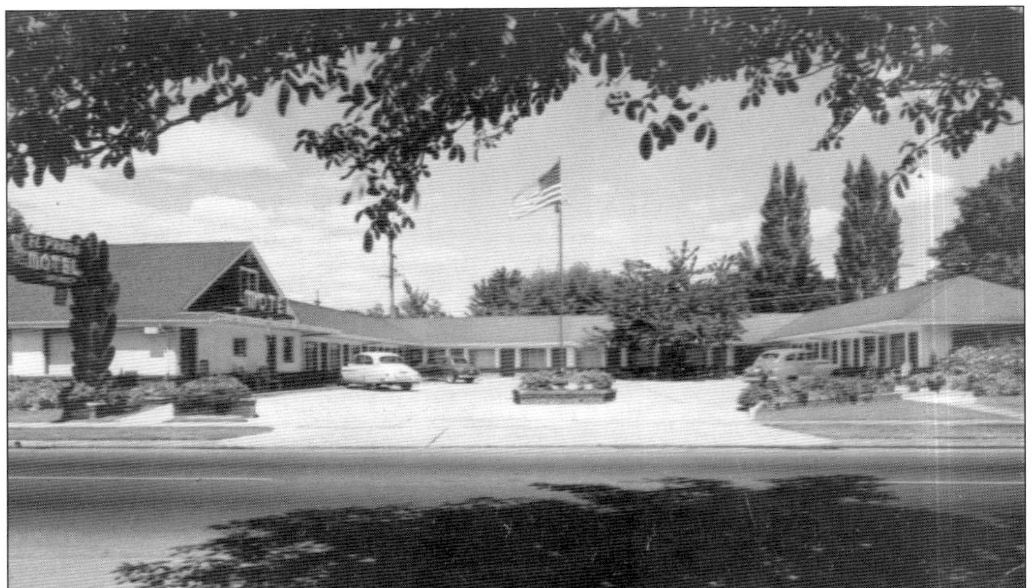

Original owners Mr. and Mrs. Walter Burkhardt sold the 21-unit El Prado Motel to Harold Boon in the late 1950s. Boon tacked his name onto the neon sign and called it Boon's El Prado. Located at 1055 W 6th Avenue, the motel's rooms—fully carpeted with tiled bathrooms and tubs—surrounded a parking area with an American flag planted squarely in the middle. Nowadays, it is a Rodeway Inn.

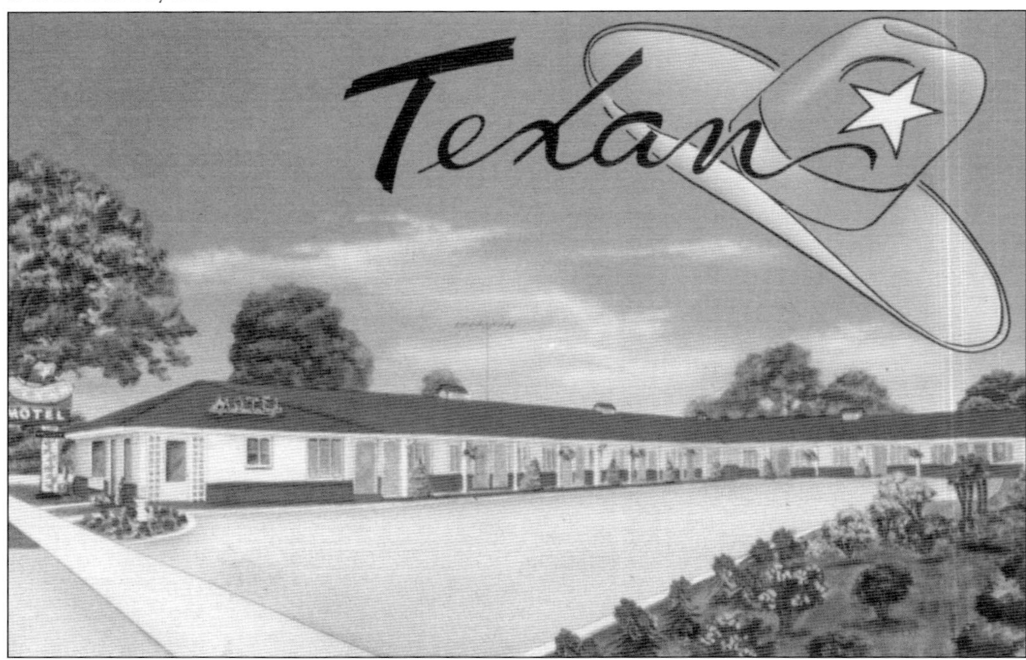

A giant cowboy hat topped the Texan Motel's neon sign at 750 W 7th Avenue. Its 17 units were arranged in an "L" with flower gardens bordering the parking lot. Owned at one time by Mr. and Mrs. J.D. Stevens, it was purchased by Mr. and Mrs. M.W. Chandler and resold in 1958 to Mr. and Mrs. Harold Ryals for $165,000. The site is a parking lot today.

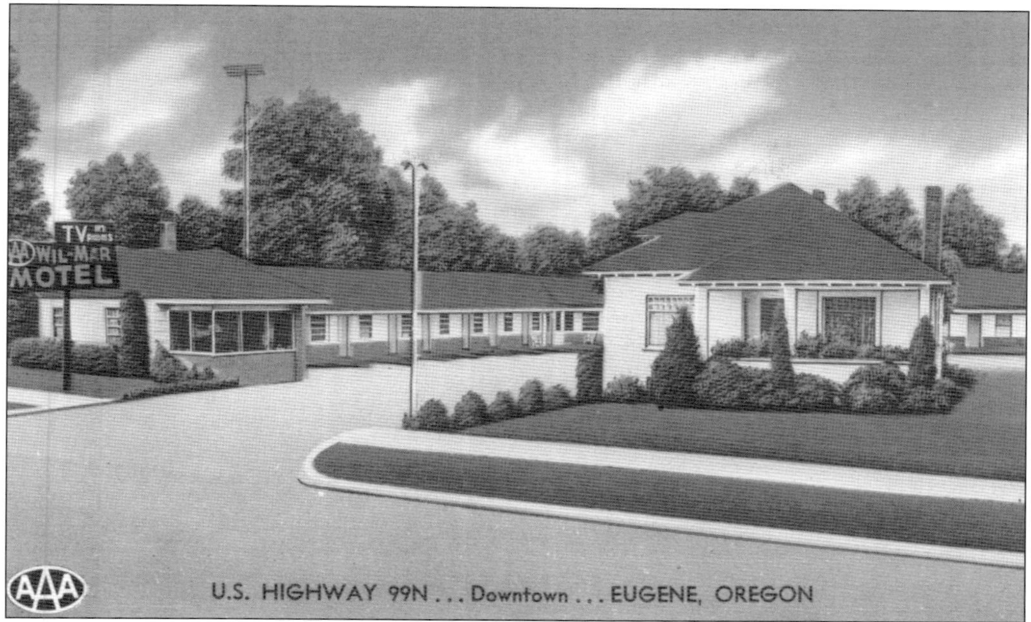

Like many others before them, Wilbur and Mary Rowe christened their motel, the Wil-Mar, using a combination of their own names. It was located at 571 W 6th Avenue, a site that in 1946 was occupied by the Radabaugh Courtel. The Wil-Mar's units were arranged around what appears to have been the owners' dwelling. The AAA-approved motel was owned by Ross and Hilda Hughes in 1958. It has since disappeared.

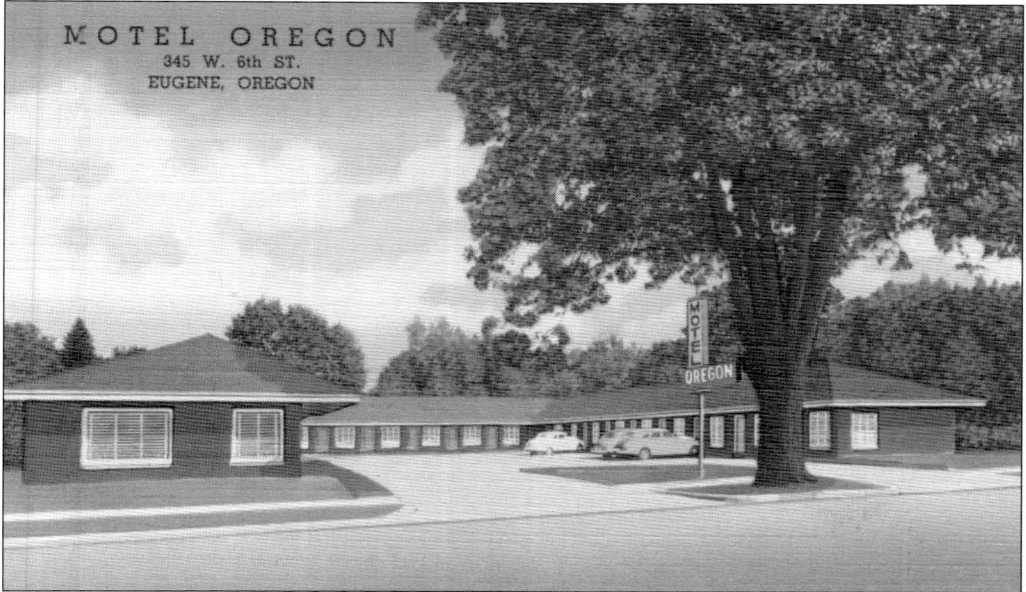

In 1944, Walter Dennis left his position as Roseburg's schools superintendent to operate the Restwell Court on Highway 99 north of Eugene. Ten years later, he was owner of the Motel Oregon at 345 W 6th Street—21 units with the customary Beautyrest mattresses, tub/shower combinations, and steam heat. Renamed Mason's Motel in the 1960s and minimally altered over the years, today it is known as Courtesy Inn Eugene.

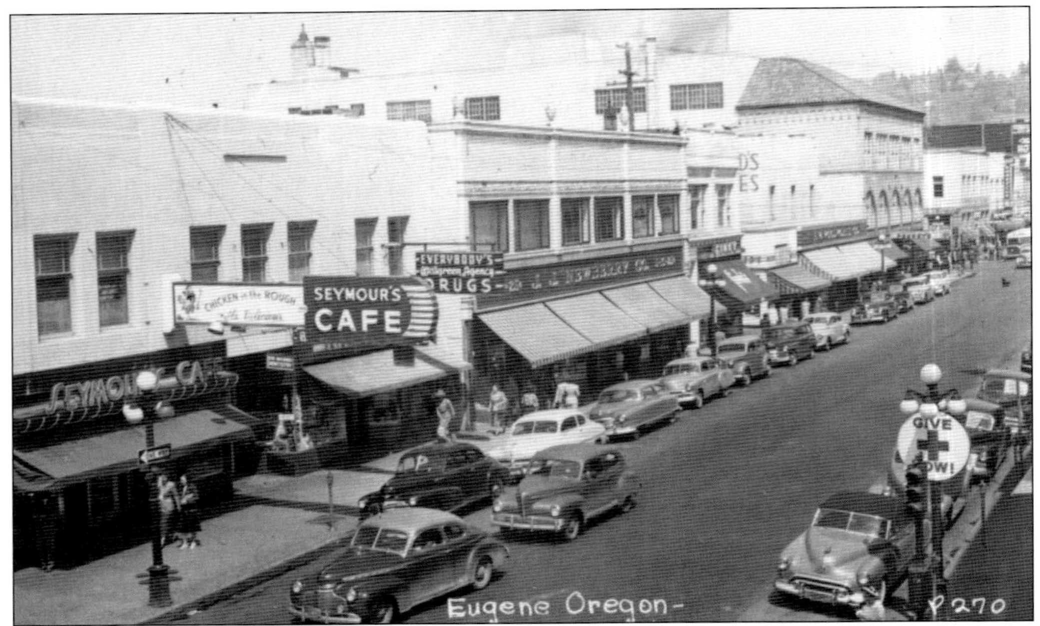

Highway travelers chose from a variety of routes through downtown Eugene. If they picked Willamette Street and happened to be looking for a meal, Seymour's Cafe would have tempted them to stop in. Darle Seymour opened his namesake restaurant in 1930 at 966 Willamette. In July 1950, a customer occupied a booth at Seymour's for 18 hours nonstop and consumed nine meals. Why? "Just hungry," he said.

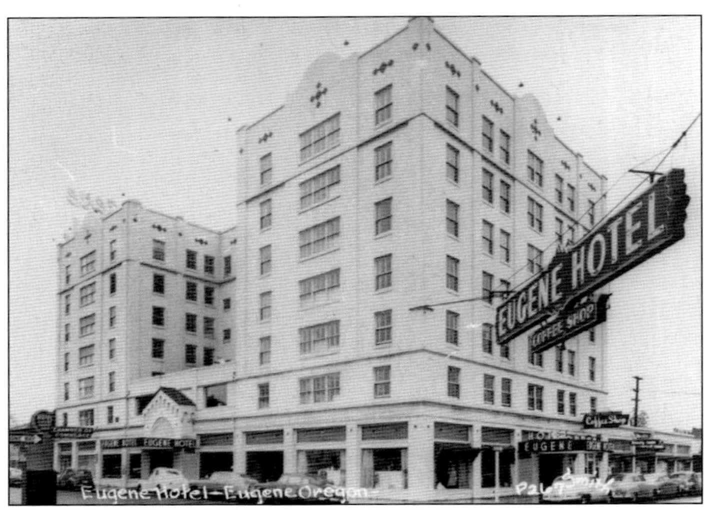

When the Eugene Hotel opened in June 1925, the local newspaper gave it 10 pages of coverage. The hotel offered 183 rooms—single rooms with shared bath, plus suites consisting of a parlor, bedroom, and private bath. A beautifully decorated lobby, ball room, main dining room seating 500, and "dainty tea room" completed the accoutrements. Located at 222 E Broadway, it became a retirement center in 1983. (JCO'D.)

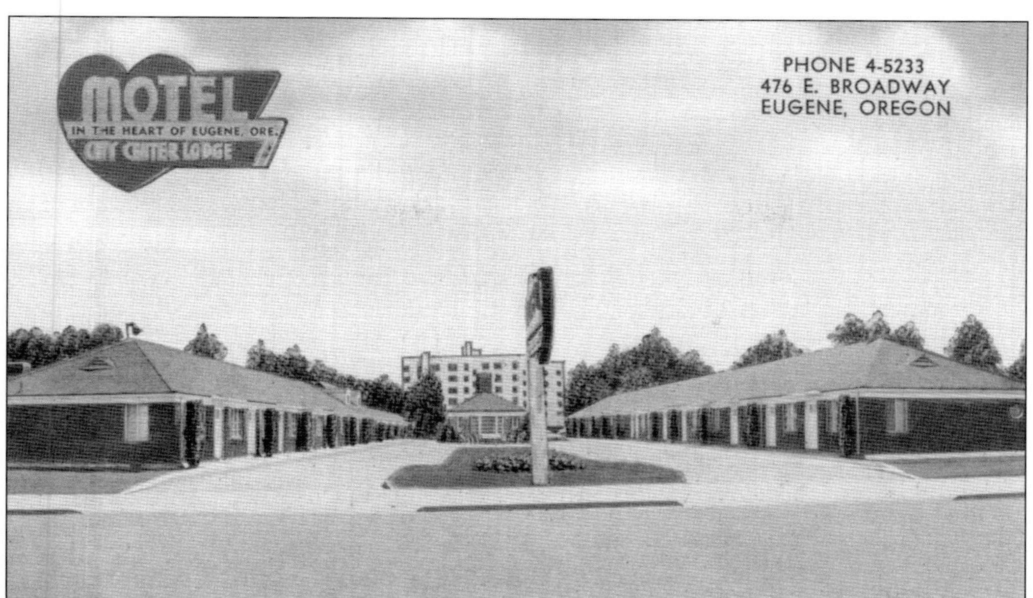

City Center Lodge, at 476 E Broadway, prided itself as being "in the heart of Eugene." Offering both housekeeping rooms and tourist accommodations, the motel's 35 rooms—two rows of units separated by a grassy median—could be had for $5.50 and up per night in 1948. The building survives as the Broadway Inn; the cottages appear remarkably intact, though the grass has been replaced by pavement.

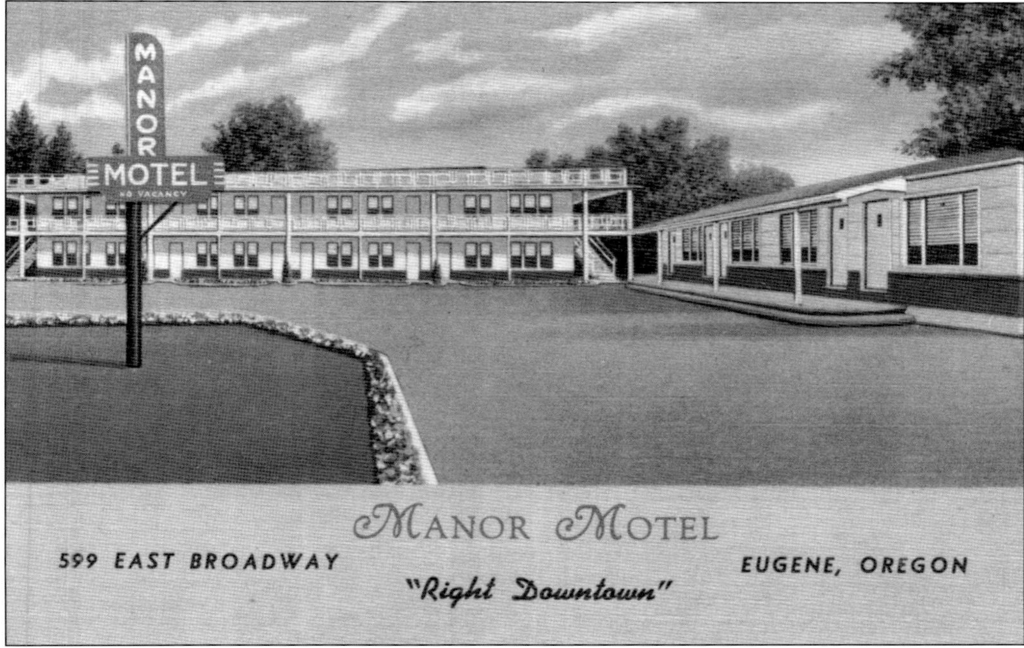

The Manor Motel advertised itself as ideal for outdoor recreationists with fishing, tennis, and bowling available within a few blocks. Located at 599 E Broadway in Eugene's quiet east side, it also offered easy access to the University of Oregon. The 24-unit motel opened in the early 1950s under the ownership of Vira and Bob Davis. Demolished in 2007, it has been replaced by a Red Lion.

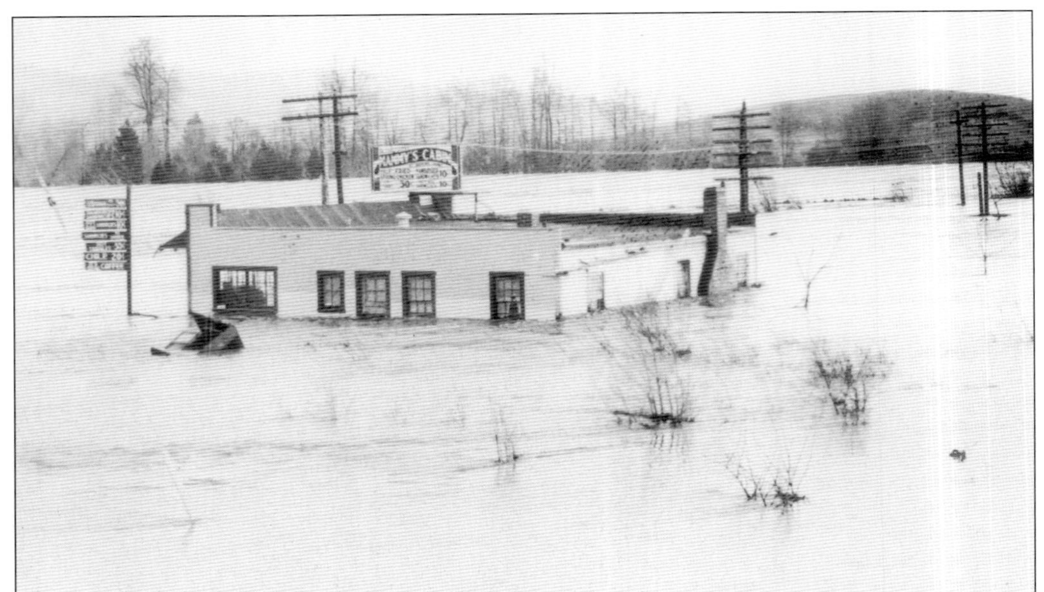

Mammy's Cabin, a chicken shack along the Pacific Highway a mile east of Eugene, opened in 1926 and is shown here when the Willamette River flooded a year later. After the water receded, the restaurant was rebuilt and featured fried chicken and steak dinners for 75¢ (1928 prices). Still in business in 1940, by that time its chief function was selling beer to University of Oregon students. (LCHM, GN6668.)

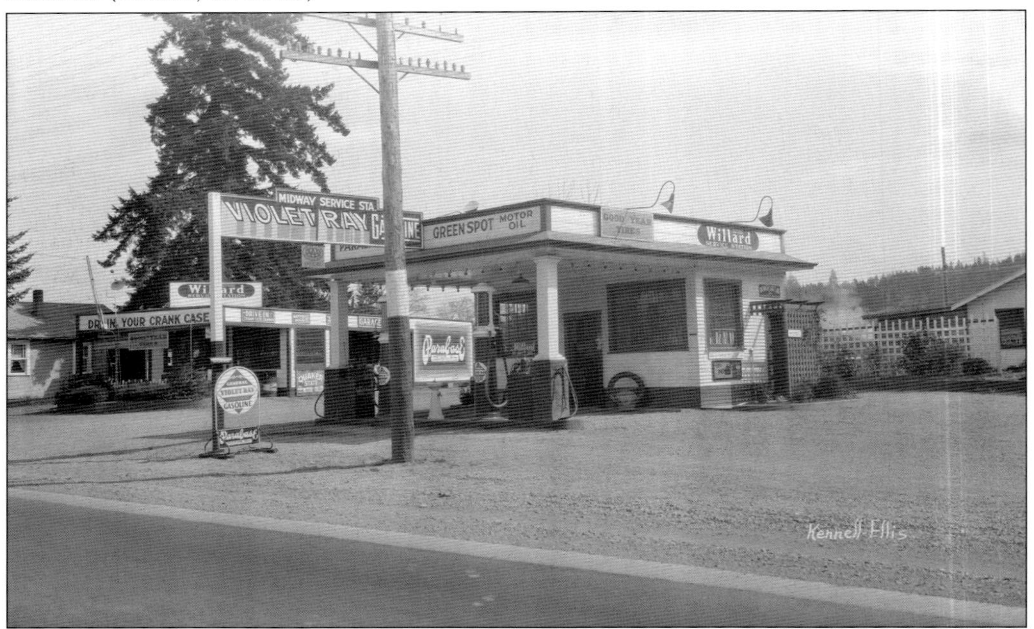

As its name implies, the Midway Service Station was located approximately halfway between Eugene and Springfield. Percy Buckman was the owner in 1925, with Jack McCune as the resident expert mechanic. Violet Ray was a brand of gasoline introduced with much ballyhoo in 1928 by the General Petroleum Company. The gas was tinted with a violet color lacking any functional benefit. Its popularity was short-lived. (LCHM, KE45.)

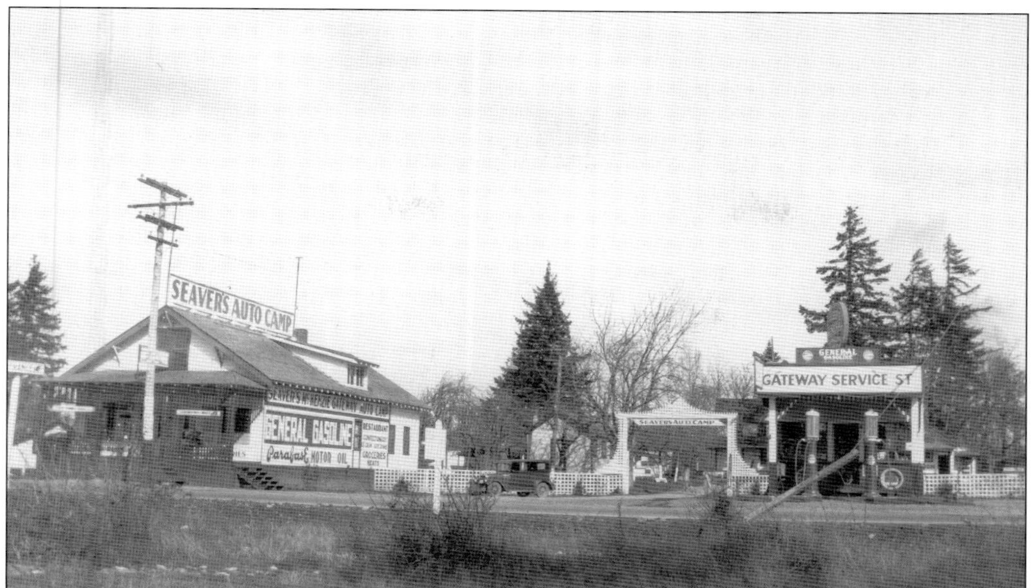

An ornate lattice entrance welcomed visitors to W.J. Seaver's McKenzie Gateway Auto Camp, located at the junction of the Pacific and McKenzie Highways just west of the Willamette River bridge into Springfield. In addition to 27 stand-alone and duplex cabins, the resort contained a restaurant, confectionery store and ice cream shop, grocery store, and service station set amidst 12 acres of beautiful, park-like grounds. (LCHM, GN6661.)

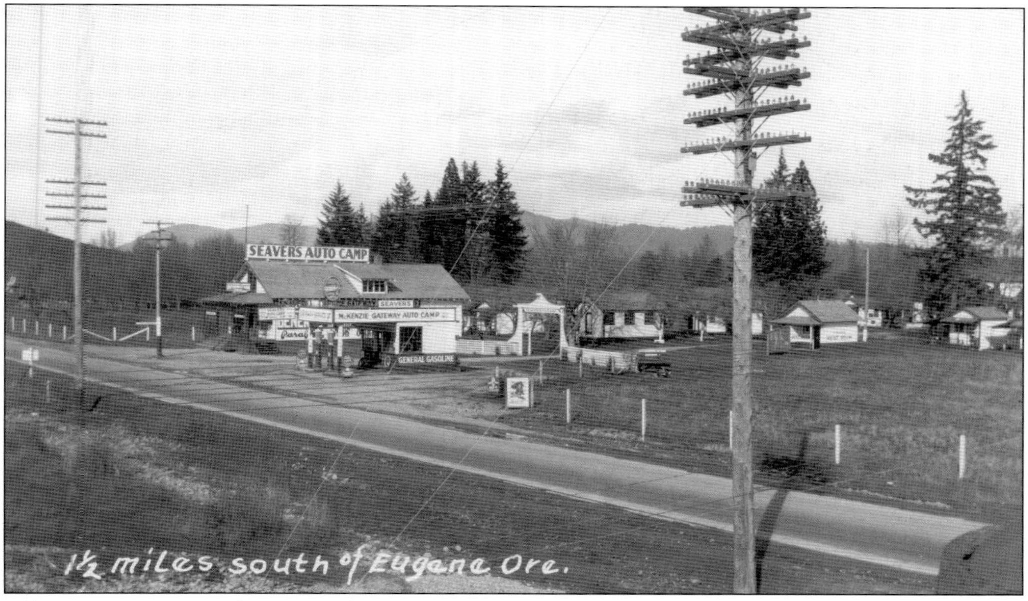

When Seaver's opened in 1925, the one-room cabins—some with showers and lavatories, all with cook stoves, folding beds, springs and mattress, tables and benches—rented for \$1 a day with wood, water, and lights all included. Each cabin had a covered carport for auto storage. For those wishing to rough it, campsites were available for 50¢ per day. The auto camp had disappeared by 1950. (LCHM, 6664.)

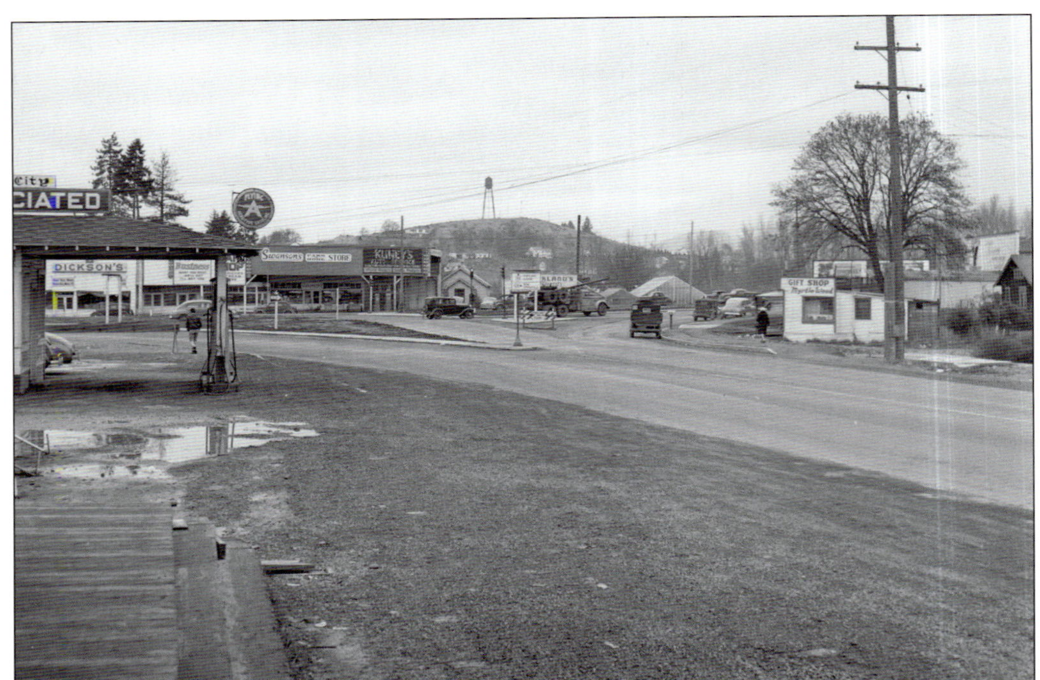

Springfield Junction has always been a busy intersection. This 1946 view looks north with Highway 99 turning left (west) toward Eugene. Highway 28 (today labeled SR126) carries eastbound traffic across the Willamette River into Springfield and on over the Cascade Mountains to Bend. Among the roadside businesses are an Associated "Flying A" gas station in the curve of Highway 99 and a myrtlewood gift shop across the road. (OSA, OHD2837.)

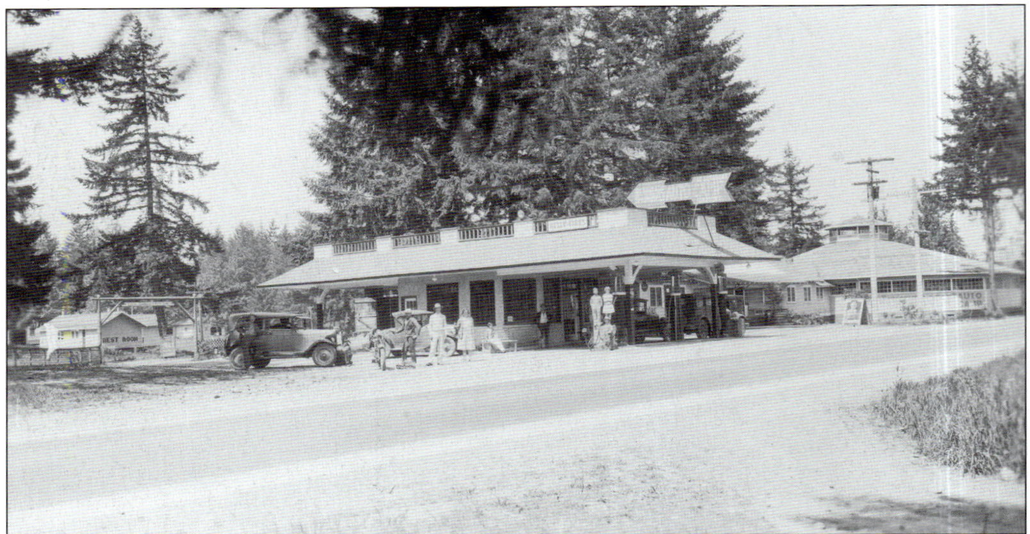

A curious crowd observes the photographer in this 1925 view of the Eugene-Springfield Auto Camp. Several of the camp's 30 cabins are visible to the left; in the center is the restaurant and service station. The circular building on the right was the Midway Dance Pavilion. Part of the service station building still stands along old Highway 99 half a mile south of Springfield Junction. (LCHM, GN10302.)

Famed photographer Dorothea Lange documented this hot dog stand somewhere in Lane County in October 1939. The dog's sheet-metal body surrounded a wooden counter, with one of its sides hinged as a window for the person behind the counter to take orders. Sitting in a field, it was out of commission when this photograph was taken. (LOC, LC-USF34-021137-E.)

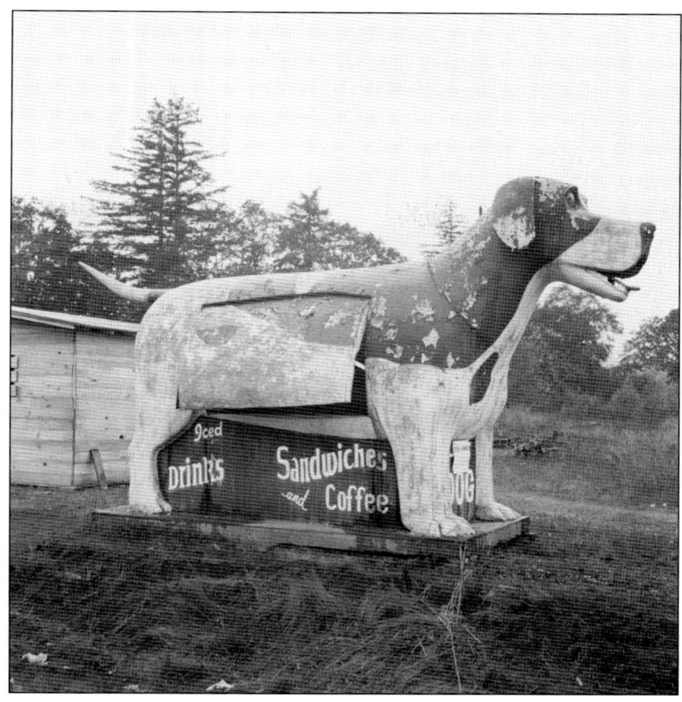

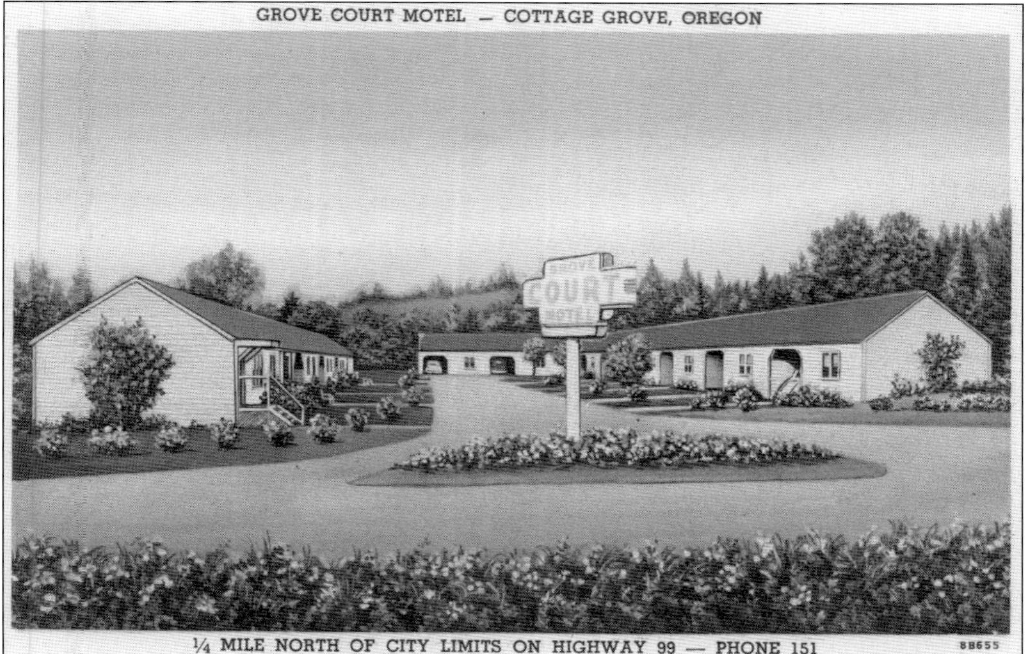

Flowers growing up walls on trellises and blooming from shrubs along the driveway heightened the homelike appeal of the Grove Court. Located half a mile north of downtown Cottage Grove, the 14-unit court opened around 1940 under the ownership of Palmer Johnson. Cottages featured Firestone Airtex mattresses (rather than the usual Beautyrest brand), kitchenettes with Magic Chef ranges, and covered carports. The site, at 1721 Pacific Highway N, is an apartment complex today.

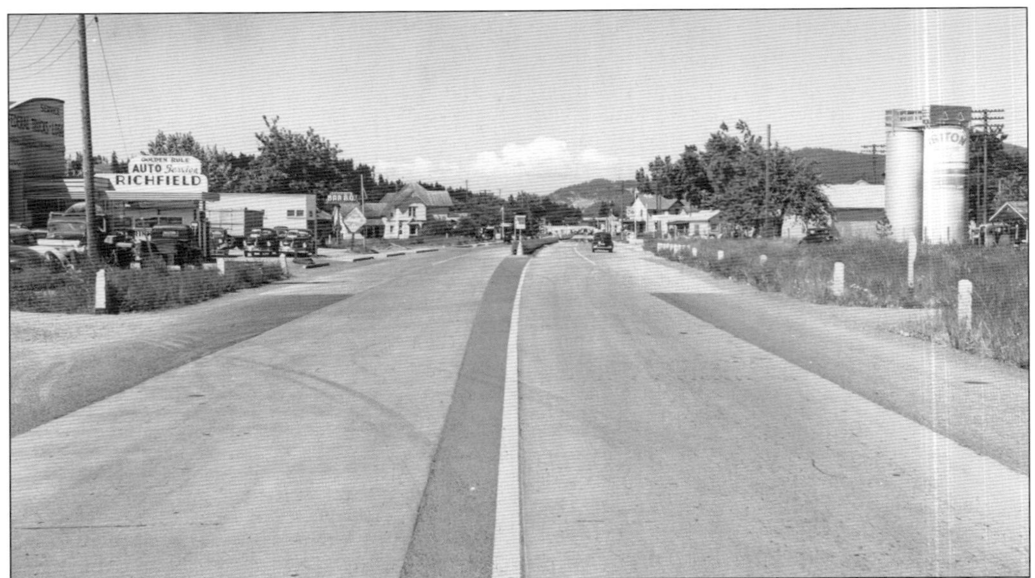

Highway 99 originally wound its way through Cottage Grove's business district via Main and 5th Streets. In 1941, a segment of four-lane highway opened, shunting motorists around the downtown core. This photograph from the following year shows that the Bar-B-Q Drive-In and the Golden Rule Richfield Service had already sprung up to serve traffic along the new highway. The view looks north from Quincy Street. (OSA, OHD1870.)

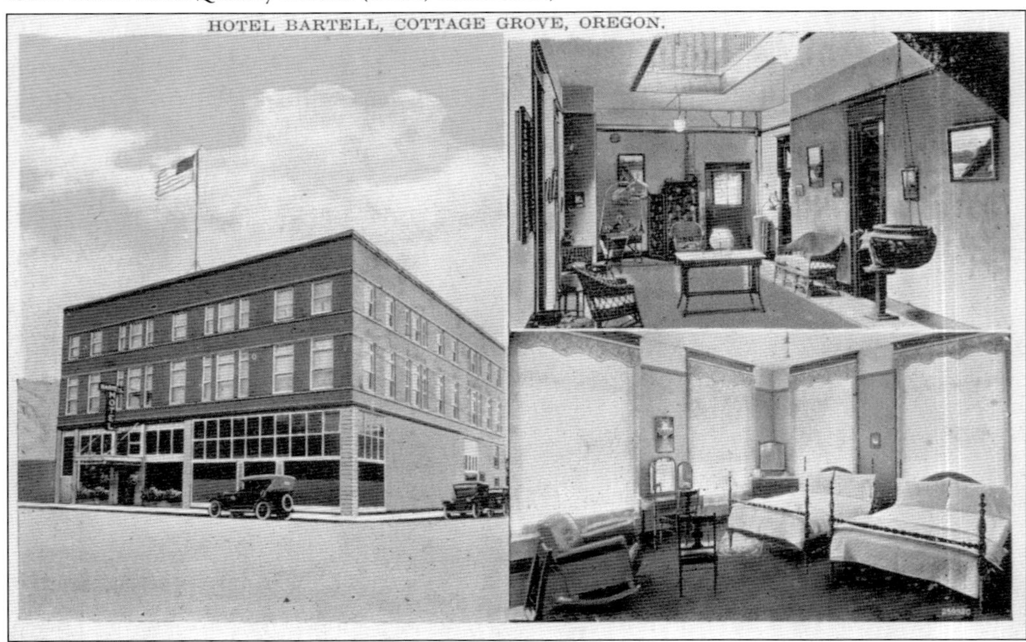

Cottage Grove's Hotel Bartell was typical of the small-city hotels catering to travelers in the 1920s—comfortable but not extravagant. Built at a cost of $100,000, the three-story brick structure offered 76 rooms (36 with baths) and a dining room complete with orchestra gallery. Buster Keaton stayed here while shooting *The General* east of town. The building, in use as apartments, still stands at 8th and Main Streets.

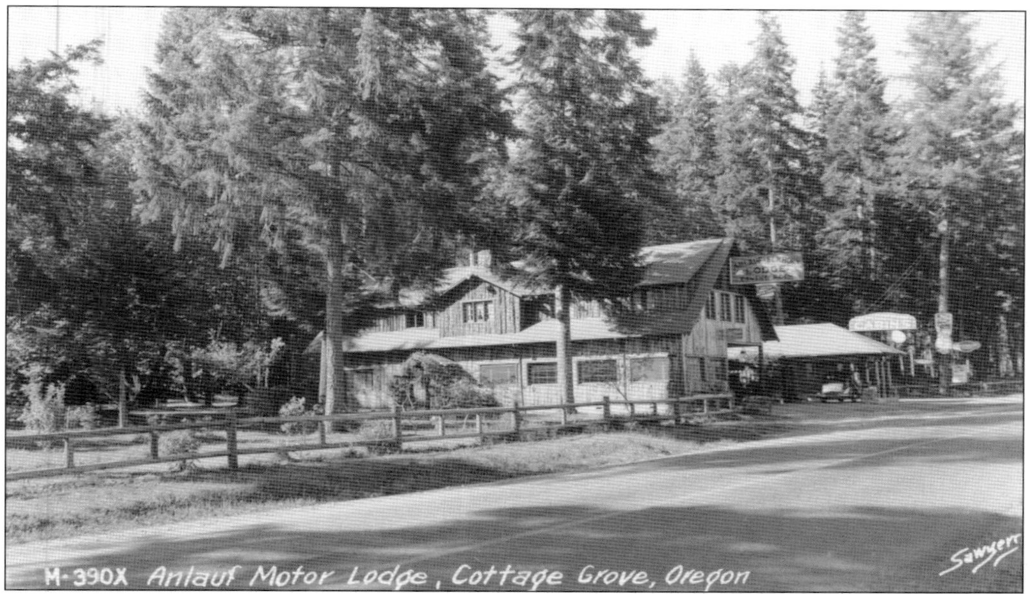

Anlauf Elkhorn Camp was an early auto campground along the Pacific Highway, 11 miles south of Drain. In the 1920s, owner C.B. Maxwell began improvements to the camp, constructing 11 cabins, a store, a service station, and an ice cream/soda fountain. Its Jolly Time Pavilion became well known for holding weekend dances. By the 1950s, the camp had become the Anlauf Motor Lodge. It was destroyed by fire in August 1960.

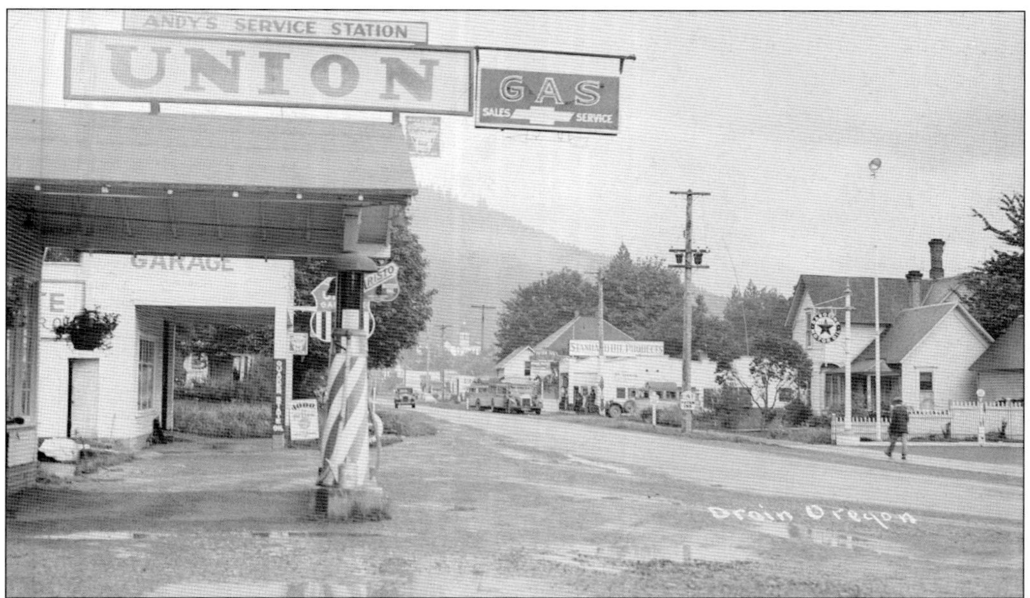

Four service stations—Andy's Union Service, a Union station next door, a Texaco outlet across the highway, and the Standard Oil station at the Totem Inn—are aligned along W B Street in Drain in this 1925 photograph. A cluster of buses (called "stages" at the time) are parked at the inn. The view looks east along B Street. Almost all of these buildings have disappeared. (LCHM, CS1008.)

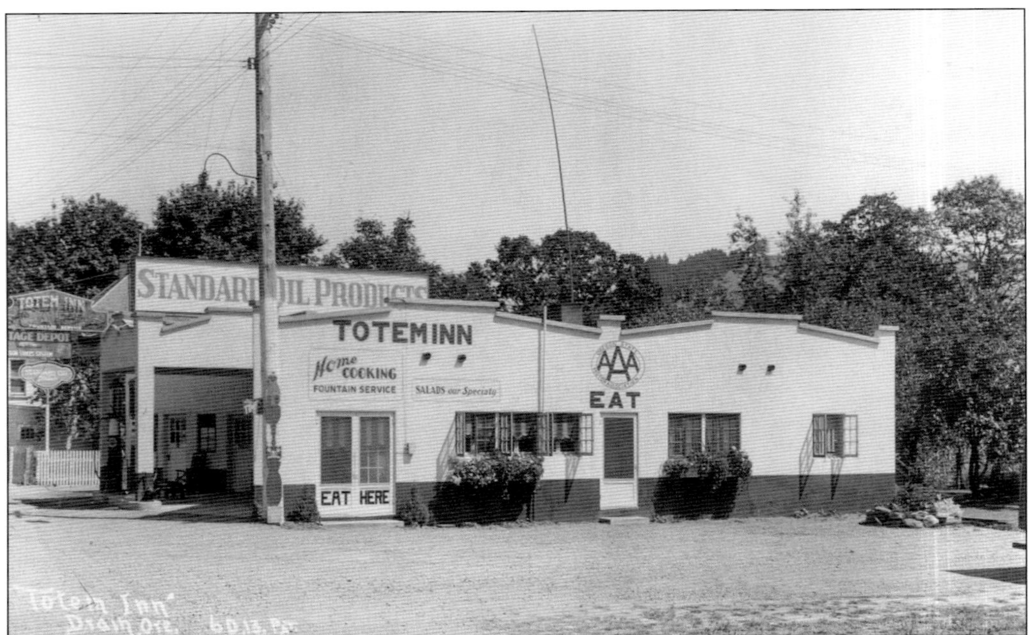

Longtime landmark Totem Inn served Drain as restaurant, gas station, and stage depot. A full dinner at Nellie Caspers's restaurant cost 35¢ in 1935; being a Greyhound bus stop guaranteed a steady flow of customers. George Thompson was proprietor of the Standard Oil service station. Located at 3rd Avenue and B Street and remodeled several times over the years, the inn was destroyed by fire in 1956.

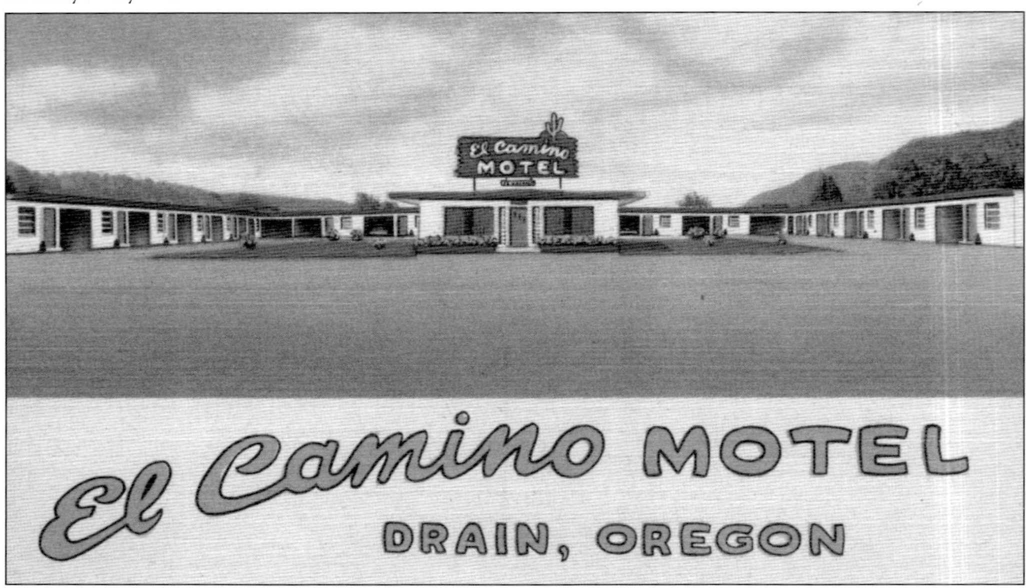

The El Camino Motel was at 525 S Cedar Street "in a fast growing town called Drain, where," says this postcard, "most folks are jolly, shine or rain." Opened in 1950, its 20 units featured electric heat, showers, and Beautyrest mattresses. Unfortunately, Highway 99 realignment in 1955 left the town off the main route and curtailed Drain's dreams of growth. Today, an EMS station is located where the El Camino was.

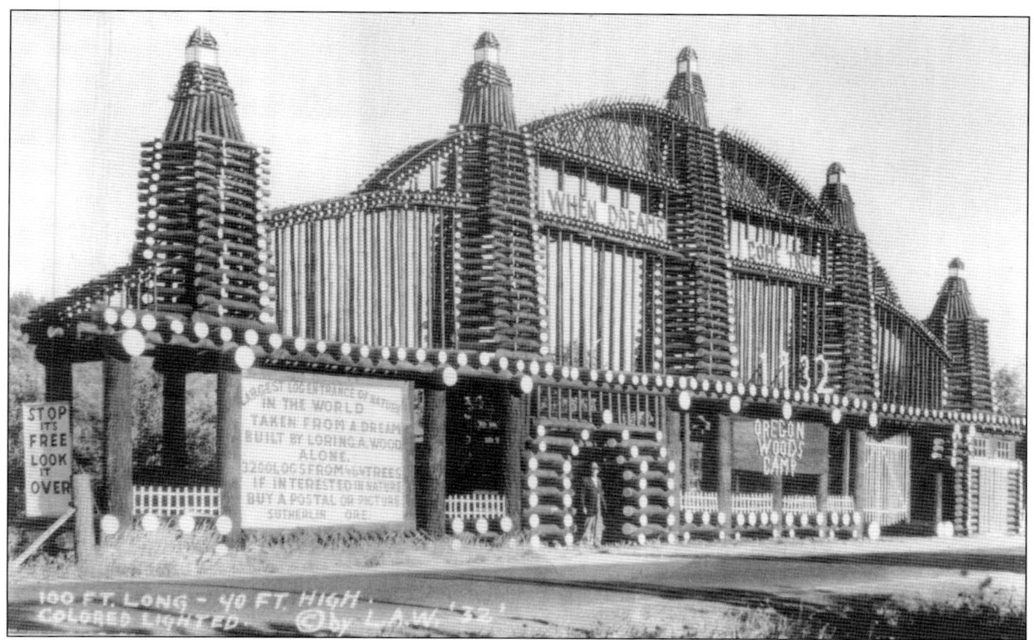

Master model-maker Loring Wood constructed this immense log facade for his roadside curio shop and museum just outside Sutherlin. At 40 feet tall and 100 feet long, it was billed as "the largest log entrance of nature in the world." Admission was free to view intricate models of such subjects as "Old Ironsides," the *Mayflower*, and the Golden Gate Bridge, details of which Wood claimed came to him in dreams.

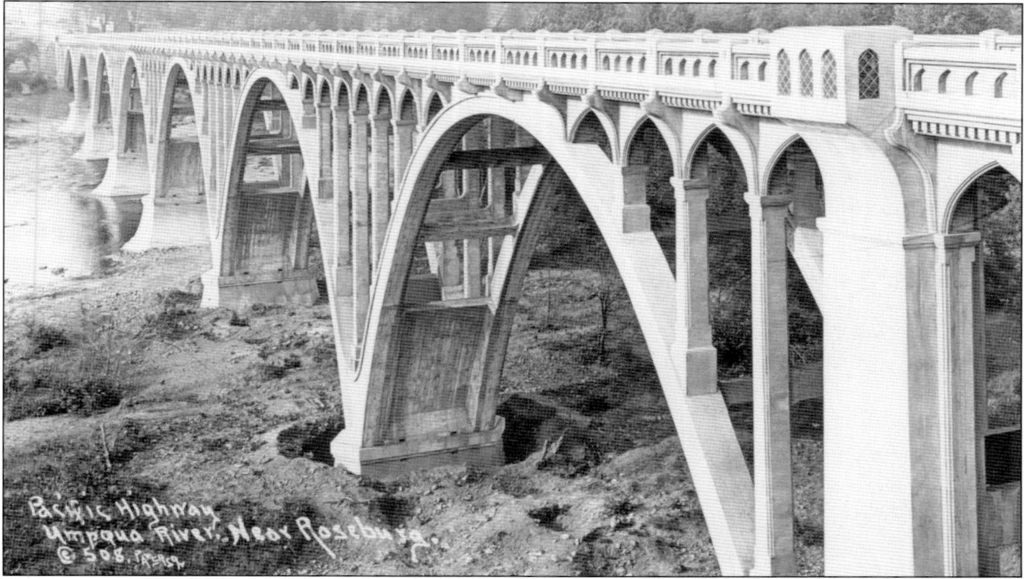

Just outside Winchester, the Robert A. Booth Bridge carries traffic across the North Umpqua River, as it has since 1924. Another creation by Conde McCullough, principal designer of Oregon's historic bridges, it consists of seven 112-foot arches, Gothic curtain walls, and alcoves for pedestrians to enjoy a view of the river. Renovated, widened, and rededicated in 2008, it is named in honor of the pioneer Booth family of Douglas County.

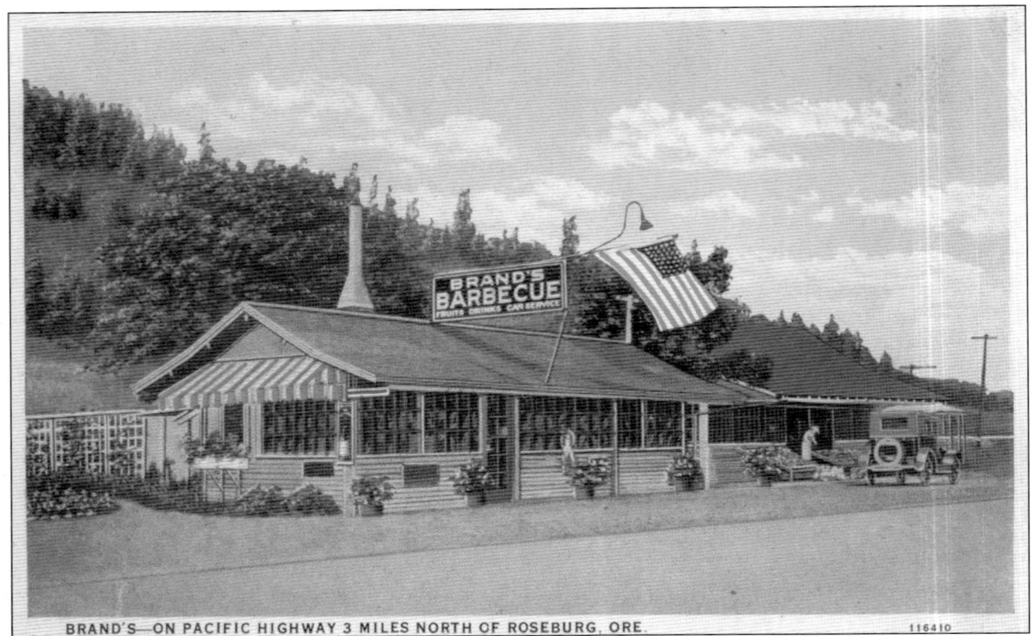

Brand's Barbecue was already an established roadside eatery and fruit stand in 1925. Owned by local businessman and civic leader Charles A. Brand, the restaurant's specialty was barbecue (their slogan: "Eat barbecue sandwiches and live forever"). They also served homemade apple pie, ice cream, and milkshakes. By 1940, Brand's had doubled in size and expanded to dinners and dancing. Located three miles north of Roseburg, it has long since disappeared.

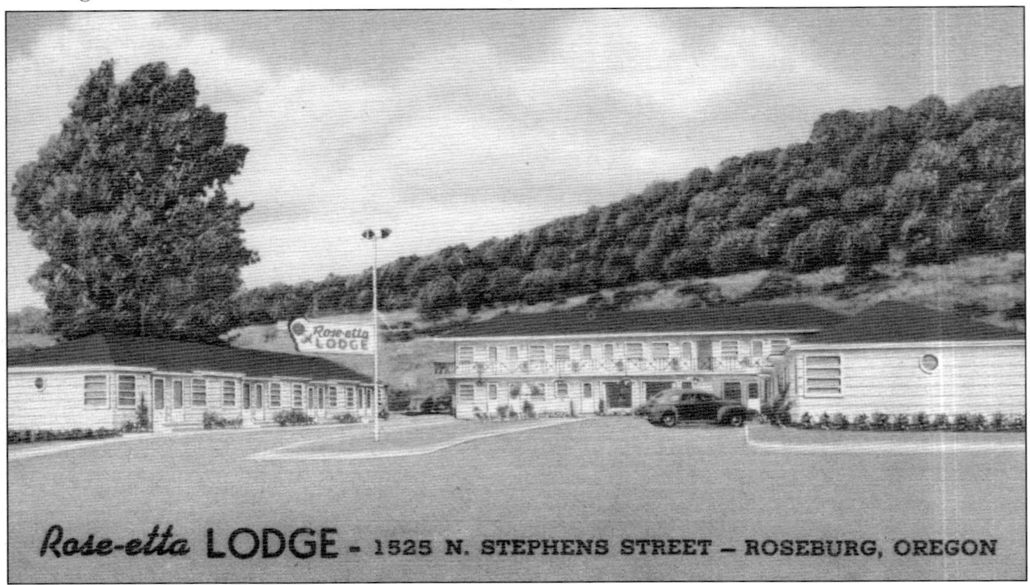

Marion and Ruby Veatch opened their Rose-Etta Lodge with 12 units in 1946, expanding that number to 47 by 1952. Over 200 attended the opening of the motel's swimming pool in 1954. The Veaches retired from the motel business in 1962. Except for a new roof, windows, and name (it is now the Budget 16 Motel, at 1067 NE Stephens Street), the Rose-Etta looks much the same as it did originally.

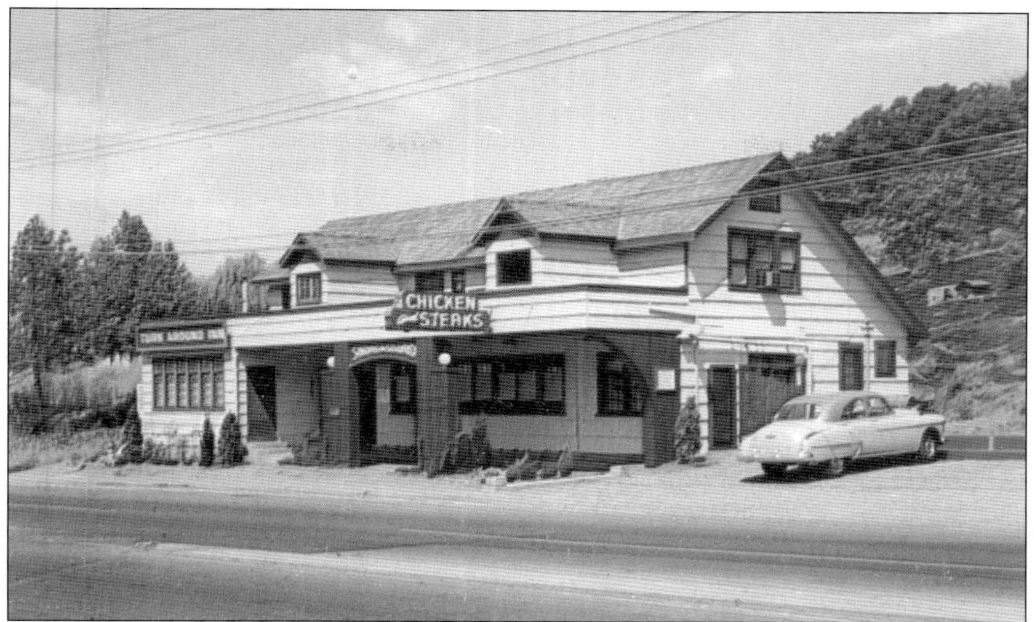

Madge and Pop Davis opened the Turn Around Inn on New Year's Day 1946. A year later, Grace and "Mac" Baker took over operations, adding smorgasbord to the menu. Madge Davis resumed control in 1948 and refocused on the dinner trade with charcoal broiled steaks and fried chicken. A lounge, the Flamingo Room, was added in 1954. The inn was located at 1023 NE Stephens Street and is still standing.

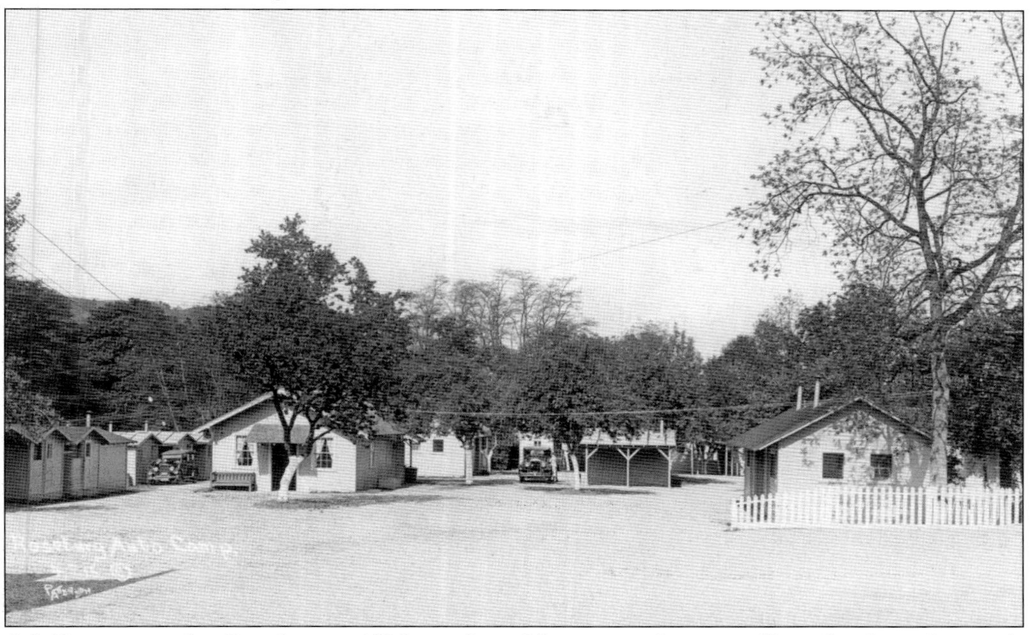

A.J. Young moved to Roseburg in 1920, purchased five acres adjacent to Deer Creek on the north edge of Roseburg, and started the Roseburg Auto Camp. In addition to its 20 cabins (each of which offered one to three rooms), the park had tent spaces and a store, lunchroom, and service station. Claimed to be the first private auto park in the state, it was still in business in 1959.

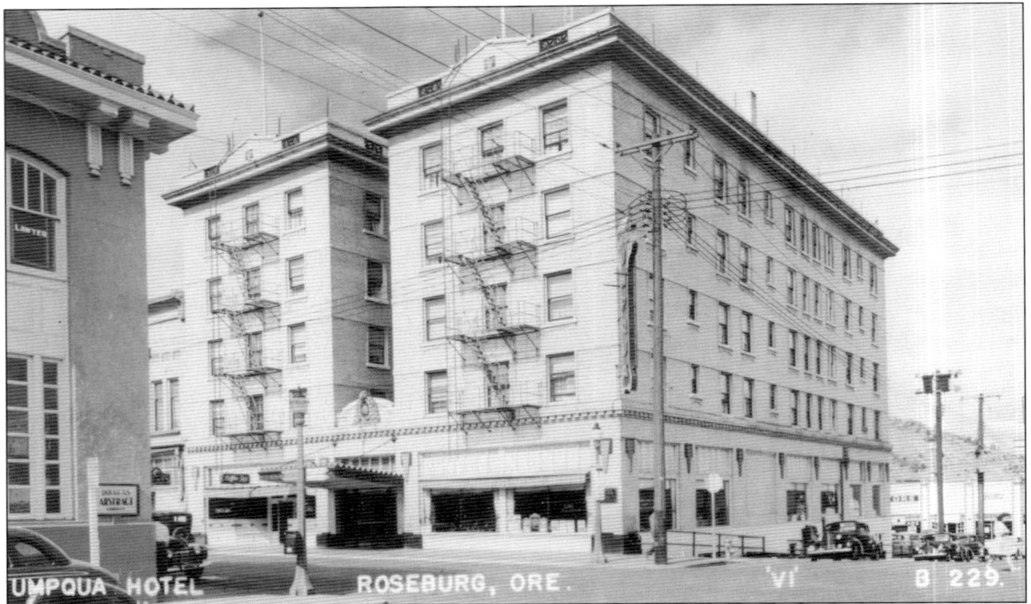

When the Hotel Umpqua opened in 1913 at the corner of Jackson and Oak Streets, it was on the Pacific Highway through downtown Roseburg. Though the route shifted to Stephens Street a few years later, the hotel still laid claim to being on the highway. Its 100 rooms rented for $4 to $6 in 1948, and it took pride in "the finest coffee shop between Portland and San Francisco" with $1.50 dinners.

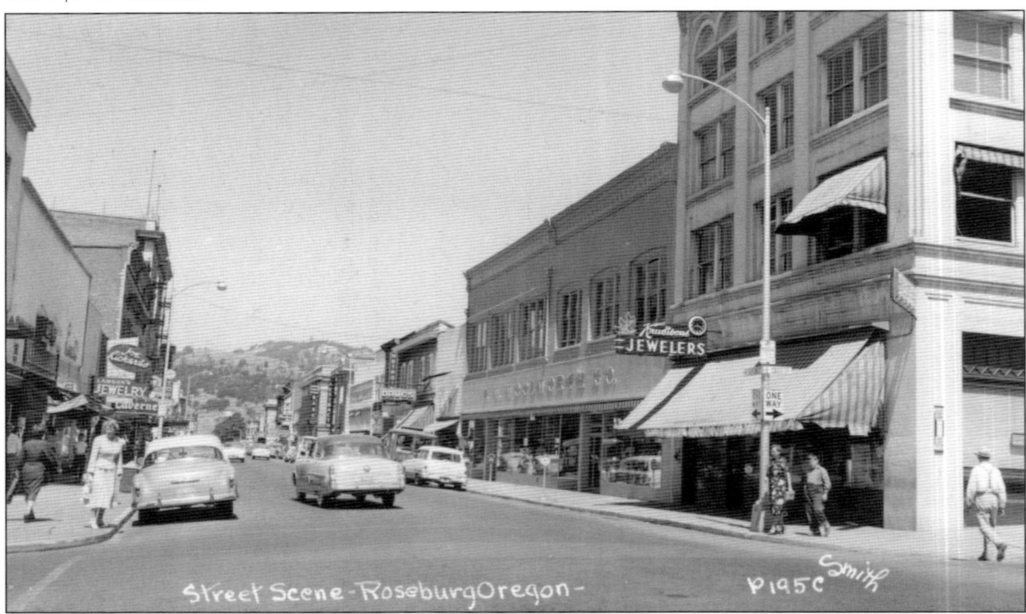

Not much traffic was moving through downtown Roseburg on the sunny morning this photograph was taken. Seat of Douglas County and heart of the "Land of Umpqua," Roseburg has long been a center of Oregon's timber industry. Signs are visible for Knudtson's and Lawson's jewelry stores, F.W. Woolworth, and Joe Richards' Men's Store. The view looks north on Jackson Street from Cass Avenue. Today's traffic flows in the opposite direction.

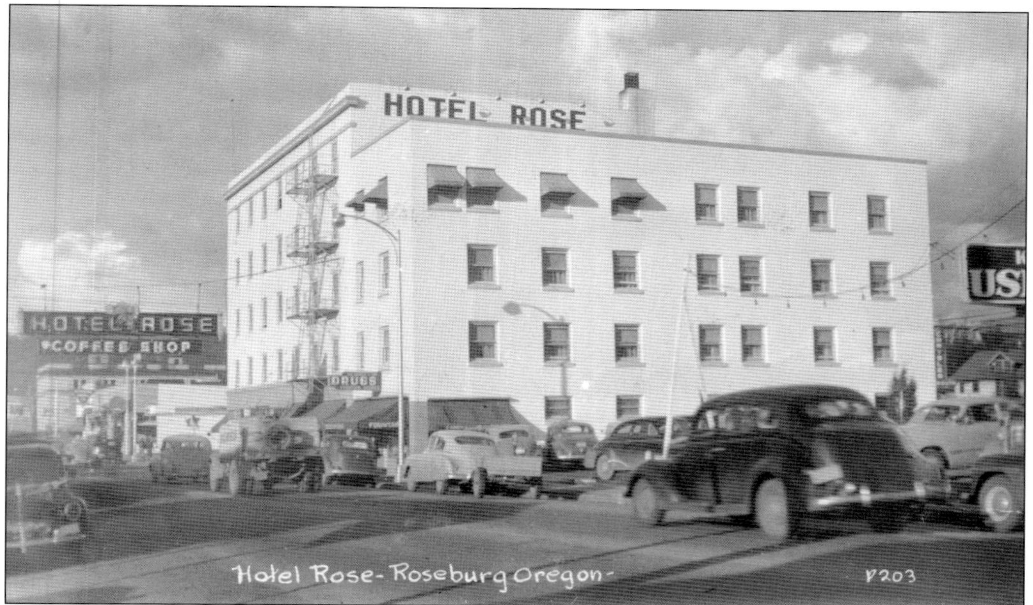

The Hotel Rose opened in September 1925 with 68 rooms, a dining room/coffee shop, and a roof garden for dancing. Furniture expenses alone reached $32,000 for the five-story hotel. When a truckload of dynamite exploded in downtown Roseburg on August 6, 1959, the hotel was heavily damaged but was back in operation within a month. Today, the building at 805 SE Stephens Street is the Rose Apartments. (JCO'D.)

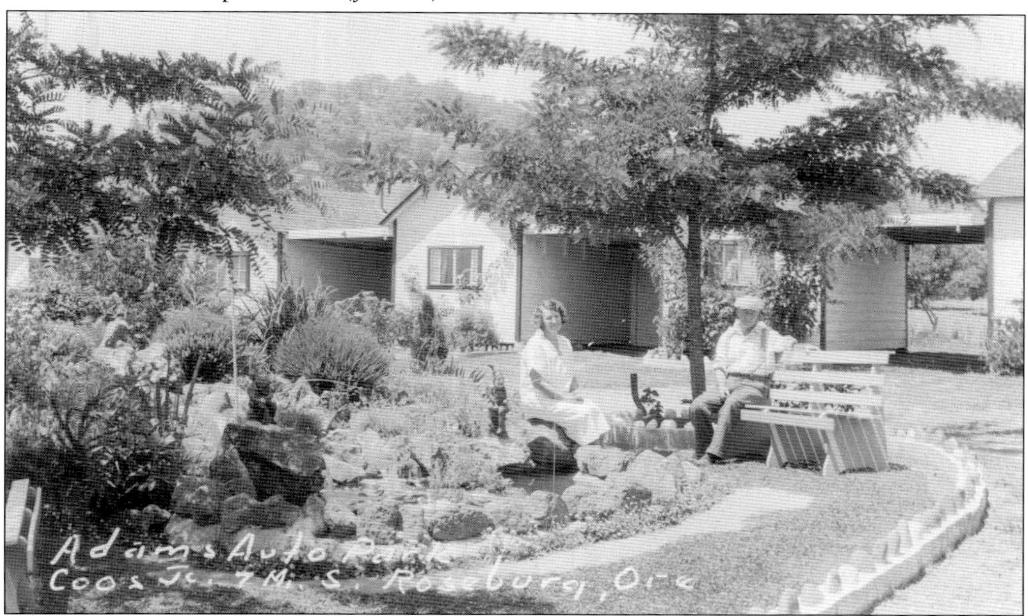

In 1928, George and Stella Adams purchased C.A. McGinnis's filling station at Coos Junction, seven miles south of Roseburg. Four years later, they had added a barbecue and Adams Auto Park, with nine cottages renting for $1 and up a night. Coos Junction, where the route to Coos Bay branched off the Pacific Highway, is called Winston today. The couple in the photograph are not identified but are likely George and Stella.

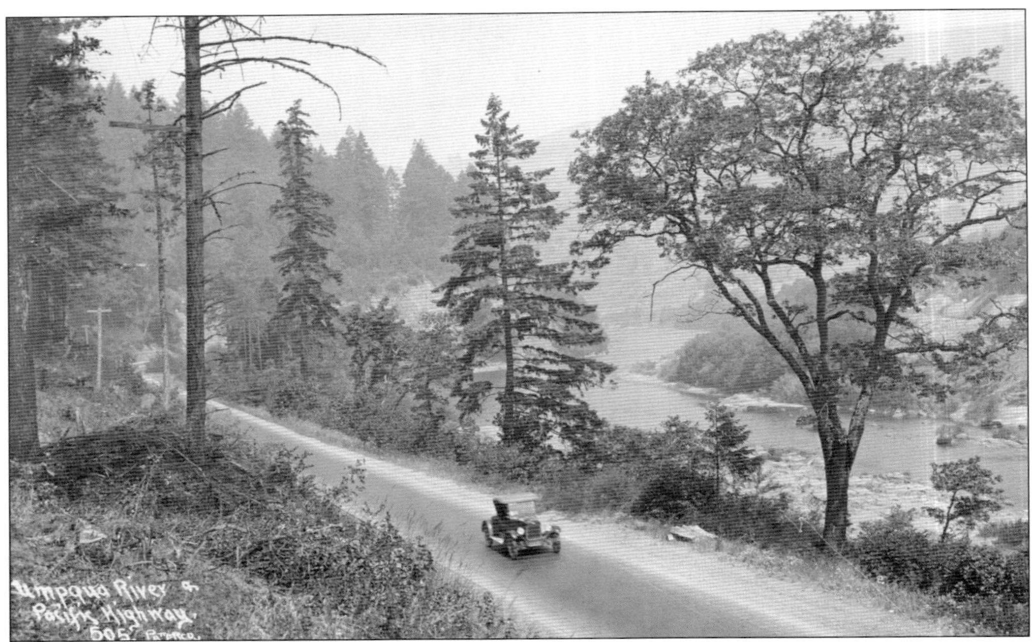

Scenery and transportation: in pre-freeway times, they often coexisted. Going somewhere was as important as arriving, and highways were often designed with an eye toward making the most of the surroundings. In this photograph, an early auto trundles along the Pacific Highway (in the center of the road, no less) with a beautiful view of the Umpqua River and no other traffic in sight. (OD.)

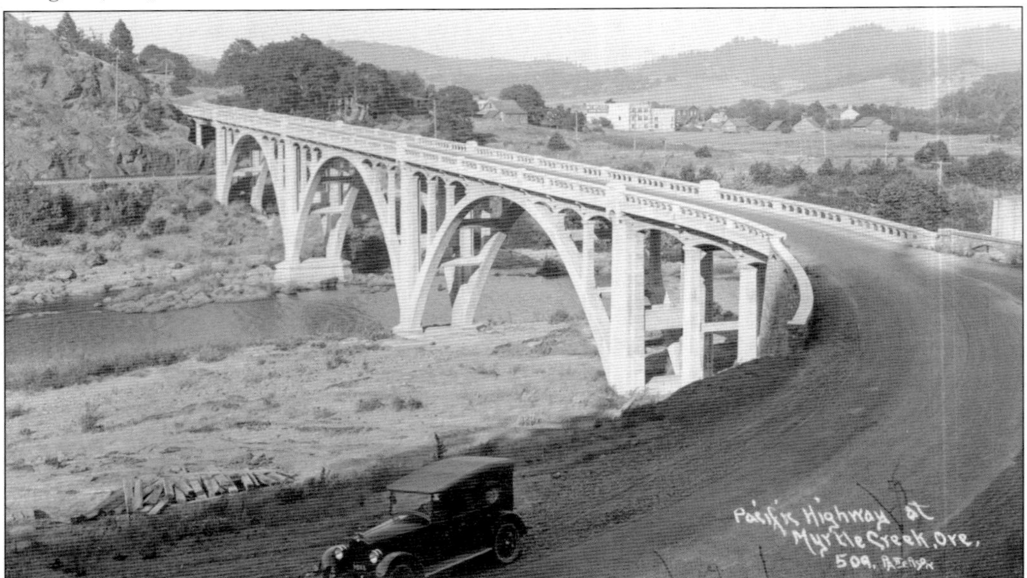

The Myrtle Creek Bridge opened earlier than planned. During construction, traffic continued crossing the Umpqua River on an adjacent older bridge. In June 1922, as the new span neared completion, a heavily loaded construction truck broke through the floor of the old bridge and dropped into the river. The new bridge was declared ready for use the next day, even though the highway leading to it was not finished.

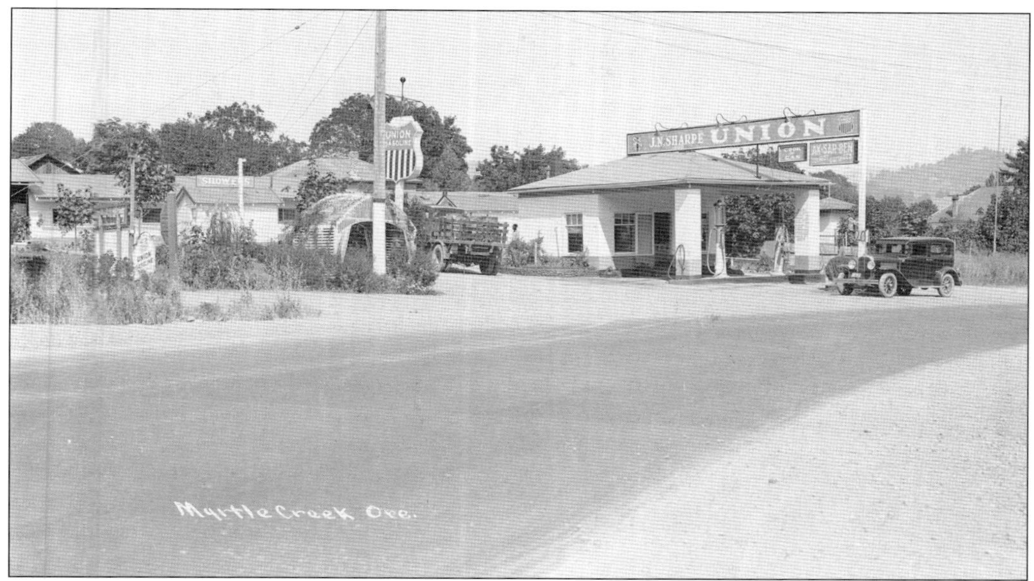

Two glass-topped, gravity-feed pumps dispensed Union gasoline at J.N. Sharpe's service station in Myrtle Creek. Behind the station, a small cabin with a "Showers" sign on its roof marks the location of the Ak-Sar-Ben Tourist Cottages. The service station and cottages were located at the north end of town. Ak-Sar-Ben ("Nebraska" spelled backwards) is a famous philanthropic organization, though any connection with the cottages is unknown. (LCHM, CS872.)

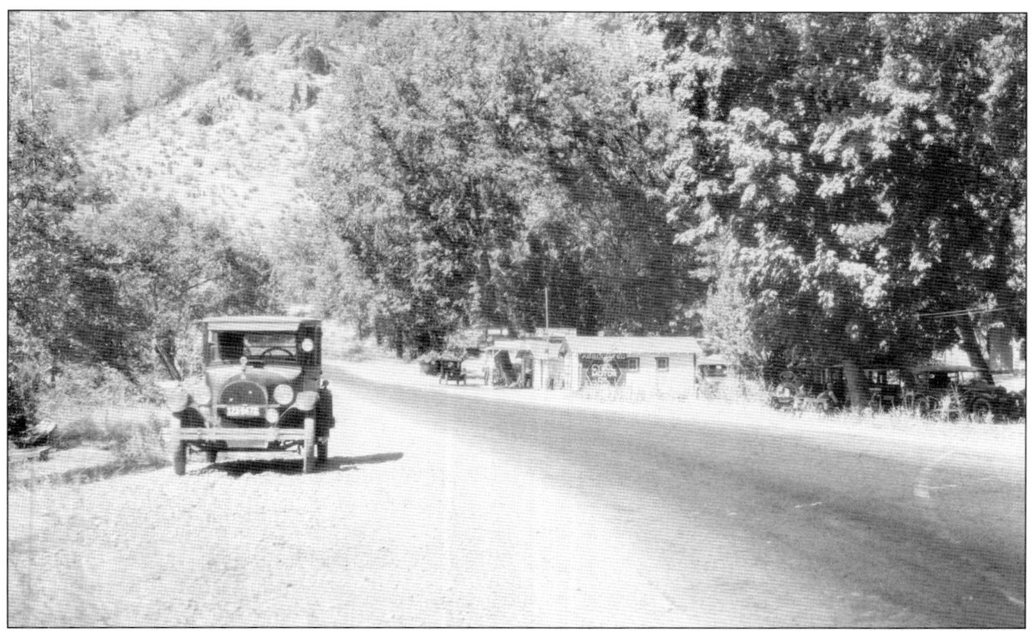

The Umpqua Auto Camp occupied a pleasant spot adjacent to the Pacific Highway bridge over the Umpqua River. In addition to 11 cabins under tall trees, the camp had a service station selling Associated gas and Cycol motor oil. Mr. and Mrs. J.W. Fitzpatrick, camp proprietors, became locally famous for hosting a well-attended annual picnic. The site, six miles south of Myrtle Creek, is buried by Interstate 5. (LCHM, CS857.)

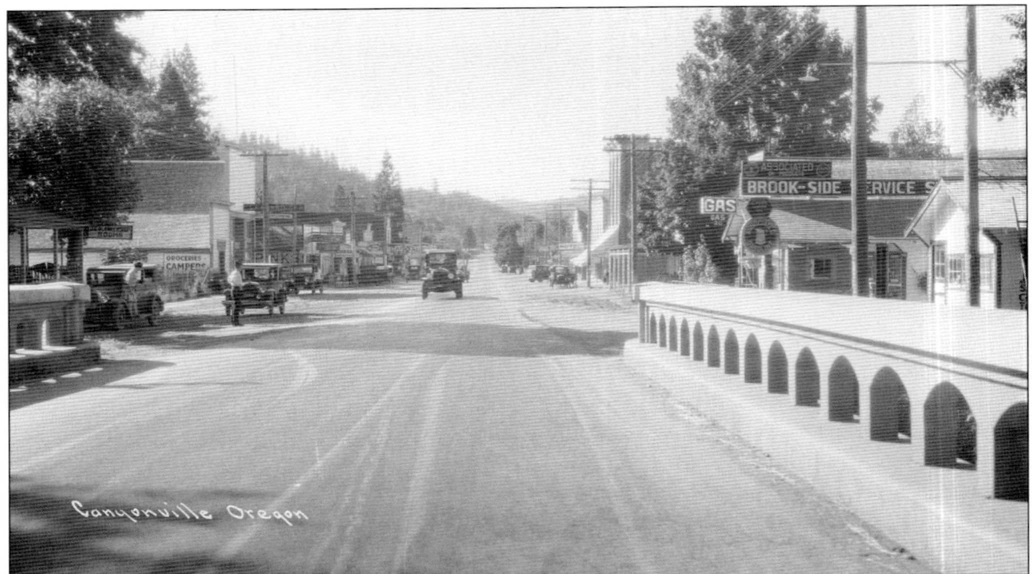

When this photograph was taken in 1925, Canyonville's business district abutted this small Pacific Bridge highway at the south end of town. In subsequent years the commercial center migrated north, but the bridge still remains on a now-abandoned section of highway. Among roadside businesses are the Brook-Side Service Station, the New Overland Hotel, and L.E. Henninger's grocery store, which also offered campsites. (LCHM, CS909.)

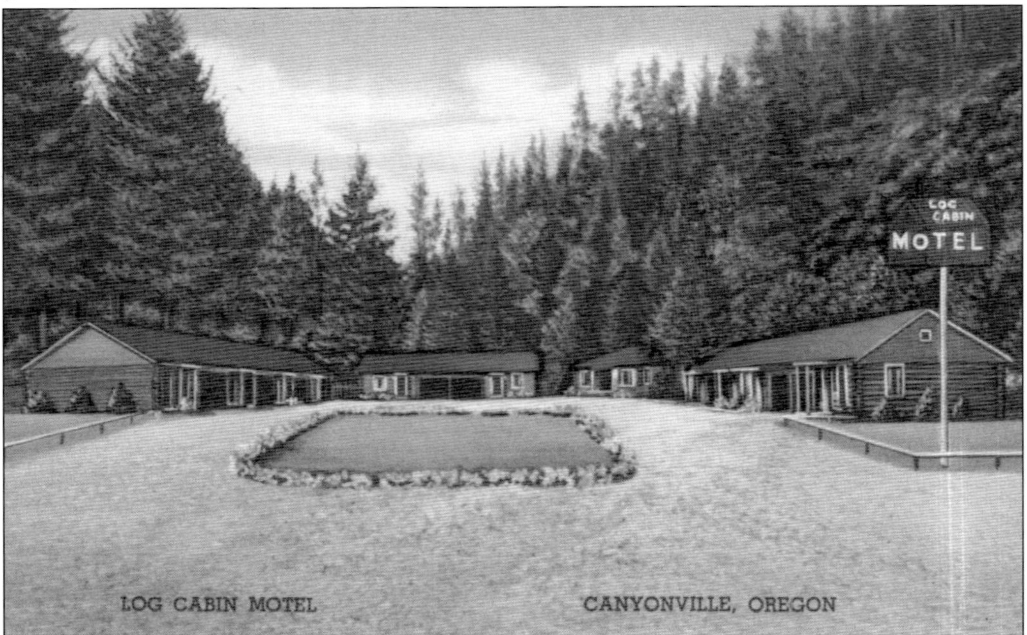

Canyonville's Log Cabin Motel consisted of 10 units with garages, arranged in a U-shape around a flowered open space and cozily tucked into a nook of woods off the highway. Cabins were supplied with Serta mattresses and were available with or without kitchen facilities. When Mr. and Mrs. J.W. Irwin owned the motel, Canyonville was a small, quiet town; it has since grown significantly thanks to the nearby casino.

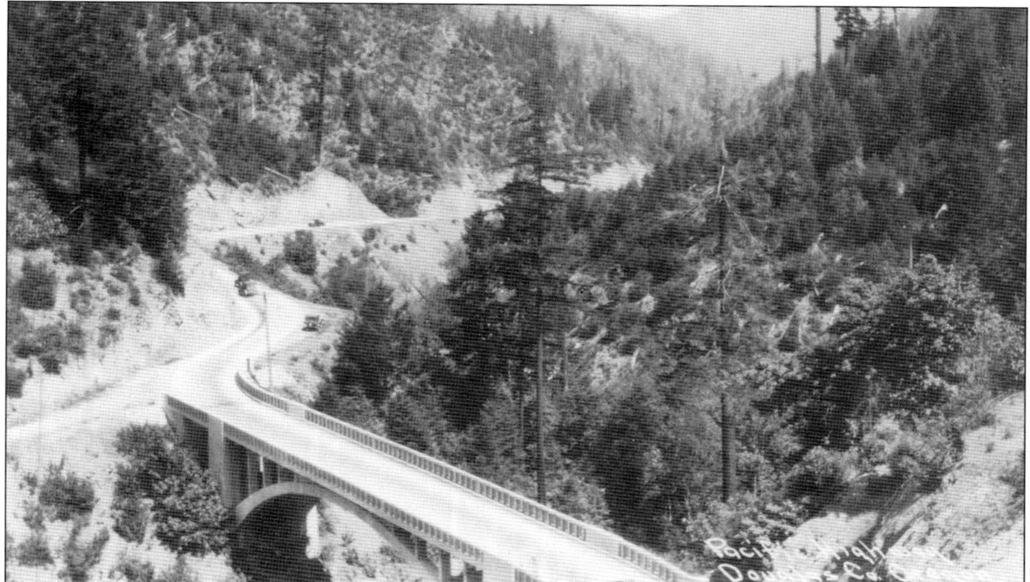

It was a 1,250-foot climb south of Canyonville to the top of Canyon Mountain. The old Pacific Highway clung to the sides of the canyon as it struggled to the top, crossing Canyon Creek on the Pioneer Bridge along the way. Highway construction in 1950 completely altered this scene: the bridge vanished, the creek's course was altered, vegetation was removed, and the canyon sides were sheared off to reduce landslides.

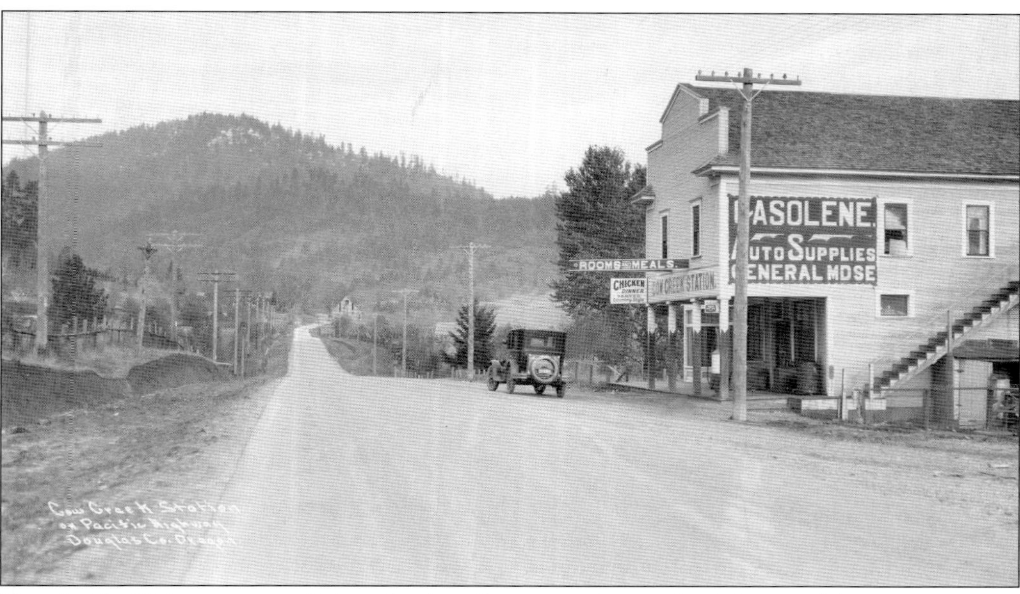

The Pacific Highway entered Cow Creek valley two miles south of Canyon Mountain summit. Here was Cow Creek Station, a full-service stopping point and home to the Canyon Pass Hotel and J.B. Hart's chicken dinner restaurant. In 1928, the Azalea post office was moved to Cow Creek Station and the place adopted the new name. Though bypassed by the freeway, Cow Creek Station continues to serve travelers. (LCHM, CS887.)

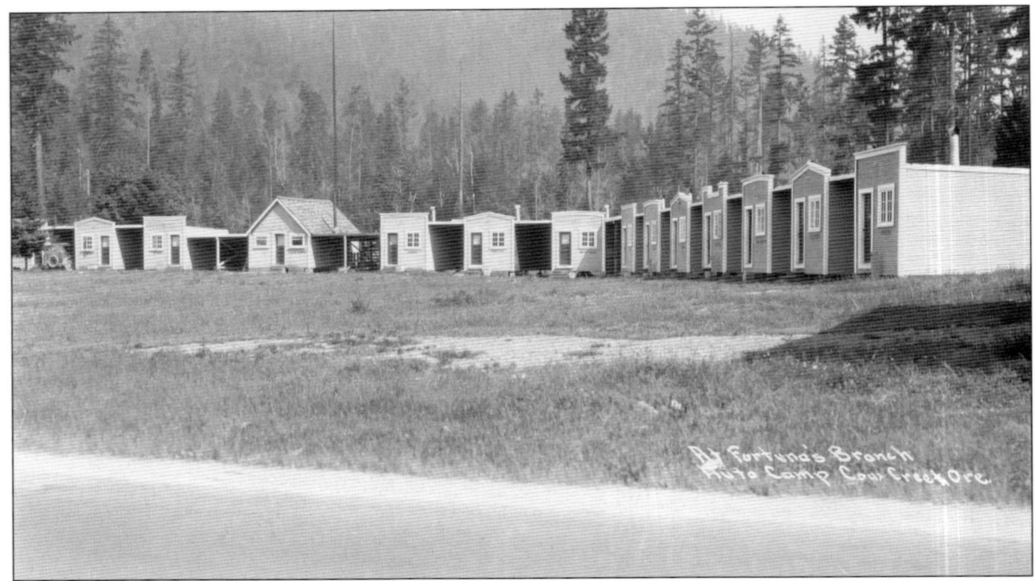

Fortune Branch Auto Camp straddled the Pacific Highway three and a half miles southwest of Azalea. The camp took its name from Fortune Branch, a small stream that empties into Cow Creek at that point. On the north side of the highway stood a gas station; behind it, 17 cabins snuggled up against wooded hills. In 1935, the cabins rented for $1 to $1.50 per night. (LCHM, CS891.)

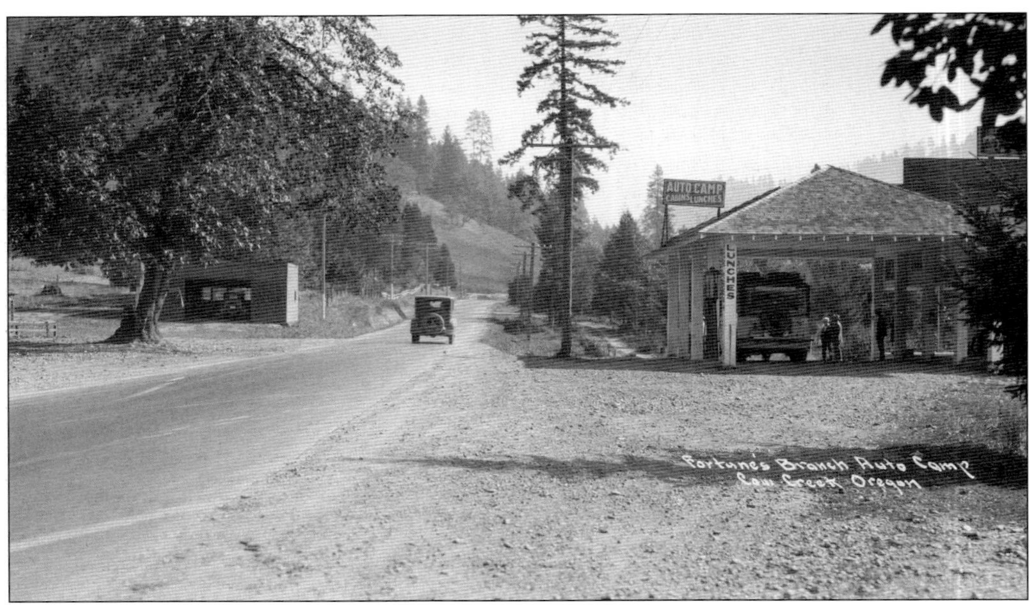

Across the highway was the Fortune Branch store and lunchroom and another gas station. Camp founder Ira Booth sold out in 1929 when he moved to Ohio, but returned in 1932 and set about updating the camp by replacing the small original cabins with modern, three-room cottages. The store was still in business in 1954. Though on a major highway, Fortune Branch did not receive electricity until 1930. (LCHM, CS893.)

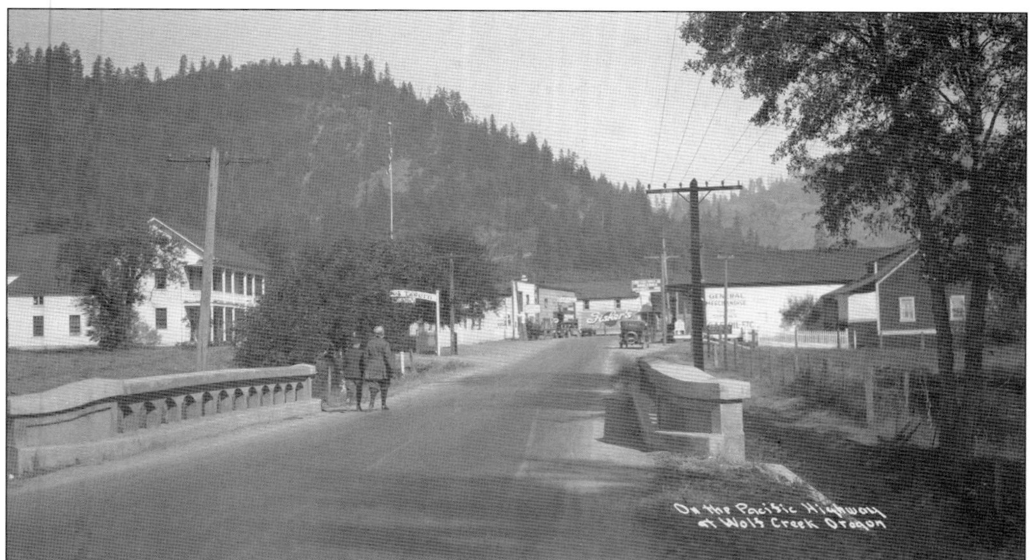

This 1925 view looks west along the Pacific Highway into Wolf Creek. The Applegate Trail, an early emigrant road, passed through here; the Roseburg–Grants Pass stagecoach line followed the same route. In 1883, Henry Smith constructed the Wolf Creek Tavern (at left). By the time the Pacific Highway came through, a small town had grown up around the hotel. The bridge in the foreground still exists. (LCHM, CS932.)

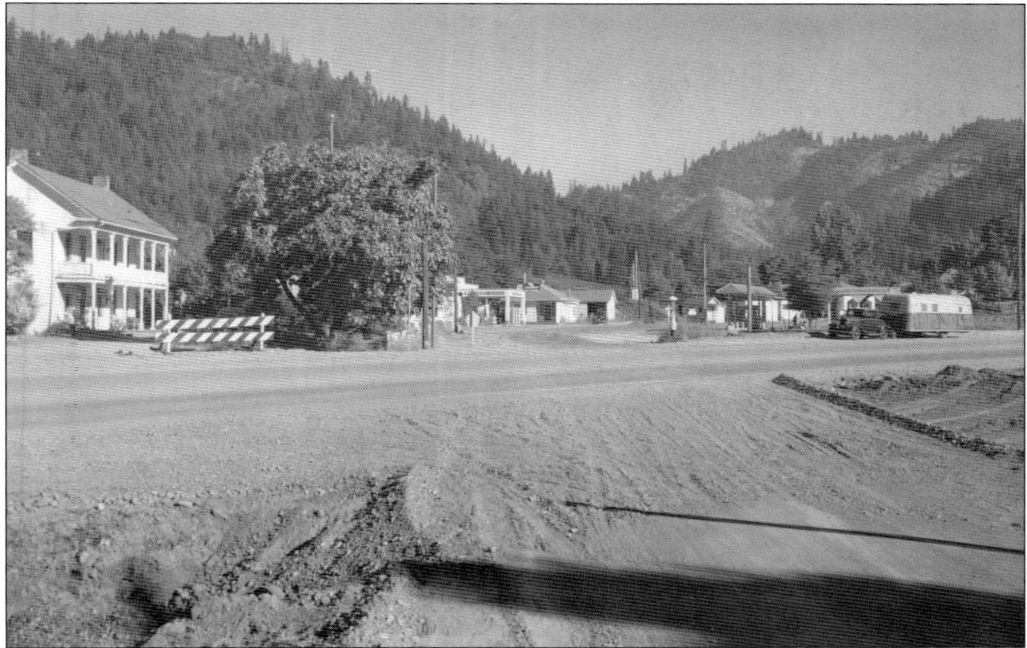

In 1947, Highway 99 was realigned around (rather than through) downtown Wolf Creek. This photograph was taken from the same vantage point as the previous image. Note the changes: part of old Pacific Highway has been converted from pavement to gravel, and several service stations have replaced the early store buildings. By the 1960s, Interstate 5 had bypassed this whole scene. (OSL, OHD3893.)

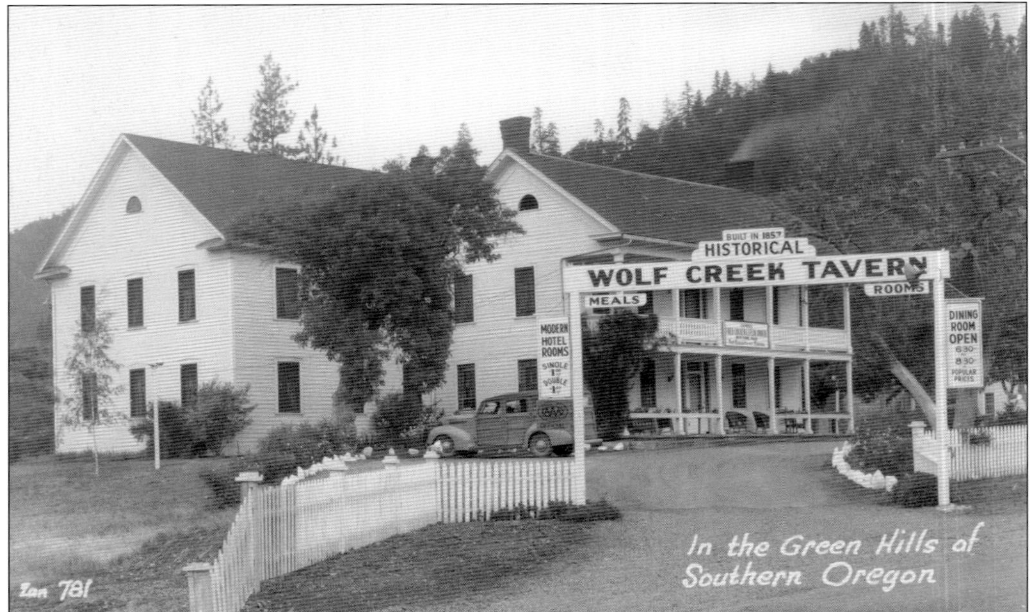

The venerable Wolf Creek Tavern, originally a stop on the old stagecoach route to California, naturally adapted to motor travel when the Pacific Highway built through in the 1910s. Many famous folks—Clark Gable and Carole Lombard, among others—have been visitors. Known today as the Wolf Creek Inn, it is the oldest continually operating hotel in Oregon, with comfortable accommodations and a fine restaurant.

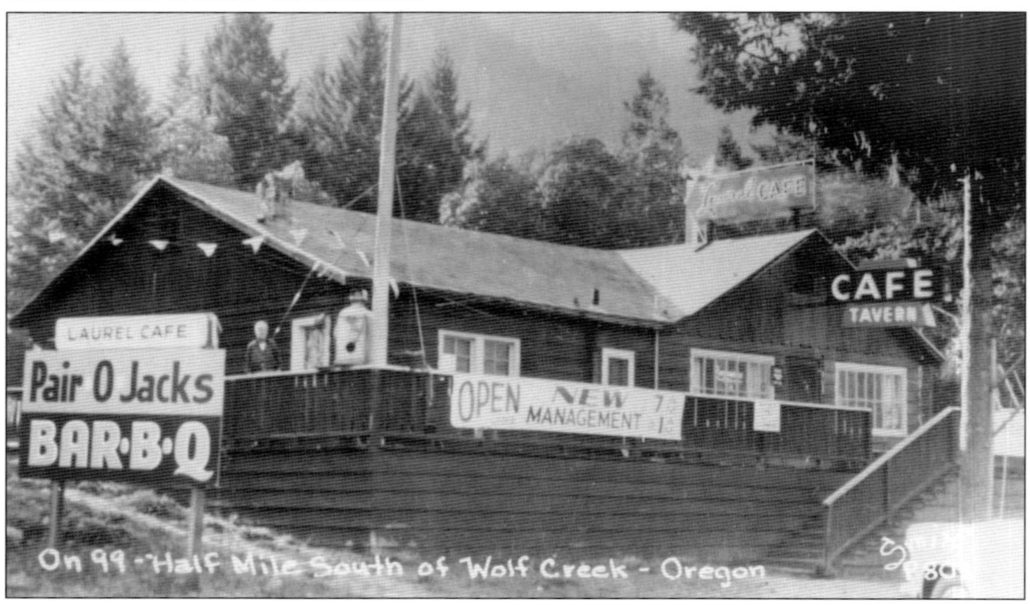

Laurel Camp opened in 1920 on 21 acres south of Wolf Creek. Originally more a park than camp, it offered large grassy lawns, flowers, and a pavilion serving light lunches and refreshments. By 1930, owner Sam Linnton had added 16 tourist cabins and a service station, store, and restaurant. The barbeque/tavern shown here appeared in the 1950s, taking its name from the new owners: two guys named Jack.

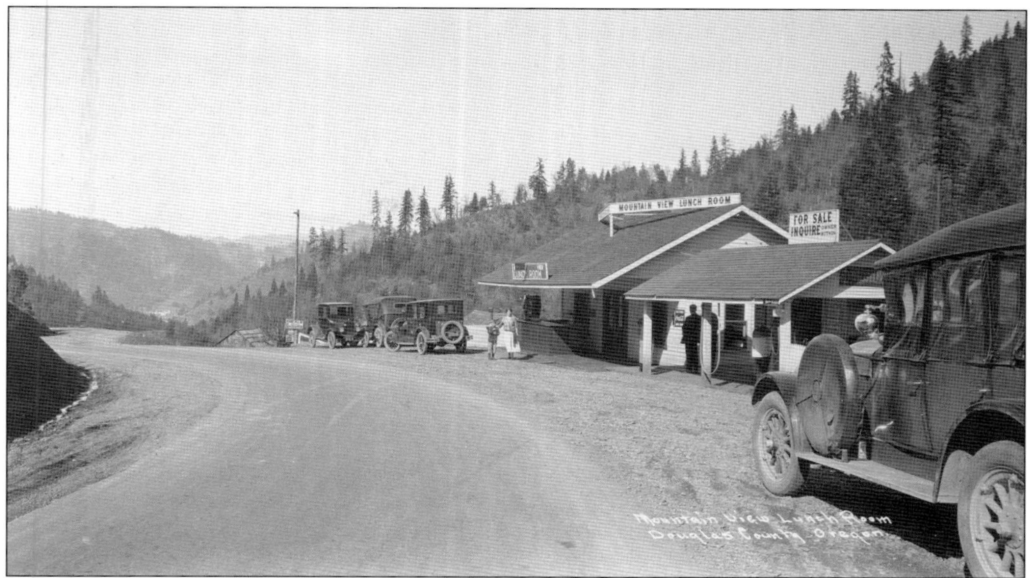

The Mountain View Lunch Room—"Meals at All Hours"—was situated atop Wolf Creek Hill. Mr. and Mrs. Henry Dassey operated both the lunchroom and the nearby Marigold Camp. An unidentified woman and boy look like they've just stopped for a meal; next door, two men appear to be conversing under a primitive gas station's canopy. This entire scene has been erased by freeway construction. (LCHM, CS819.)

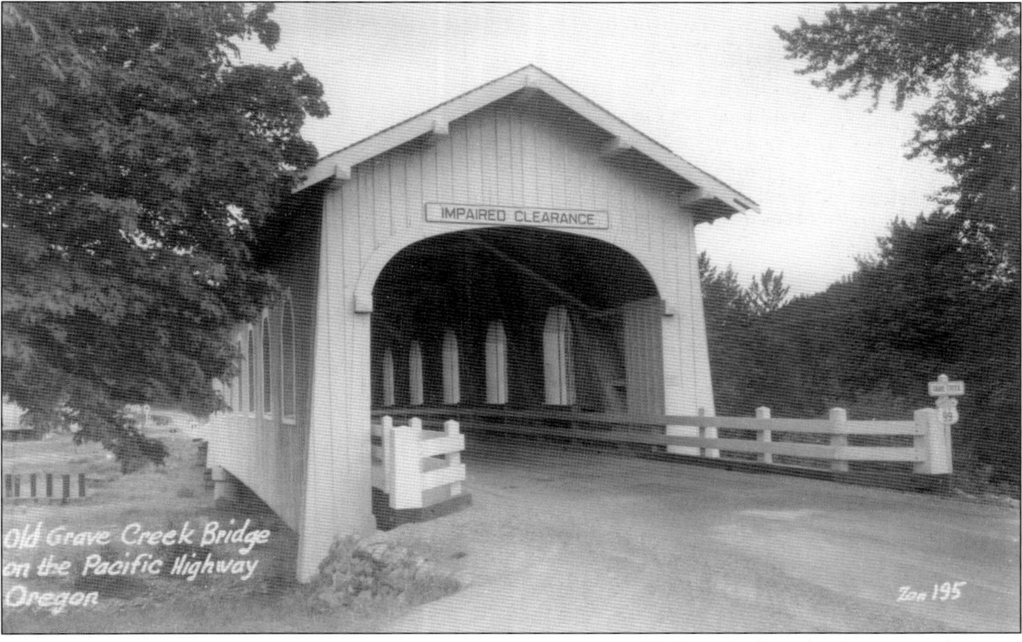

Covered bridges, though not uncommon in Oregon, are usually found along backcountry byways rather than main highways. Grave Creek Bridge, located in Sunny Valley, is an exception. Constructed in 1920, it carried Pacific Highway (and Highway 99) traffic for years until being isolated on a stretch of bypassed pavement by construction of Interstate 5 in the 1960s. Grave Creek was named for a pioneer grave along the old Applegate trail.

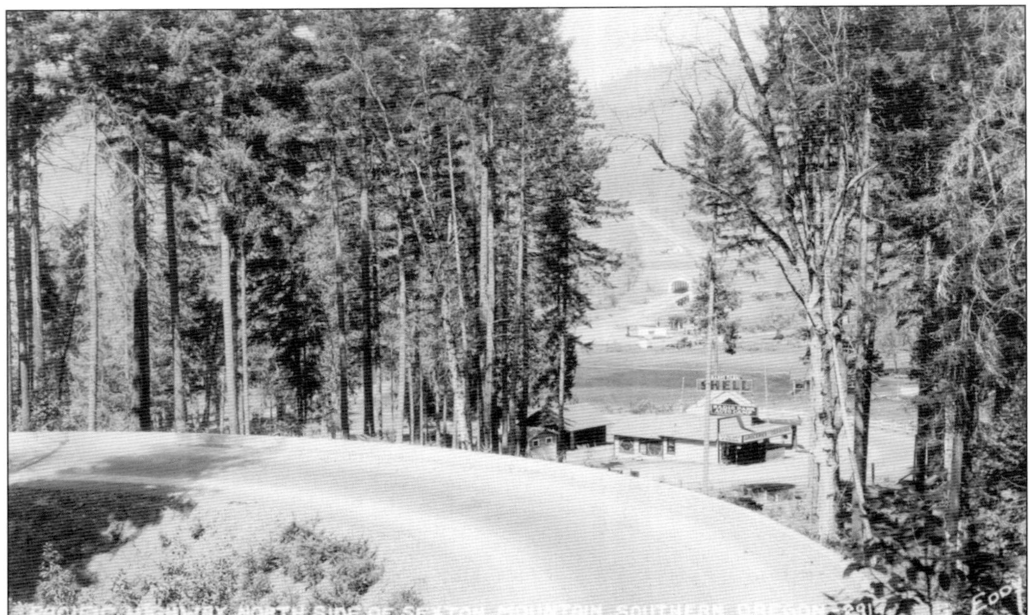

Although the elevation gain crossing Sexton Mountain was not great—about 500 feet—the mountain's steep north side demanded that the Pacific Highway negotiate a twisting, hairpin-curved climb to the top. The Sexton Loops, as they were called, became infamous among early travelers. This view looks north from the Loops to Radio Park Auto Camp. The Grave Creek covered bridge is in the middle distance, with Smith Hill beyond.

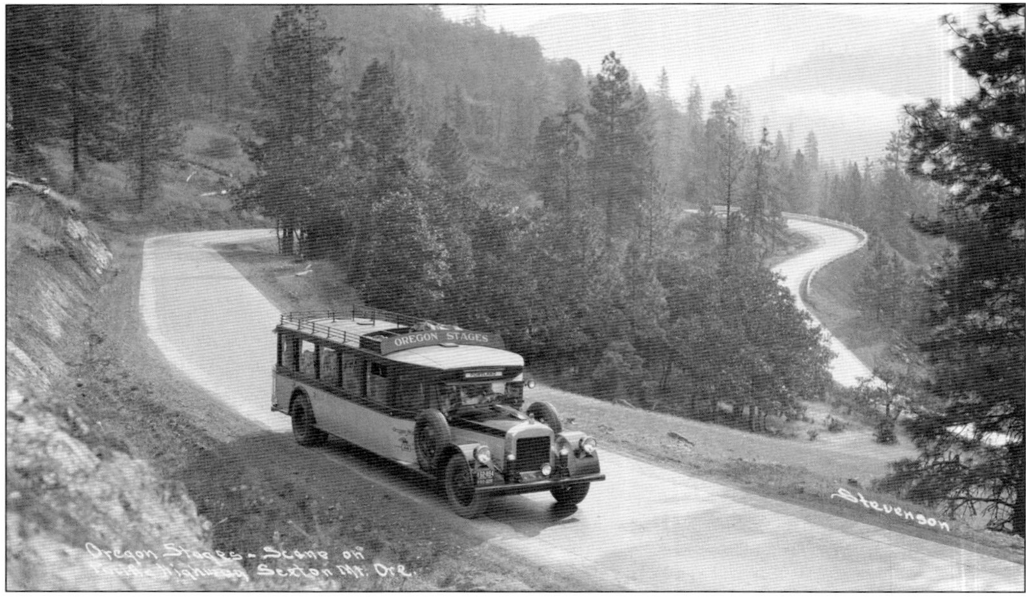

The south slope of Sexton Mountain was more gentle—loopy, but not as steep as the north side. In this 1927 view, a bus of the Oregon Stages Company trundles up the highway heading north. Oregon Stages came into being in 1925, with frequent service connecting all the Pacific Highway cities between Ashland and Portland. Their warm, comfortable safety coaches were an appealing alternative for highway travelers. [LCHM, CS946.)

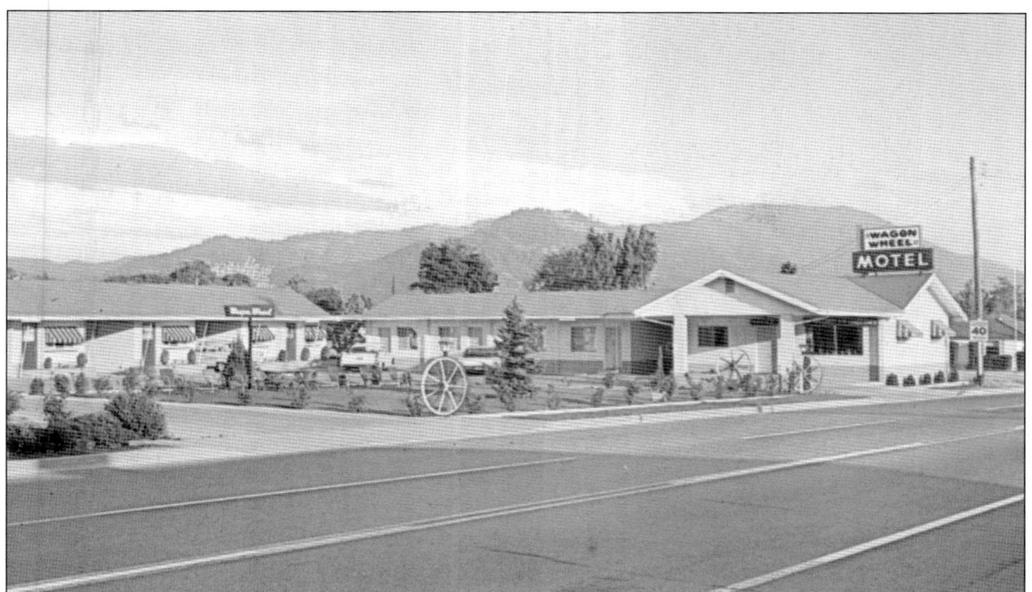

The Wagon Wheel Motel greeted visitors at the northern entrance of Grants Pass. Owned by Mr. and Mrs. John Phillips, its 11 clean, attractive units (some with kitchens) included carpeting, radios, and televisions. A second leg containing the motel office was later added to the original "L" shaped configuration. Now home to a variety of small businesses, the Wagon Wheel building still stands at 1439 N 6th Street.

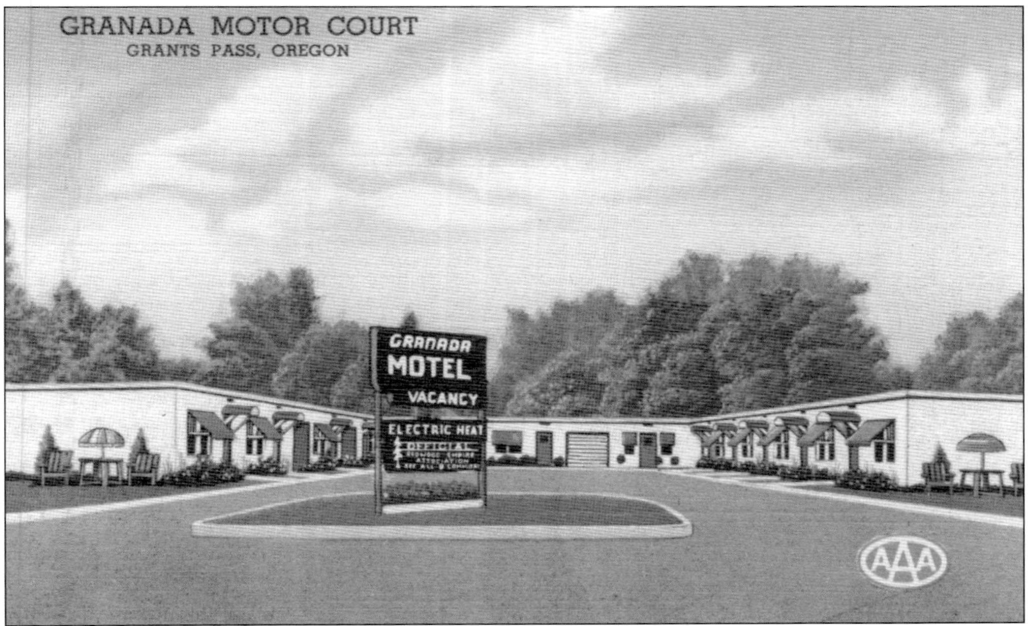

The Granada Motor Court, at 850 N 6th Street, consisted of nine units with kitchen facilities. Owner Frank McKenzie provided several areas of street-side lawn with chairs, tables, and umbrellas for guests' enjoyment. The Granada was a proud member of the Redwood Empire Association, a trade group promoting tourism in southern Oregon and northern California. As with the Wagon Wheel, the Granada Motel building is still in use hosting several businesses.

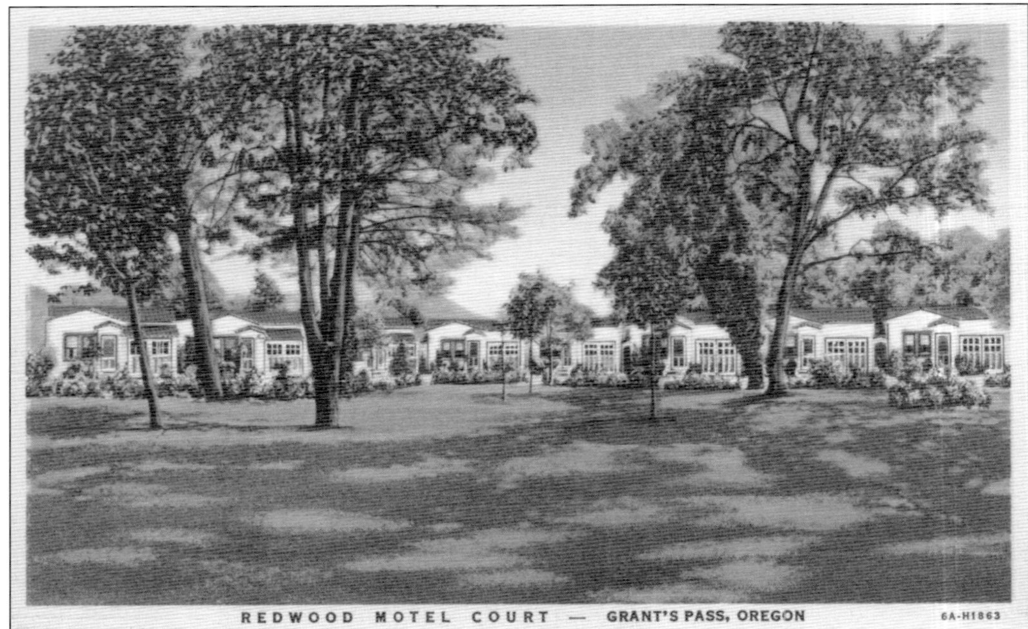

The Redwood Motel Court opened in the early 1930s under the management of Hugh Johnson. Billed as "a distinctive automobile tourist motel" with quiet, detached cottages, for years it was located at 707 N 6th Street. By 1953, the Redwood Motel Court had relocated to 815 N 6th Street and the original location became the Wee Houses Motel. It currently operates as the Redwood Hyperion Suites at the later address.

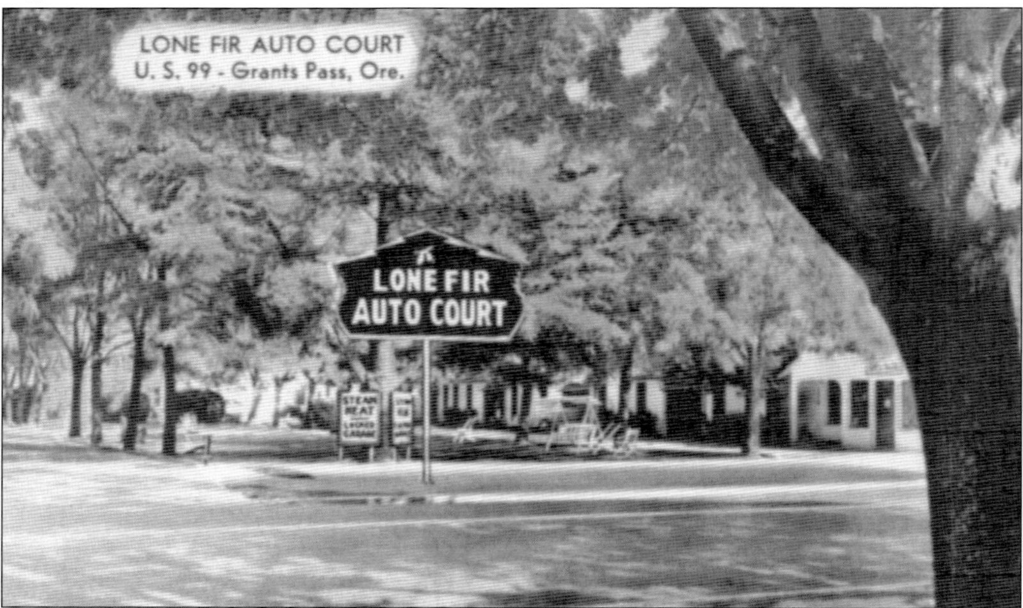

Perhaps there was only one fir at the Lone Fir Auto Court, but many trees shaded the grounds. The 14-unit court was in business prior to 1935. September 1948 saw tragedy here: two children were stabbed to death by their mother in unit 3. The Lone Fir added a modern two-story wing in the 1950s but is gone today; a medical building occupies the site at 741 N 6th Street.

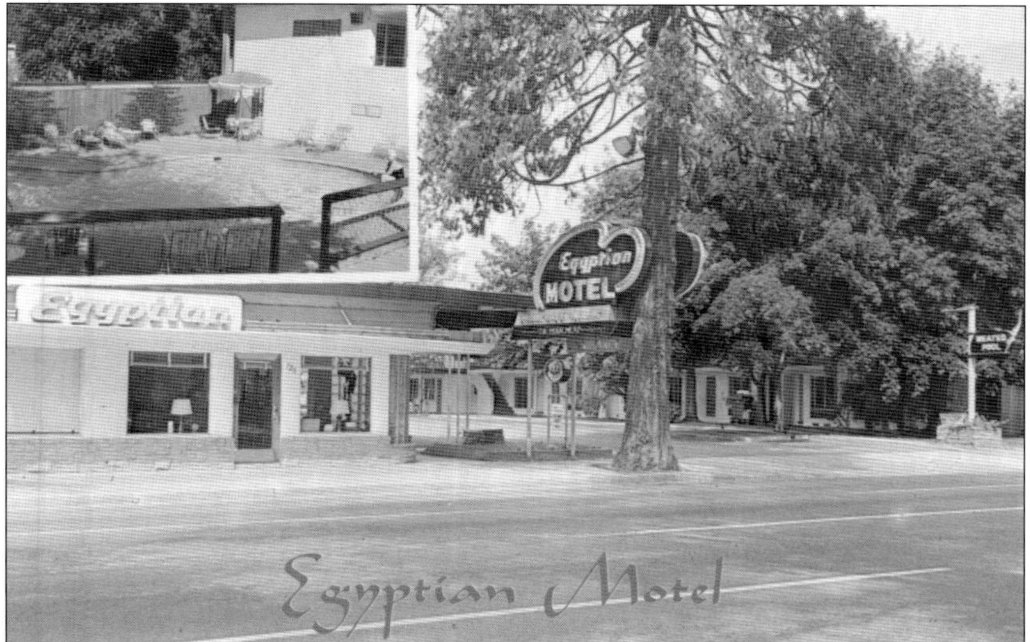

Dating to 1935, the Egyptian Motel described itself as "an oasis of hospitality." Its 27 units were arranged in two rows in an attractive garden setting; each unit ($5 single, $8 double per night in 1954) featured carpeted floors, combination tub/shower baths, and TV in air-conditioned comfort. A longtime member of United Motor Courts, the Egyptian is the Flamingo Inn today. It is located at 632 N 6th Street.

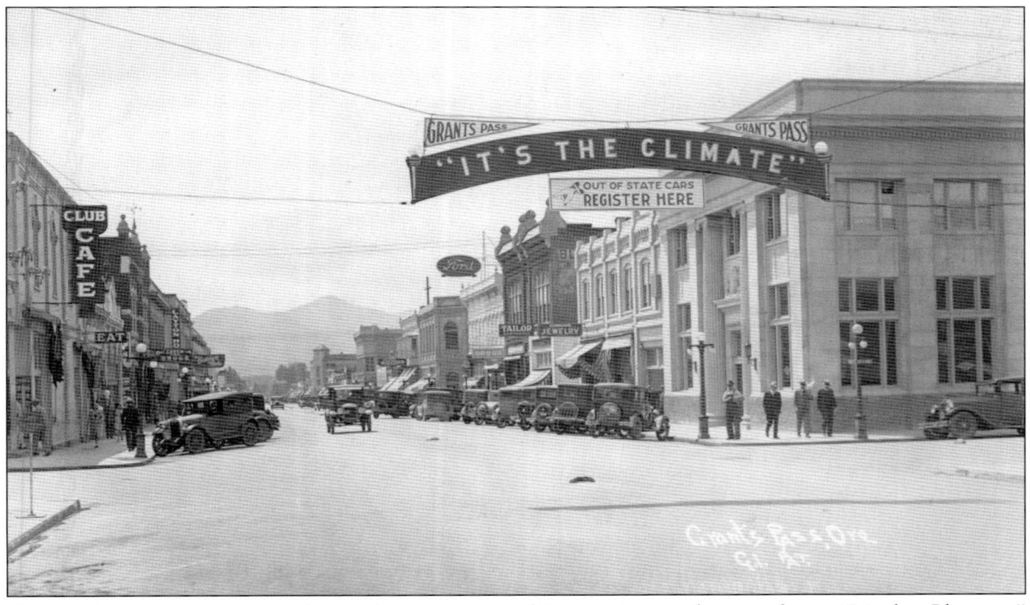

For nearly 100 years, this arch sign has announced Grants Pass's claim to fame: "It's the Climate." Actually, the city has much more going for it—seat of Josephine County, a center of the timber industry, hub for recreationists on the Rogue River, a prosperous downtown, and a 2010 population of nearly 35,000. First erected in 1920, the sign still hangs above 6th Street.

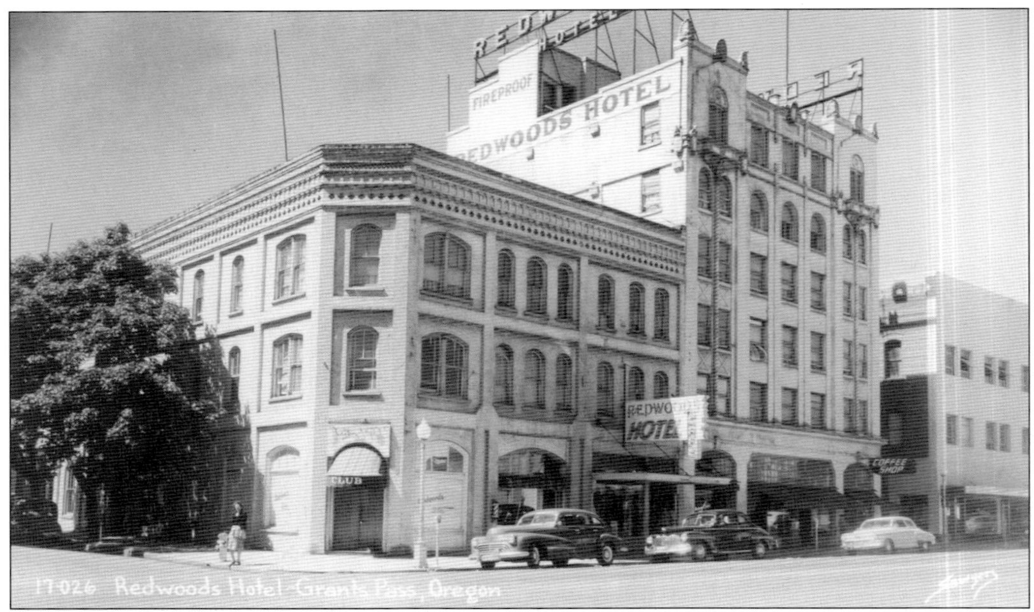

The Redwoods Hotel opened in 1926 as an expansion of the older Josephine Hotel, shown here to its right. With 45 rooms, a coffee shop, and the Brass Ring restaurant, the Redwoods maintained a steady clientele well into the 1950s under resident owners Virginia and Pete Good. Preserved but not functioning as a hotel, today it contains a bookstore and office spaces. It is located at 306 NW 6th Street.

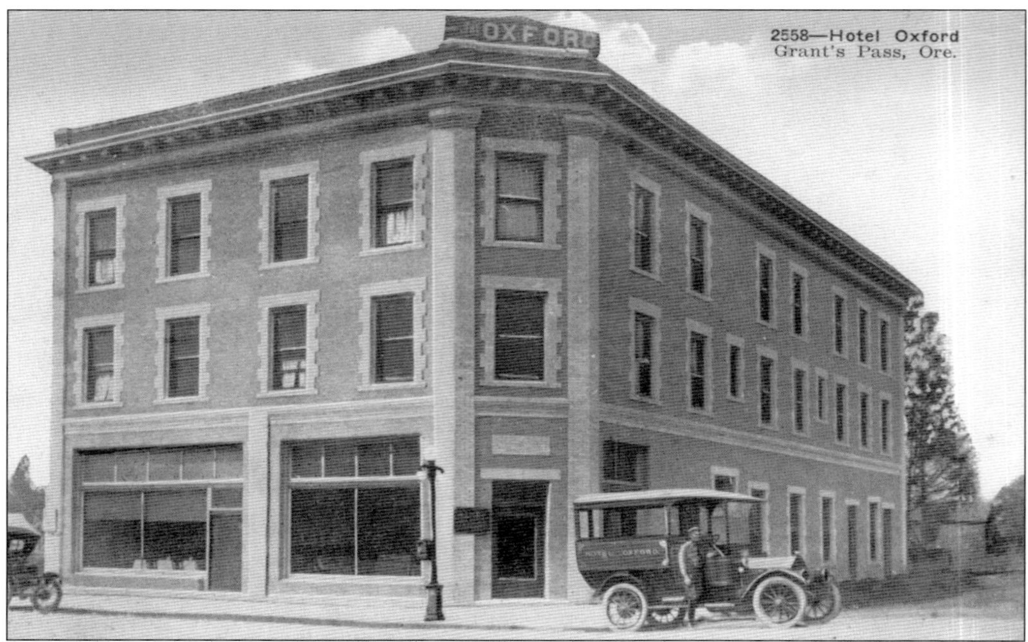

The Oxford Hotel is mentioned as early as 1913, when manager B.C. Dunlap installed an "auto bus" to convey guests back and forth from the local railroad depot. By 1915, the Oxford—"a quiet, refined house, tastefully furnished," with hot and cold running water in each room (but shared baths)—was owned by F.W. Streets. Edward Miller assumed management and eventual ownership in 1922.

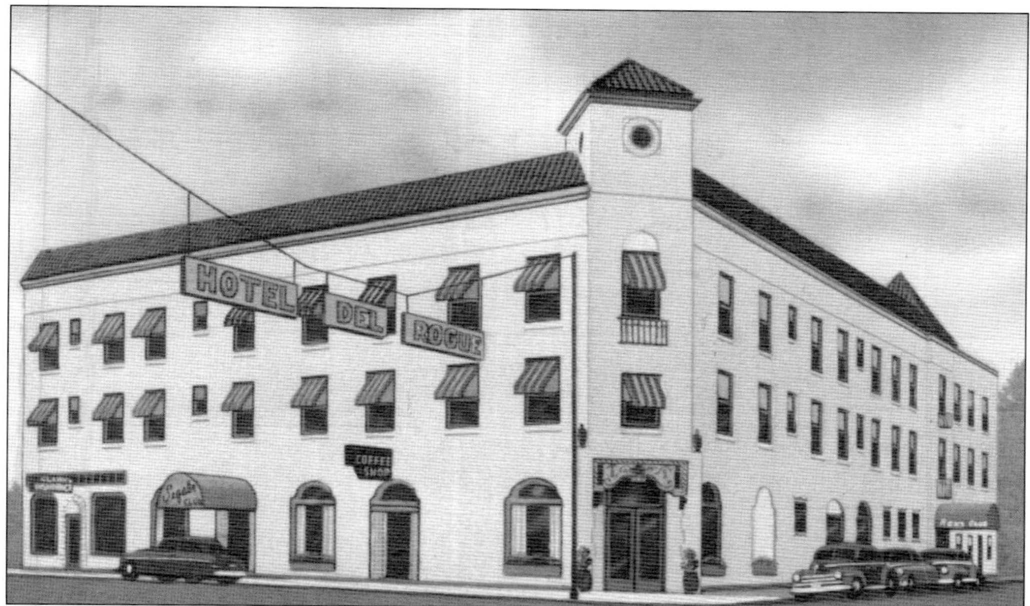

By the end of 1926, Edward Miller was a state senator, the Oxford Hotel had been renamed the Del Rogue, and a major remodel was underway. Additions were built on the hotel's west and south sides, and a Spanish Mission–style facade—more Californian than Oregonian—overlaid the original brick exterior. For years, a suspended sign over the highway announced the Del Rogue's location at 6th and K Streets.

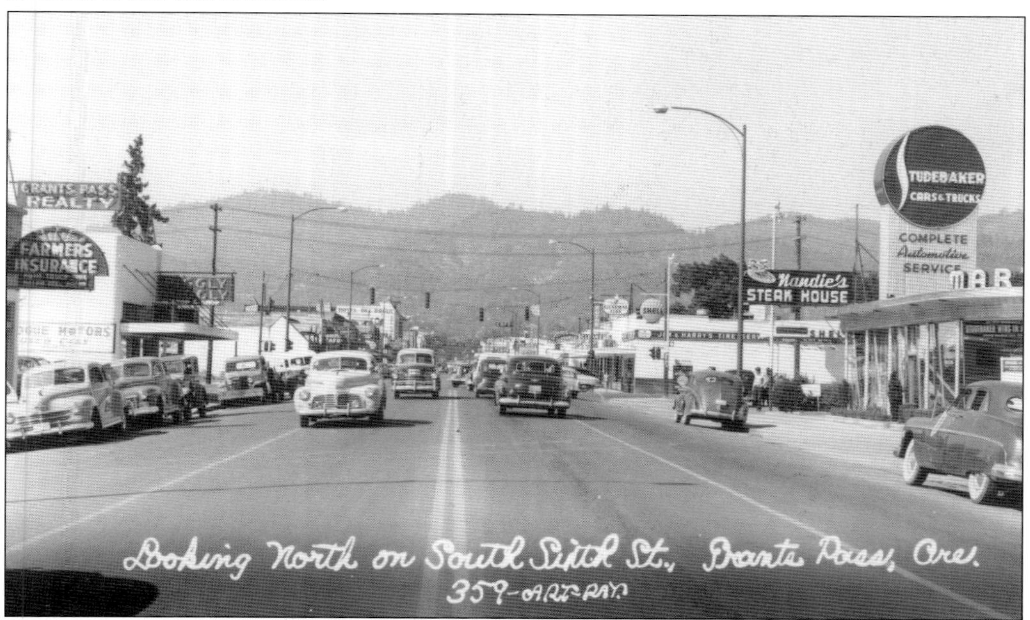

This is a view north on busy 6th Street from the vicinity of M Street. At that time, 6th carried two-way traffic through downtown; today, southbound vehicles use 6th, and those heading north use 7th. Signs include a Studebaker dealer, Nandie's Steak House, a Piggly Wiggly market, a Shell station, Jim and Harry's General Tire Service, several cafés, and, in the distance, the Hotel Del Rogue and its suspended sign.

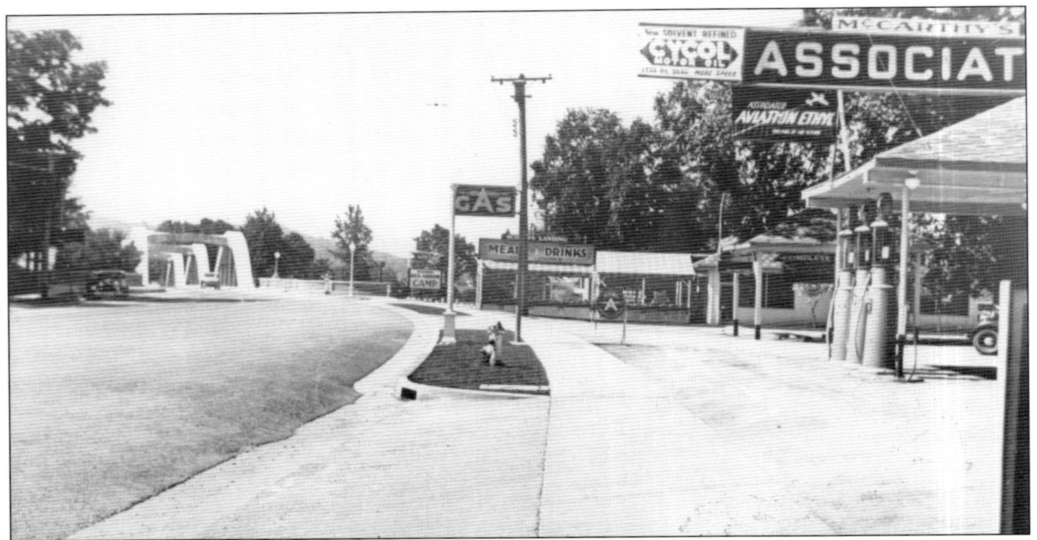

In this 1930s view, 6th Street is seen curving toward the Caveman Bridge southbound from downtown Grants Pass. McCarthy's Associated Oil station, shown at far right, was owned by Andy and Maude McCarthy. Right next door was another service station selling Flying A gas, then came Scotty's Landing and the Red Arrow Auto Camp. The only thing in this photograph that still remains is the bridge. (JCHS.)

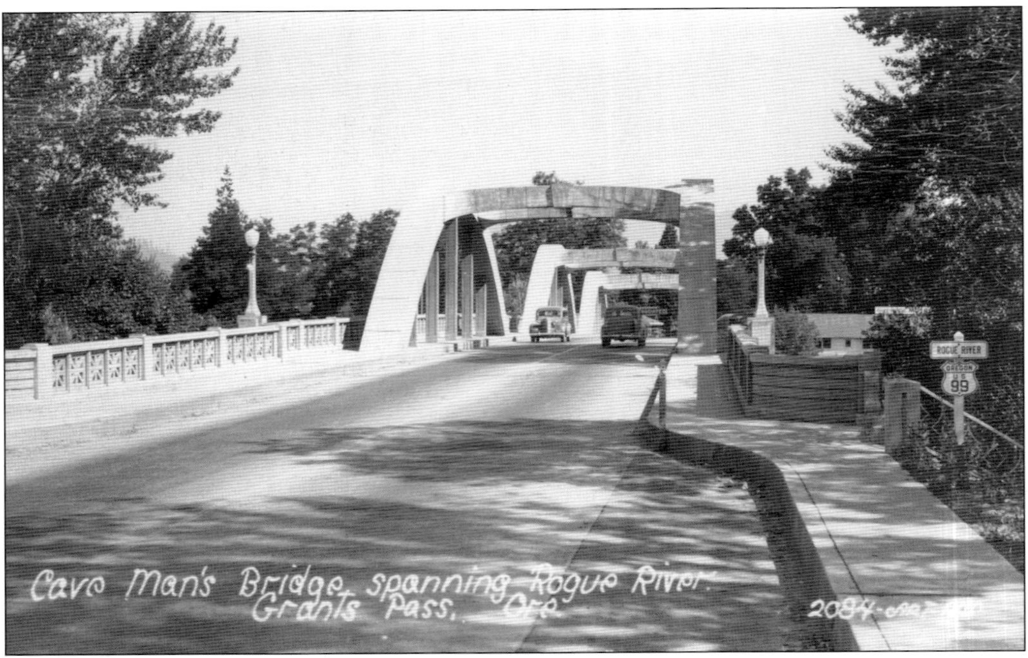

The Caveman Bridge takes its name from a local civic organization; their name in turn is derived from the nearby Oregon Caves. When it was dedicated in 1931, the Cavemen participated in full regalia. Another Conde McCullough design, the bridge consists of three 150-foot partial spans ornamented with lampposts and railings with inset floral patterns. A parallel bridge across the Rogue River opened in 1960 to carry northbound traffic.

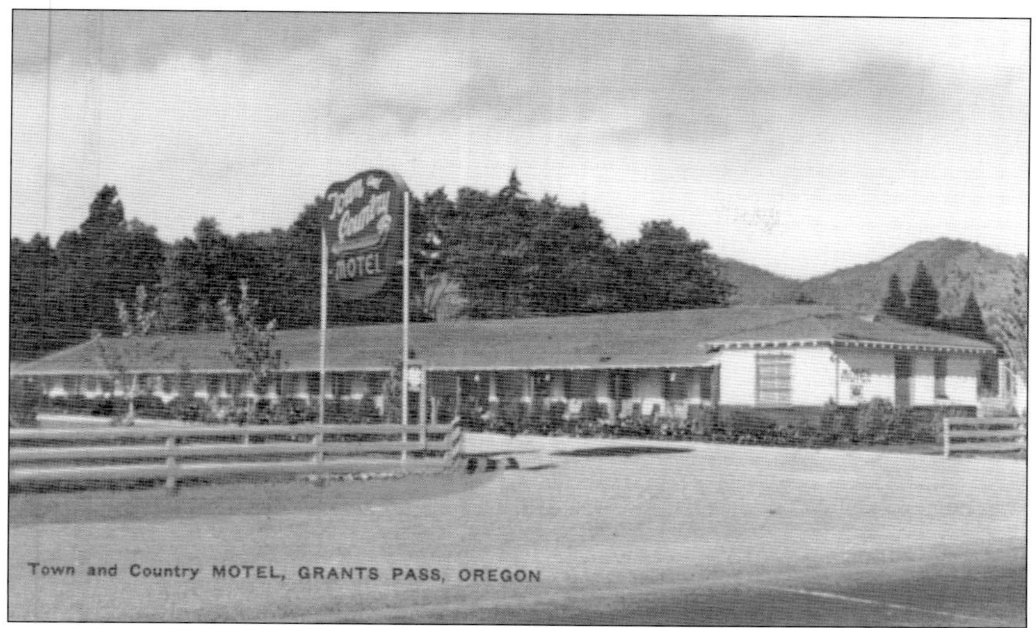

Town and Country MOTEL, GRANTS PASS, OREGON

Just south of the Caveman Bridge, Highway 199, the Redwood Highway, branched off toward California while Highway 99 swung east and paralleled the Rogue River to Gold Hill, 15 miles distant. This scenic stretch of highway was a recreation magnet, and numerous motels sprang up along the highway to provide accommodations for vacationers and highway travelers. The Town and Country Motel, at 1130 Highway 99 S, was a typical example.

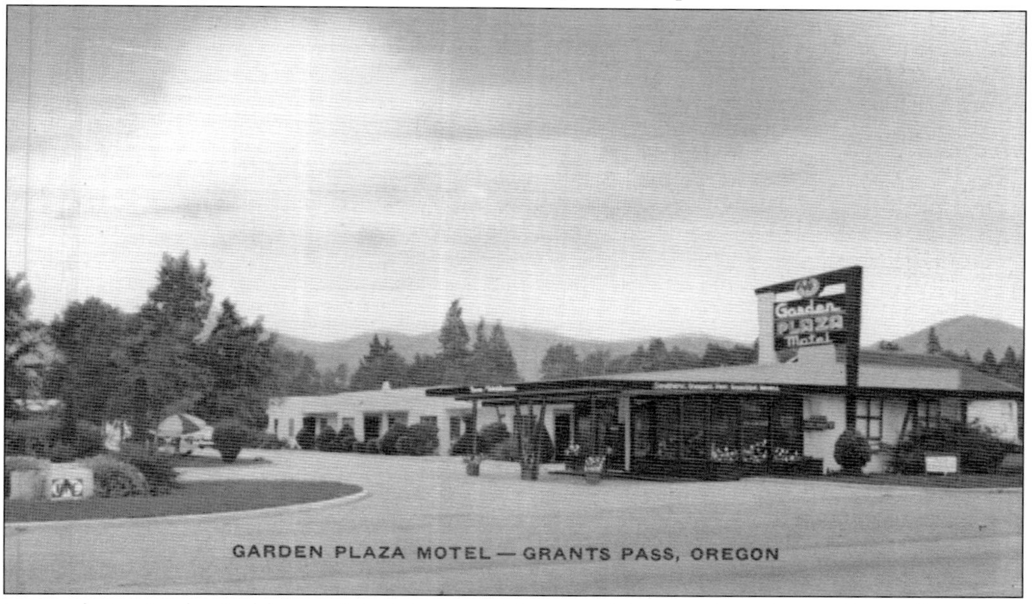

GARDEN PLAZA MOTEL — GRANTS PASS, OREGON

Mr. and Mrs. Leslie Parkhurst of the Town and Country Motel took pride in offering "Southern Oregon's most beautiful rooms"—21 air conditioned units, radios and telephones in each, and optional TV and kitchenettes—for nightly rates of $4.50 single, $7 double in 1948. Set in a parklike atmosphere with a children's playground, the motel was located at 1142 Highway 99 S and is still in use as long-term apartments.

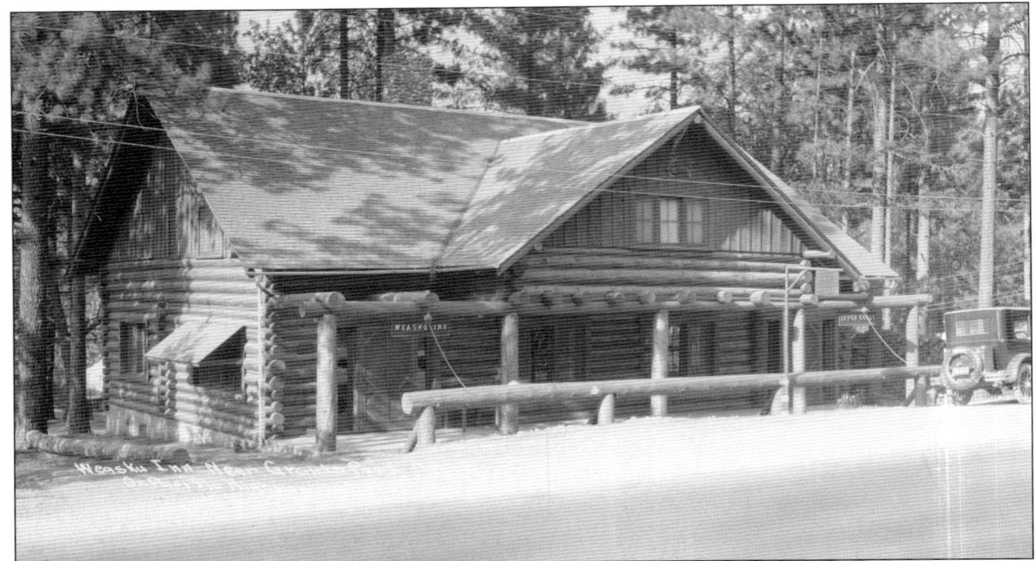

A world-renowned fishing resort since 1924, the Weasku Inn has welcomed such famous guests as Walt Disney and Zane Grey. In 1928, the inn passed from original owners Bert and Sarah Smith to "Rainbow" and Peggy Gibson. For years, the Gibsons had the honor of catching the first salmon of the season on the Rogue River. The Weasku Inn was restored in 1998, its historic character fully preserved. (LCHM, CS968.)

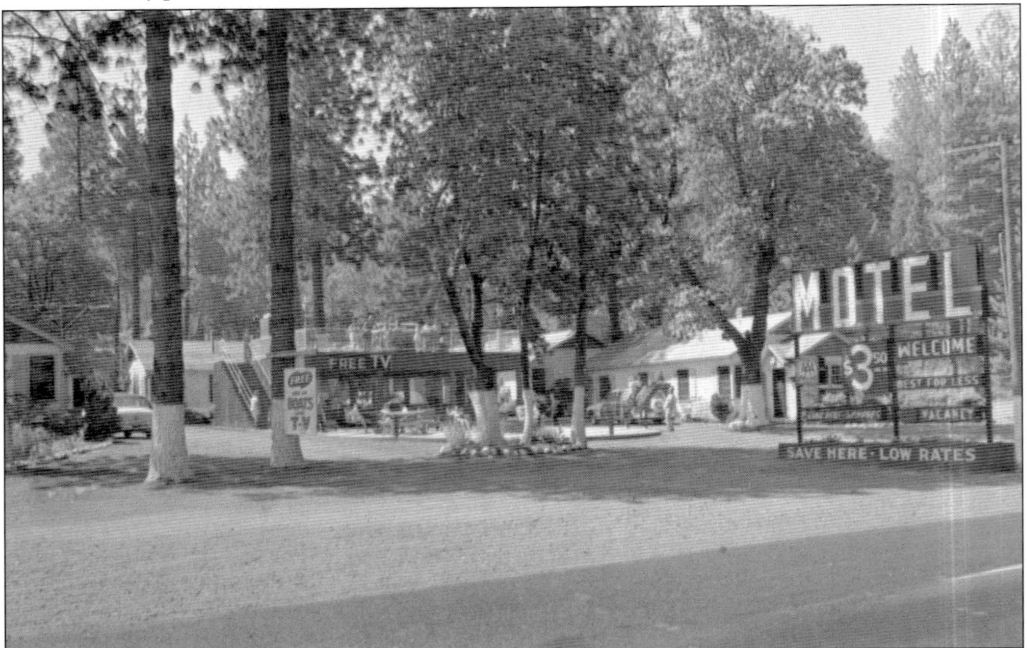

Six miles down Highway 99 from Grants Pass was the Welcome Motel, opened by former Klamath Falls boxing promoter Mack Lillard in early 1947. With 18 deluxe units and low rates, the Welcome appealed to outdoor enthusiasts—it had its own dock for swimming, fishing, and rowboating on the Rogue River. A member of AAA and the Oregon State Motor Association, it was located at 3949 Highway 99 S.

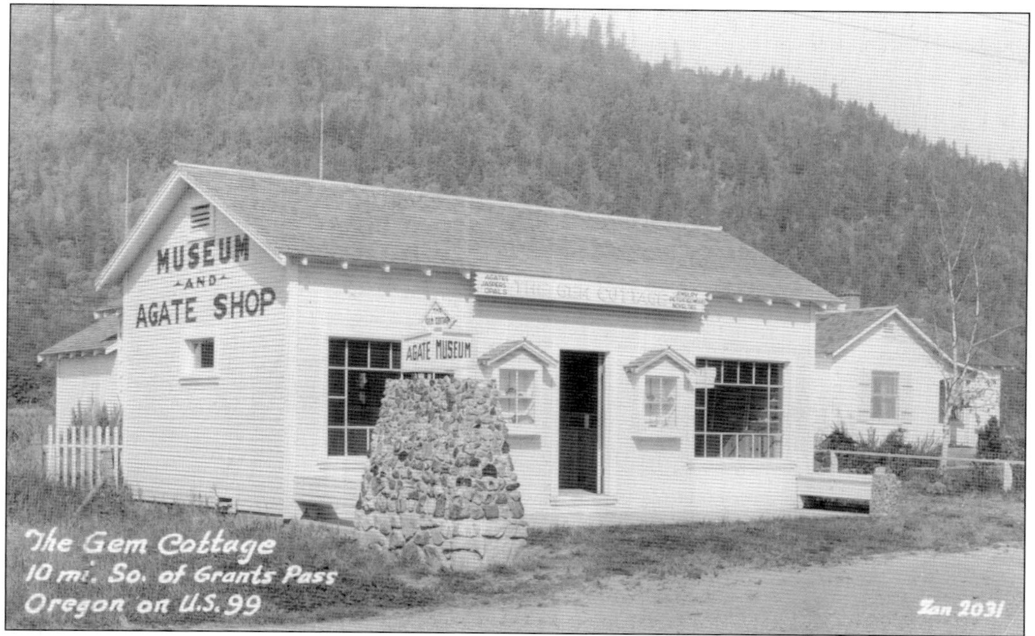

The Gem Cottage opened for business before 1940, specializing in cutting and polishing Oregon agates and creating custom jewelry from locally found semiprecious stones. When Dixon sold out in 1950, the new owners enlarged the building, expanded their wares, and even stayed open until 10:00 p.m. on weekends during the Christmas season. No longer selling gems, the Cottage still stands along Highway 99 seven miles west of Gold Hill.

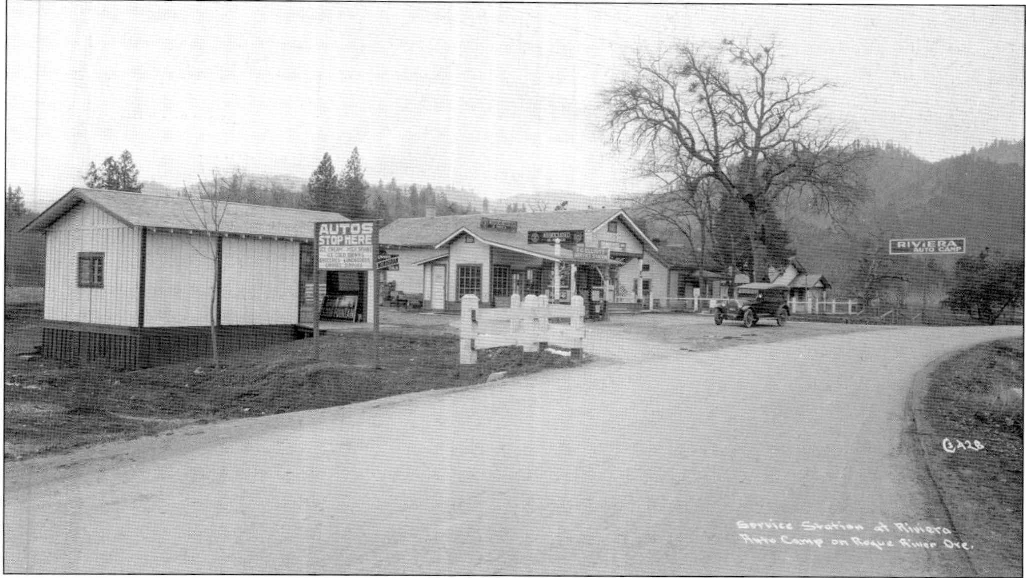

F.C. Elliott's service station was located where Foots Creek Road meets the Pacific Highway, about five miles west of Gold Hill. In 1922, Elliott added a campground—Riviera Park, claimed to be the oldest in southern Oregon—and expanded again a few years later with a combination grocery store/confectionery shop and tourist cottages to cater to the increased tourist traffic. This photograph dates to 1925. (LCHM, CS762.)

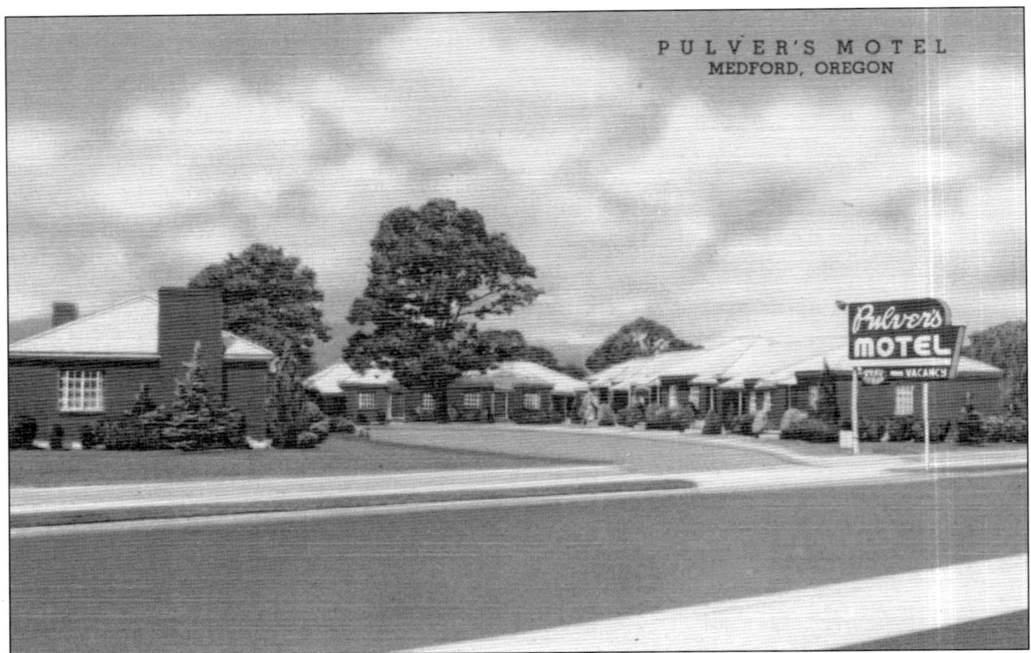

The solid brick-built, 30-unit Pulver's Motel opened at 1237 N Riverside Avenue in 1946. Owner James Pulver described his motel as providing "hotel-style accommodations," a euphemism for lodging that did not include cooking facilities. In 1948, a single room rented for $5 ($7 double); all rooms were electrically heated and provided telephone service and free radio. An insurance company claims office now occupies the site.

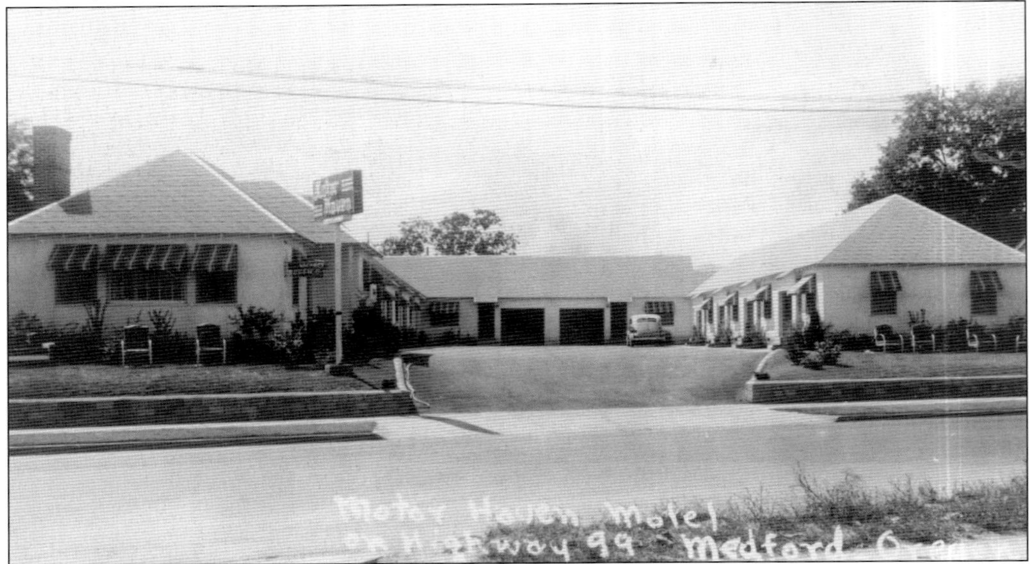

Pulver's closest competitor was literally right next door—the Motor Haven Motel, at 1225 N Riverside Avenue. The two motels opened nearly simultaneously, were very similar in style, offered the same amenities, and had virtually identical nightly rates. Mr. and Mrs. Clarence Partch were the original owners of the Motor Haven, with Mr. and Mrs. Fred Farrar taking over in the 1960s. It is a parking lot today.

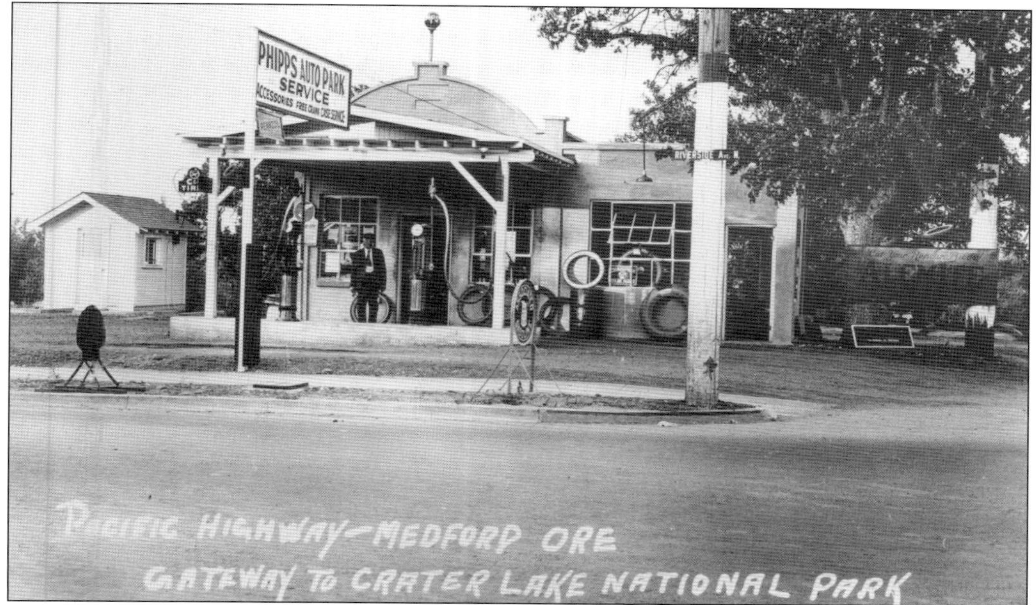

Phipps Auto Park was among the first built along the Pacific Highway, mentioned as early as 1924. Owned by Medford dentist Ira Phipps, it was operated by Albert Shaw for many years. The park featured 23 cabins available furnished or unfurnished, a service station, and shaded campsites along Bear Creek. Phipps's self-described "five acres of tourist's paradise" was still in business in 1947 at 404 N Riverside Avenue. (SOHS, 08138.)

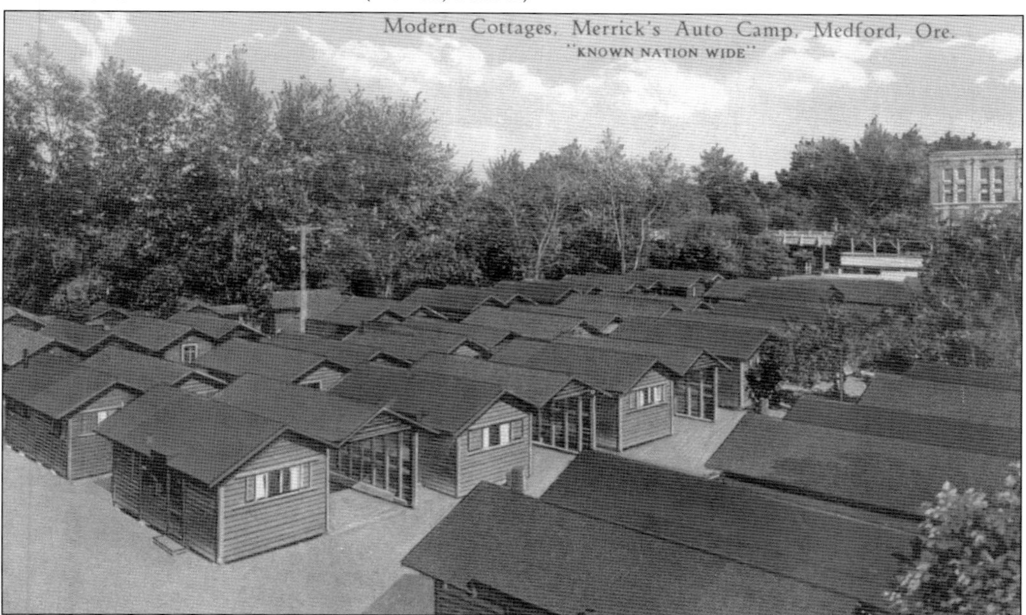

Sitting on bare ground and looking almost military in their precise alignment, the 68 cabins of Merrick's Auto Camp do not appear particularly appealing in this view, but—according to their advertising—Merrick's was "Known Nation Wide" for comfortable surroundings. Luckily, the city natatorium was right next door, so guests had a place to cool off from southern Oregon's summer heat. Merrick's was located at 112 N Riverside Avenue.

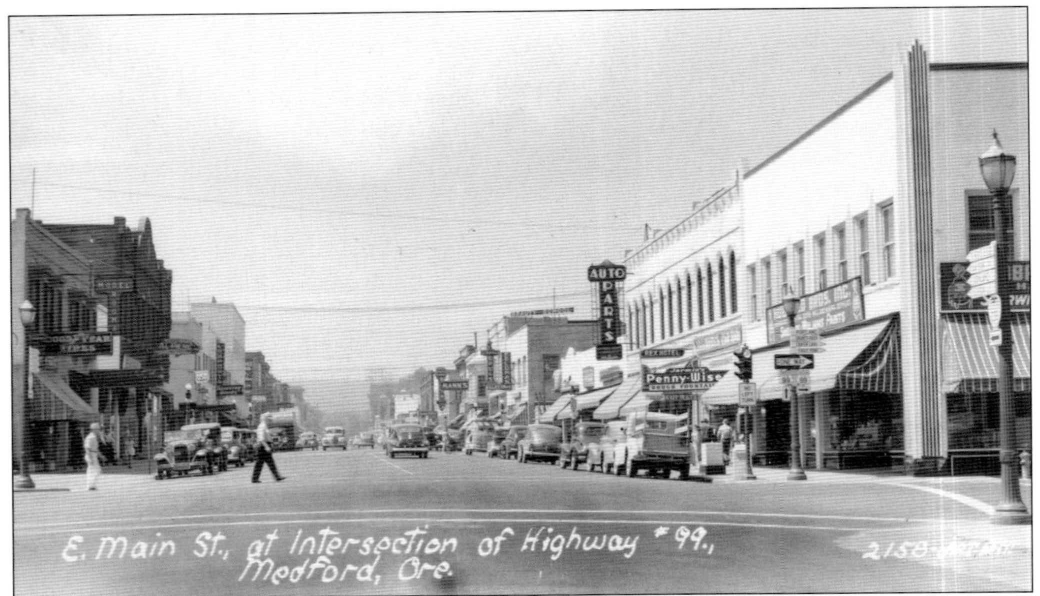

Highway 99 jogged southwest at the corner of Riverside Avenue and Main Street, passing through downtown Medford before turning south again at Central Avenue and out of the city. The numerous signs include the Rex Hotel, Jarmin's Penny-Wise Drugs, Goodyear Tires, The Shack Restaurant, and Al Piche's and Lamport's Sporting Goods stores; the Hotel Medford can be glimpsed in the far distance. Though altered, many of these buildings remain.

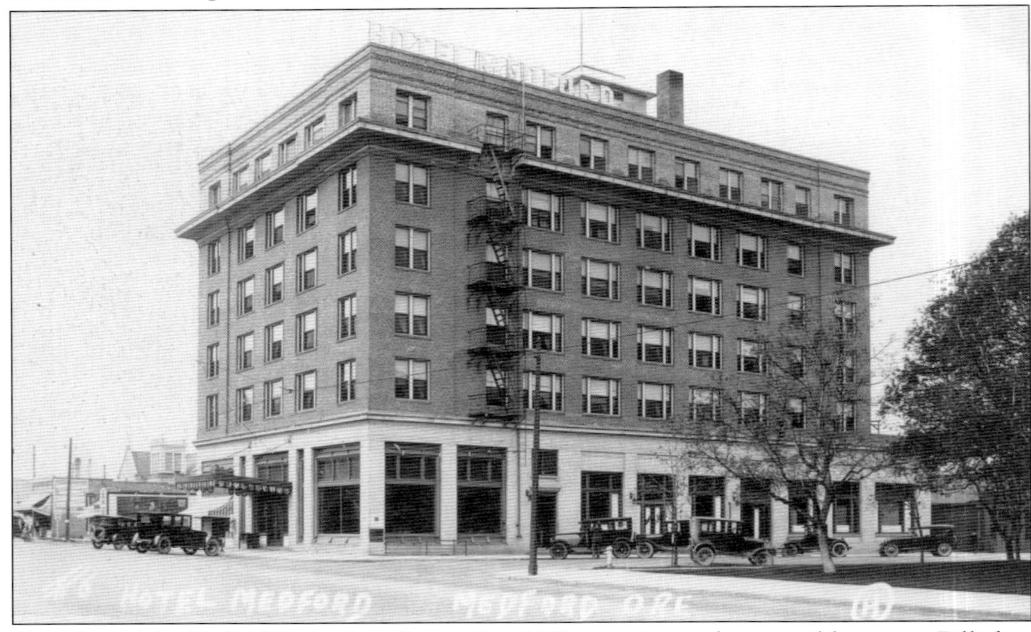

The Hotel Medford celebrated its September 1911 opening with a grand banquet. Billed as Oregon's finest outside of Portland, the five-story brick and terra cotta hotel, modern in every detail, cost $200,000 and contained 127 rooms (90 with private baths) and a coffee shop, lounge, and dining room. A sixth story was added in 1925. Though no longer used a hotel, the building still stands at 410 W Main Street.

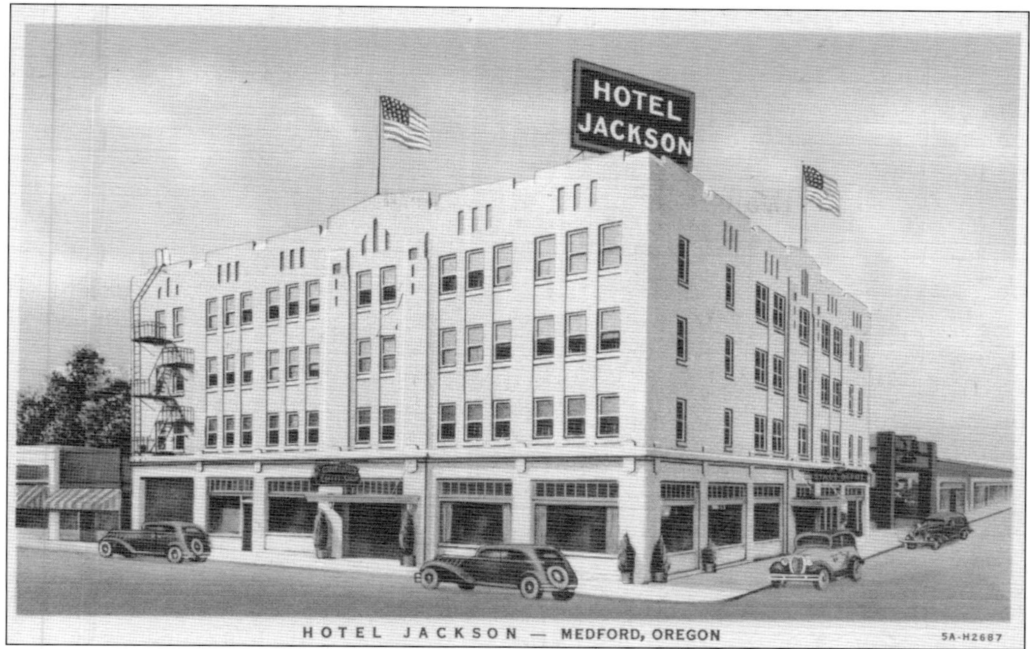

The Hotel Jackson was one of several operated by Chadwick Hotels, which also had hotels in Salem, Eugene, and Grants Pass. Known as "the traveler's home and haven," it opened in September 1926 at the southwest corner of Central Avenue and 8th Street. The hotel was refurbished in July 1949 with a new coffee shop and the Pioneer Room, a banquet facility. The site is a parking lot today.

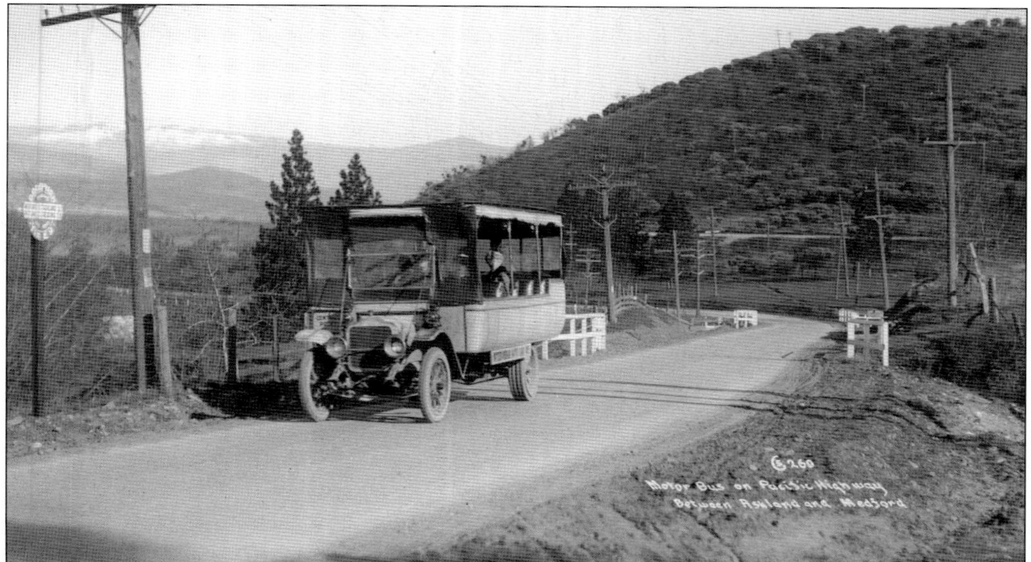

Grading had barely been completed on the Pacific Highway before the Interurban Auto Car Company started autobus service between Medford and Ashland. In 1921, a round-trip fare cost 40¢. The company expanded service to Jacksonville and Roseburg the following year. The sign on the left, advertising Goodrich Tires, pinpoints the location where the photograph was taken: nine miles from Medford, just south of Talent. (SOHS, 11671.)

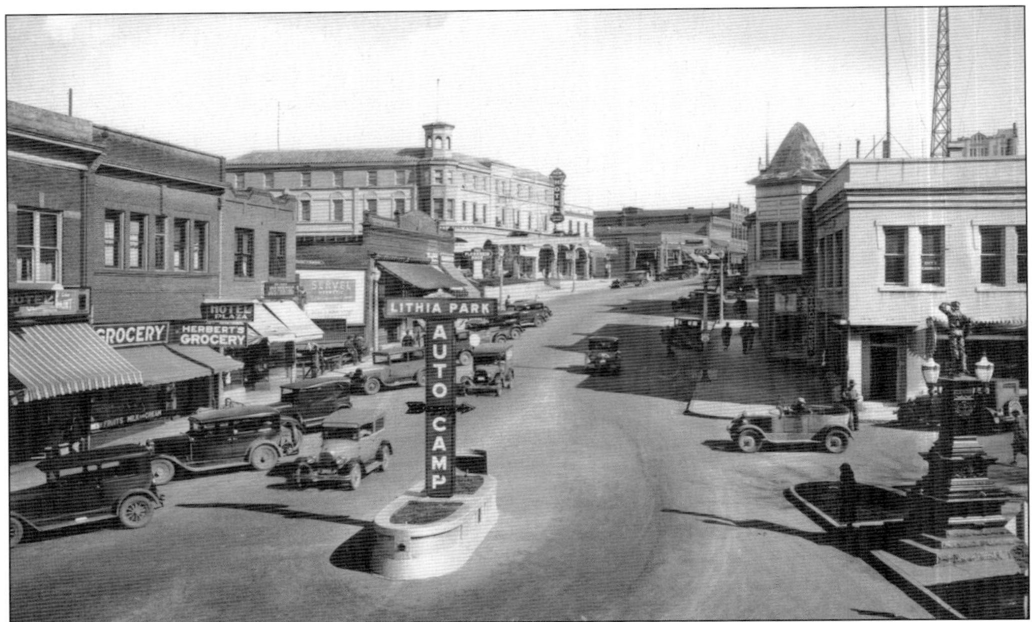

The Pacific Highway approaches the Plaza at the north end of Ashland in this 1920s photograph. A prominent sign—protected by a concrete barricade—points motorists to the Lithia Park Auto Camp up a side street to the right. In the background looms the massive New Ashland Hotel. Other signs advertise Herbert's Grocery, the Hotel Plaza, Florsheim Shoes, Associated gas, Nininger's Cafe, and Franklin's Bakery. (OSL, 21295.)

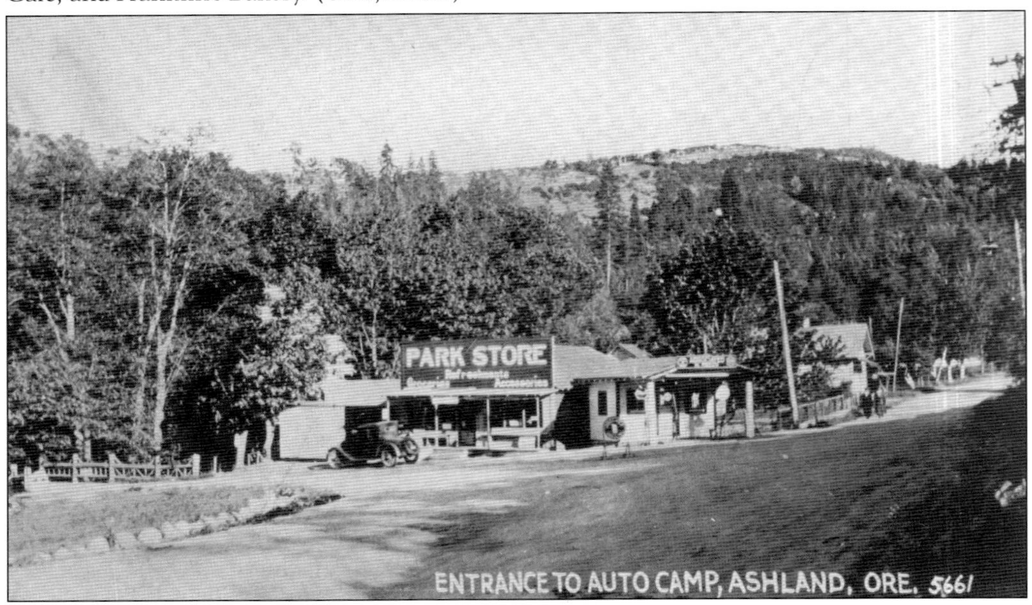

In 1908, Ashland set aside 90 acres of city-owned property along Ashland Creek as a public park. A pipe was built to convey mineral waters from a nearby spring into the park; a health resort developed to cater to health-seekers (the name "Lithia" derives from the mineral lithium). In 1915, a municipally operated auto camp, with its own store, opened within the park nearly a mile off the main highway. (SOHS, 05663.)

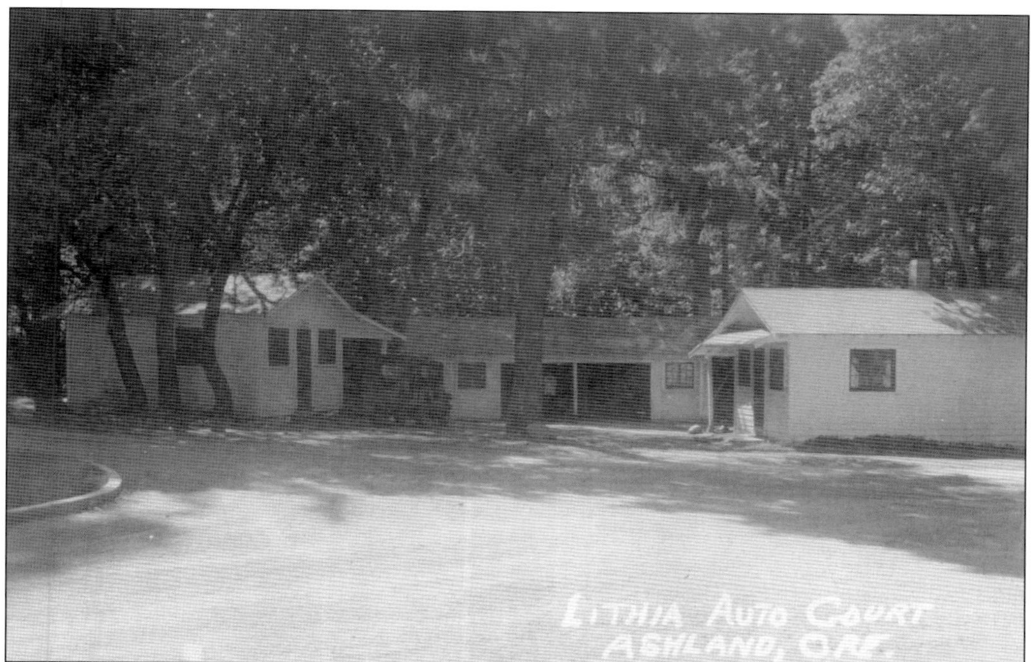

In early days, the Lithia Park Auto Camp was simply a campground with free overnight camping, cooking facilities and bathrooms, and a community house. The first cabins went up in 1926, and 20 more cabins were added in 1930. The camp (later called the Lithia Park Auto Court) survived into the 1950s. One original cabin has been restored, and the community house is now the Ashland Parks and Recreation Department headquarters.

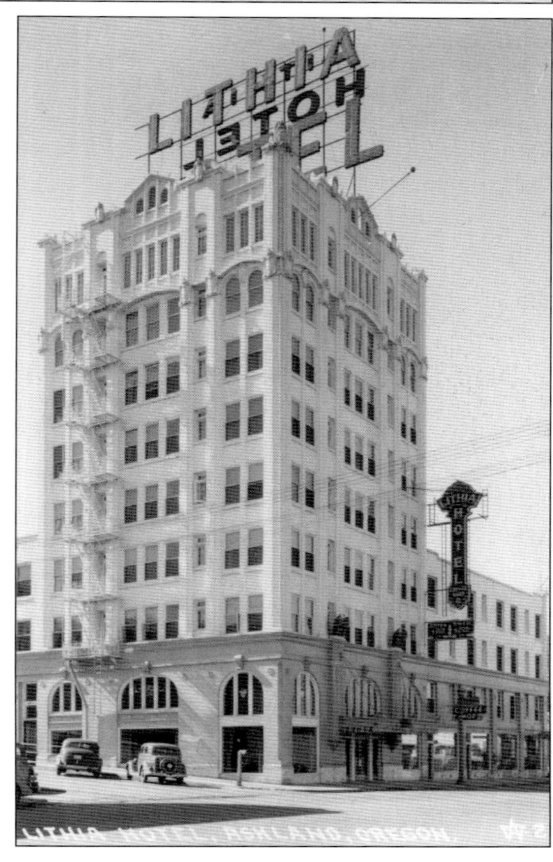

The Lithia Hotel's nine stories of Beaux Arts grandeur tower above downtown Ashland. Constructed in 1925, it was the tallest building between Portland and San Francisco for years. Its 80 rooms with tub baths rented for $3 nightly in 1948 ($5.50 double). It became the Mark Antony Hotel in 1960. Restored in the late 1990s and renamed the Ashland Springs Hotel, it continues in business as southern Oregon's most elegant hotel.

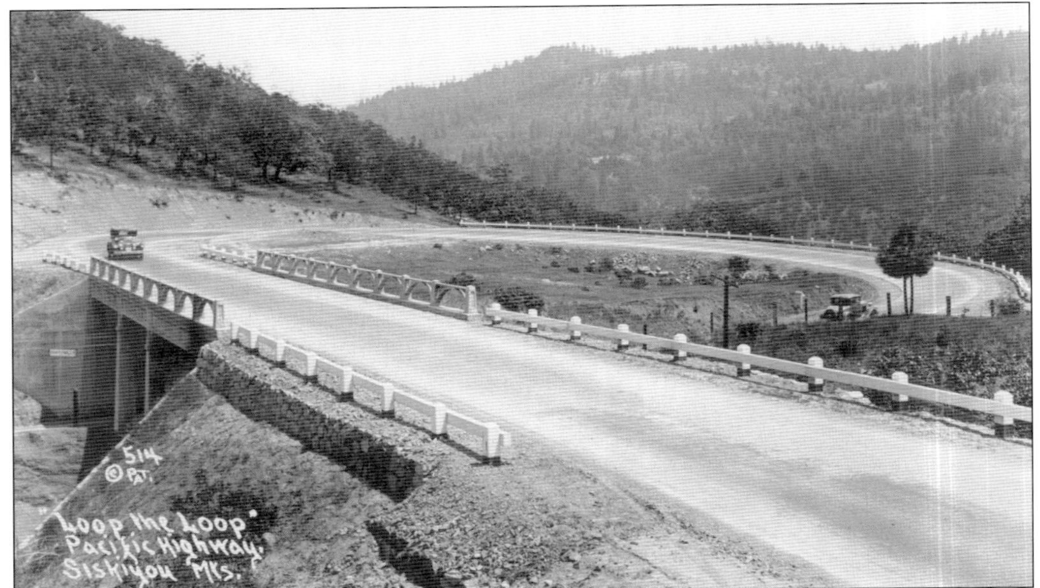

Nine miles south of Ashland, the Pacific Highway curved back over itself—a complete 360-degree loop to gain sufficient elevation to cross over adjacent railroad tracks. The Loop-the-Loop, as it was called, became a familiar landmark on the old highway, much of which (now labeled Old Siskiyou Highway) is still drivable between Ashland and the California border.

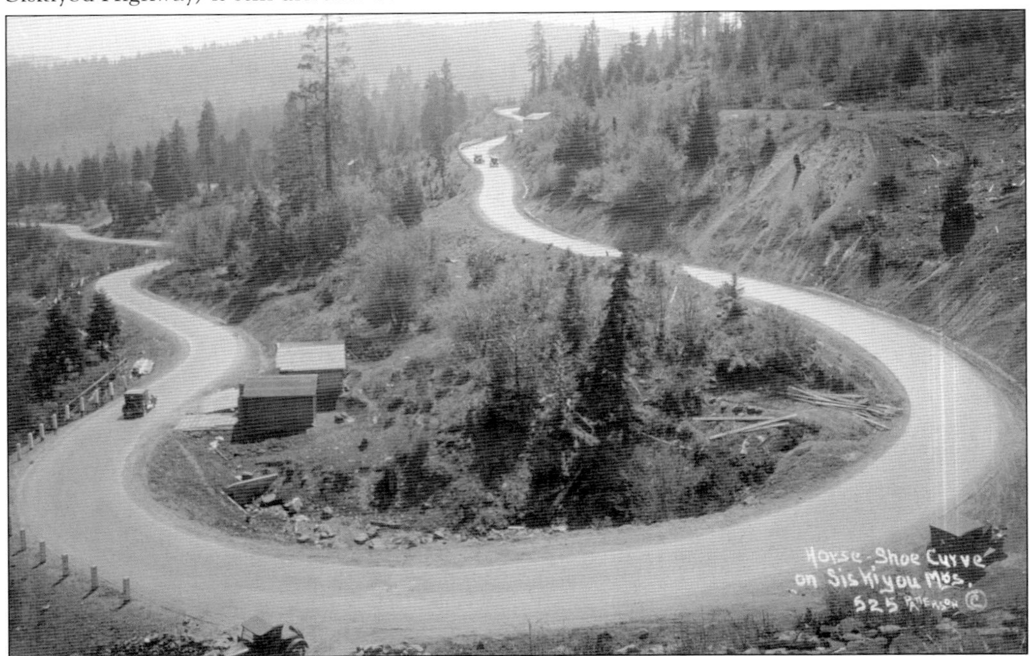

Once past the Loop-the-Loop, the Pacific Highway began its long 2,500-foot climb to Siskiyou Summit. This often-photographed view of one of the numerous curves and switchbacks shows the elevation gain the old autos had to contend with. Highway realignment, begun in the late 1930s but not completed until a decade later, eliminated practically all the twists and turns but made the drive less exciting.

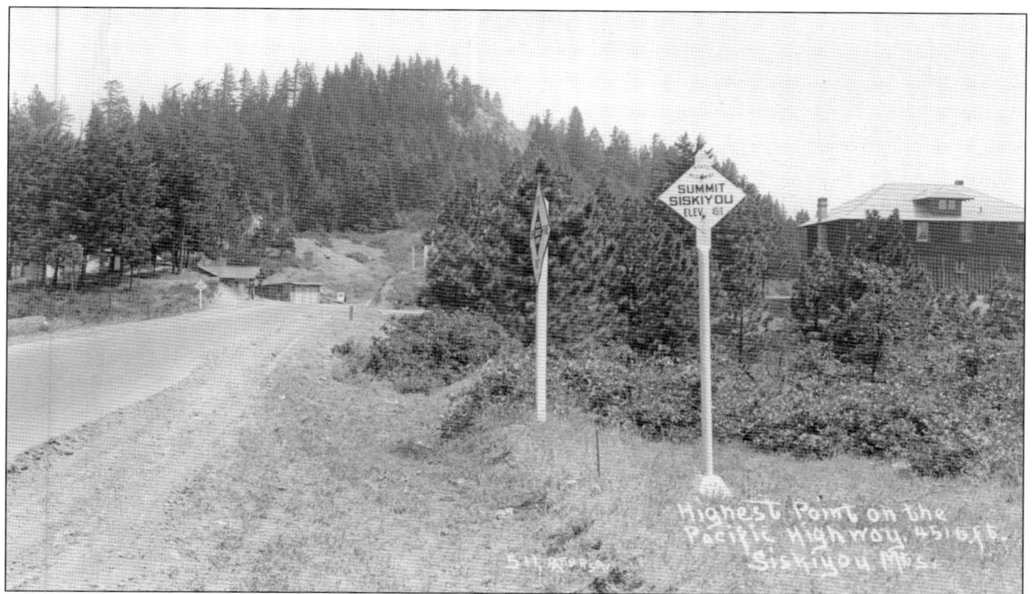

At 4,516 feet, Siskiyou Summit was the highest point on the Pacific Highway in Oregon. Winter often saw four feet of snow on the highway, with plow crews making every effort to keep the route open. Despite the rugged conditions, by 1923, several roadside businesses had built up at the summit. This view shows the Summit Lodge on the right and the Summit Ranch Service Station ahead on the left.

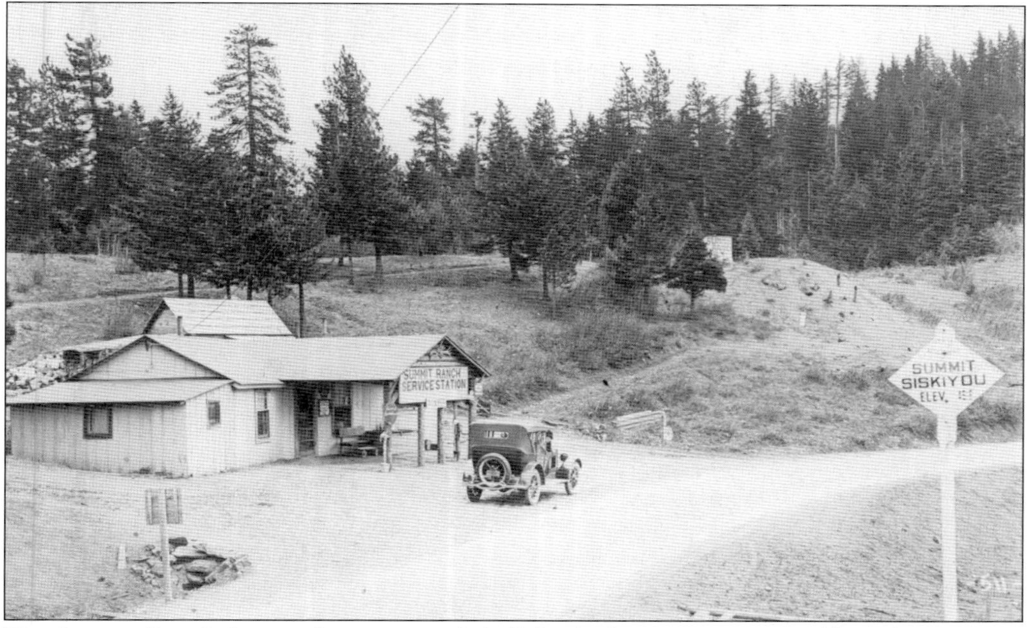

The Summit Ranch Service Station provided all the facilities a motorist could need—gas, tires, auto supplies and repair, camping space, and home-cooked meals "direct from ranch to table." Elk antlers decorated the rustic canopy overhanging the station's single gravity-feed gas pump. For those not wishing to camp, indoor accommodations were near at hand across the road at the Summit Lodge.

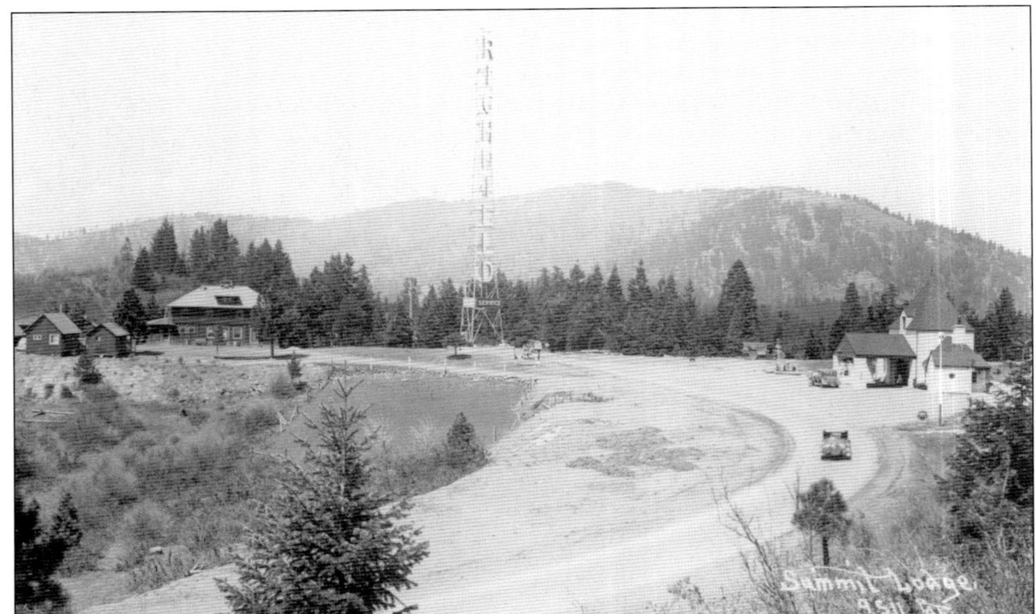

In 1929, Richfield Oil leased the land at the Summit Ranch, demolished the old station, and erected another of the Great White Way beacons the company was building along the West Coast—a total of 34. These facilities paired a Tudor-style service station and a 125-foot airplane beacon tower, the latter flashing an eight-million-candlepower light and sporting eight-foot-tall neon letters spelling RICHFIELD on its sides.

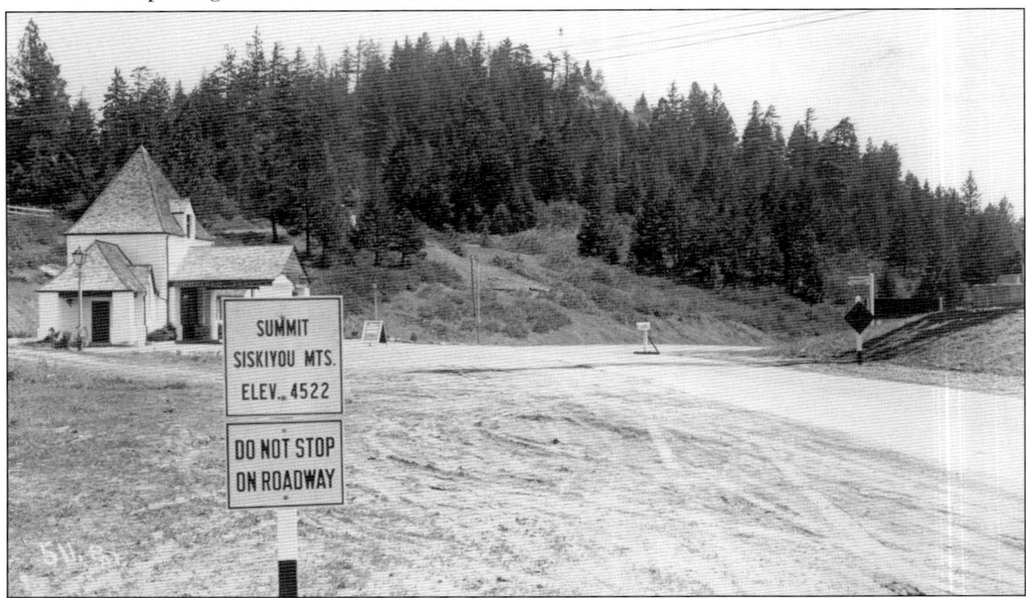

The Richfield Beacons only lasted a few years. The company went bankrupt in 1931; the towers—more of an advertising gimmick than an actual aid to aviators—were outpaced by modern developments in aerial navigation and soon disappeared. Though a few of the service stations survive elsewhere, all the buildings in these two views disappeared when Highway 99 was widened, straightened, and lowered in the 1940s.

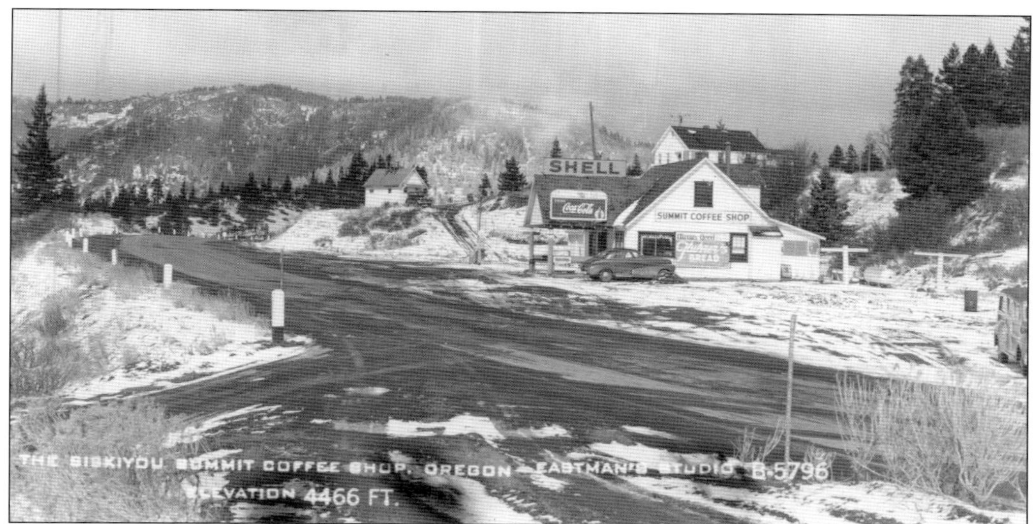

Reconstruction of Highway 99 carved away so much hillside that the highway elevation was lowered by nearly 50 feet and a new summit created south of the old. The Summit Coffee Shop opened at the new high point sometime around 1946 and was a welcome stopping point for weather-weary travelers. It closed in the 1960s after losing business when the interstate was built on a new alignment a quarter mile west.

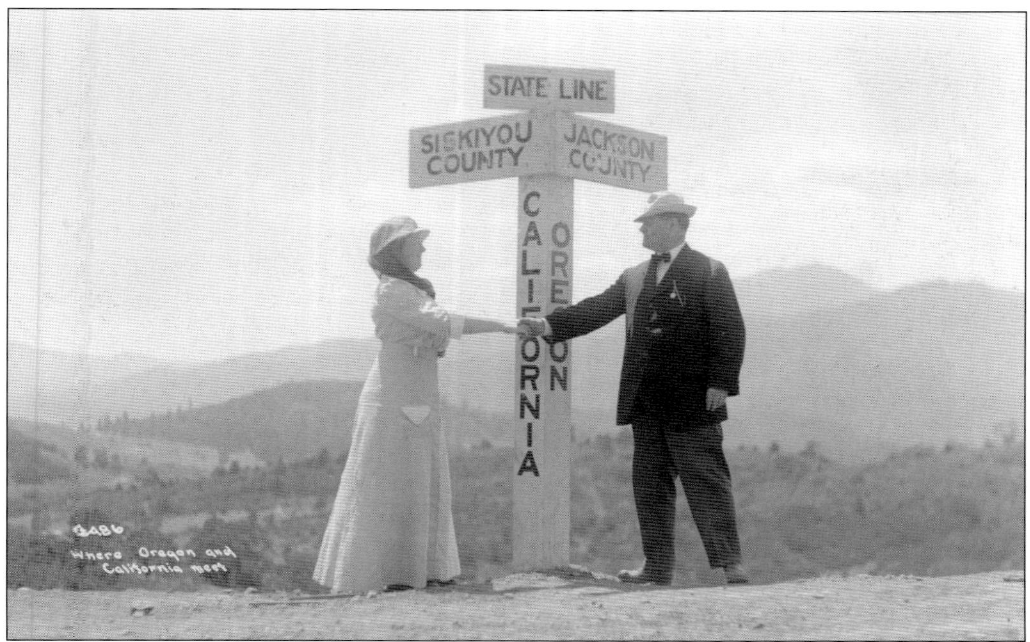

A well-dressed tourist couple—she in long, flowing skirt, hat and veil; he debonair with waistcoat, watch suspended from lapel, bow tie, and jaunty hat—congratulate themselves on having arrived at the Oregon/California state line; no mean feat, considering the nature of highway construction and automobile engineering of the day. Beyond them, looking west from Siskiyou Summit, are miles upon miles of virtually empty, unsettled territory.